handbook of

plant forms

FOR BOTANICAL ARTISTS

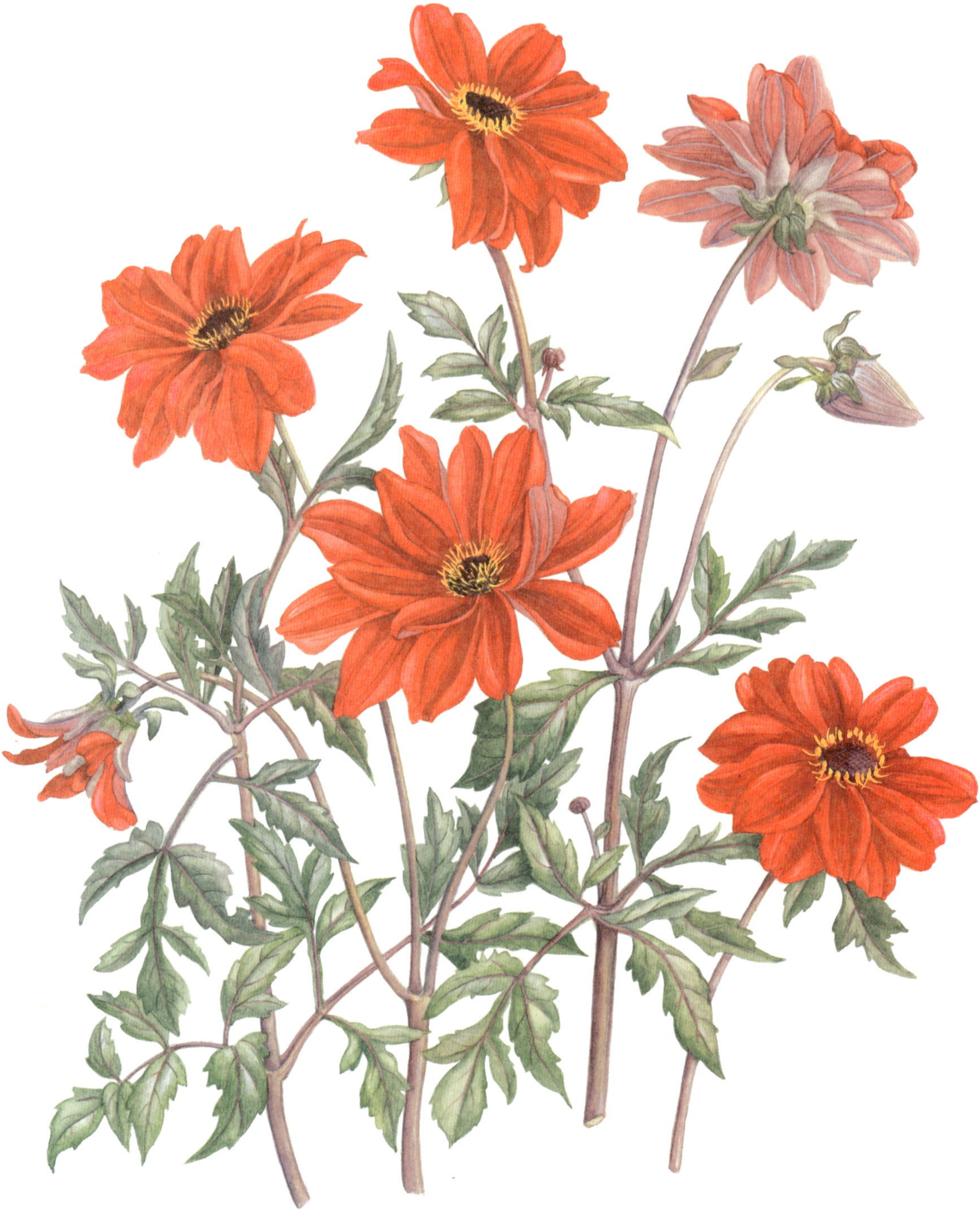

handbook of

plant forms

FOR BOTANICAL ARTISTS

Ernest E. Clark
& Margaret Stevens

BATSFORD

ACKNOWLEDGEMENTS

My sincere thanks to all the artists, both students and tutors, who have allowed their work to be included in this book. Special thanks to Vickie Marsh, President of the Society of Botanical Artists, for her support; and to Kay Rees-Davies, who was gallantly still painting illustrations less than a week before the publisher's deadline.
Margaret Stevens

The botanical text and drawings from author Ernest E. Clark (EC) are the original text and drawings from the 1909 edition of the book *A Handbook of Plant Form*. This botanical text has not been updated so reflects the botanical understanding and nomenclature of the time.

First published in the United Kingdom in 2013 by
Batsford
10 Southcombe Street
London W14 0RA

An imprint of Anova Books Company Ltd

ISBN-13: 9781849940726

A CIP catalogue record for this book is available from the British Library.

10 9 8 7 6 5 4 3 2 1
20 19 18 17 16 15 14 13

Reproduction by Mission Productions, Ltd, Hong Kong
Printed by 1010 Printing International Ltd, China

This book can be ordered direct from the publisher at the website: www.anovabooks.com, or try your local bookshop.

Distributed in the United States and Canada by Sterling Publishing Co., 387 Park Avenue South, New York, NY 10016, USA

Page 2: *Dahlia* 'Bishop of Llandaff'. Watercolour, Jenny Jowett.

CONTENTS

INTRODUCTION

When I was asked to update Ernest E. Clark's *A Handbook of Plant Form* (Batsford, 1909) and make it relevant for today's botanical art students – or indeed anyone who appreciates fine botanical paintings and wishes to learn more about their creation – I realized this was quite a difficult undertaking. Drawing on my experience as Course Director for the Society of Botanical Artists' Distance Learning Course, I decided that my starting point would be to address the continuing need for observation and drawing, without which students are unlikely to progress far; in order to paint a magnificent sunflower, for example, one needs to be able to draw and understand the structure of the simple daisy, both of them members of the Compositae (Asteraceae) family. Those who join our courses find that basic drawing is a key requirement if they are to emerge after 27 months with a credible diploma.

Just as relatives within a human family can be very different in appearance and character, so it is in the plant world and by altering the format of Ernest Clark's book to list the plants in alphabetical order of botanical family, I hope to raise awareness of this. The student who concentrates on producing a simple line drawing of a bluebell may well go on to receive a Royal Horticultural Society Gold Medal for an exhibit of tulips, all of them members of the Liliaceae family.

We are sometimes asked why we need Latin names in botanical art and it may be thought pretentious. However, without them it would be much harder to communicate worldwide, since all countries have their own common names for many flowers. Even within the United Kingdom, there are local differences – the bluebell of Scotland is the harebell of England, for example, but if they are referred to as *Campanula rotundifolia* and *Hyacinthoides non-scripta* there is no mistaking them.

Reading the words of Ernest Clark, written over a century ago, one can only marvel at the discipline and order which he conveyed to his students. Apart from the actual teaching methods, there are two very important differences between that time and the present day. Now one would be forced to hunt high and low in search of an establishment offering botany as part of a degree course, as it is no longer treated as a subject in its own right. Unless there is a radical change before too long, Society of Botanical Art Members holding a BSc in Botany will be as extinct as the dodo.

Secondly, when Clark was teaching the principles of design to his students in Derby, there was a real hope that those who made the grade would find employment. Fine printing by independent publishers such as William Morris's Kelmscott Press flourished, along with others influenced by the Arts and Crafts Movement. As well as books, magazines and journals provided an outlet for the graphic artist. One such, *The Studio*, continues to this day in print and online under the name of *Studio International*, and is still an important conveyor of information to the art world.

In the United States, printing took its lead from the UK and many exquisite examples of the designer's art were produced. Covers, end papers and title pages made free use of botanical designs, in some cases without reference to the actual designer back in Britain. Anyone interested in this aspect of design should hunt down examples of the books published by Thomas Bird Mosher of Portland, Maine.

Beyond the printed page, there were other outlets for artists. The newly extended Victoria and Albert Museum gave pride of place to decorative tiling and, from the Doulton factory in Lambeth to Della Robbia in Birkenhead, botanical subjects dominated the decoration, although the latter firm was commercially unsuccessful and went into voluntary liquidation. In 1913 the highly successful Staffordshire potter William Moorcroft set up his own company, Moorcroft, which still survives and is a name revered among collectors of fine art pottery.

Underlying this interest in botany was the fact that young people had the opportunity to study nature from their earliest school days. The nature table held pride of place in the infants' classroom and children were taken on nature walks, where their eyes were opened to the quiet beauty around them. Children also benefited from the art lessons at school, where many hours were spent drawing and painting repeat patterns, which gave a grounding in symmetry and balance, as well as adding discipline and patience to the mix. Forty years after Clark wrote the book, I was enjoying nature walks and adding objects to the nature table, from prickly conkers to a pearly shell found in a rock pool.

Today, the world moves faster in all respects. Many people want instant results and resent time spent when there is little to show for it, but luckily there are exceptions and among them are aspirant botanical painters and designers prepared to put in hours of effort in the hope of achieving perfection. So this book is all about tutors and students, from the wonderful work of Ernest Clark, doing his best to prepare his students for a very tricky government examination, to the work by SBA tutors who strive to pass on their skills. Some paintings here are by Distance Learning Diploma Course students past and present and all have one thing in common: they had to learn to draw before they could paint just as they learnt to toddle, walk and then run.

Margaret Stevens

LEAF FORMS

In the illustration opposite, a number of different leaf forms occurring on different plants is given. The variety that exists also in the way they are notched or toothed along their margins is illustrated, and the various ways in which they attach themselves to the main stems. It must be borne in mind that the endless variety of forms to be found in leaves is due to the degree of development to which the leaf has been carried; all leaves, to begin with, are similar in form, but some are arrested in their growth earlier than others, and undergo less modification on that account thus becoming *simple* and *entire* leaves, or other simple forms: degree in development also carries us to *decompound* and *supra-decompound* leaves. The various names attached to the illustrations are explained in the list of botanical terms. A reference to fig. 1, and to the leaf of the Columbine will explain the difference between a *simple* and *entire* leaf and a *decompound* leaf. Fig. 1 is entire because its edge is not notched or divided in any way. Fig. 2 is orbicular in form, and its edge is *crenate*. It is also called *peltate*, from the way the stalk is attached to the underside of the leaf, from which point the veins radiate. Fig. 3 is a Wild Rose leaflet, is elliptical in form and its edge is *serrate*. Fig. 4 is *spatulate* in form and likewise serrate.

Fig. 5 is *oval* or egg-shaped, and *entire*. Fig. 6 is *ovate* or in versely egg-shaped, with serrated margin. Fig. 7 is another rounded leaf, with serrated edge. Fig. 8 is rather an elongated heart-shape, with a *toothed* edge. Fig. 9 is *oblong*, with a fringed edge or margin. Fig. 10 is the Fir-tree foliage and is called *acicular*, or needle-shaped. Fig. 11 is *cordate* or heart-shaped, and serrated. Fig. 12 is *obcordate*, or inversely heart-shaped. Fig. 13 is *reniform* or kidney-shaped and serrated. Fig. 14 is an example of the *capillary* or hair-like form. Fig. 15 is the *linear* shape, seen also in the leaves of grasses. Fig. 16 is the *linear-lanceolate* leaf of the Willow. Fig. 9*a* is lanceolate. Fig. 17 is arrow-shaped or saggitate, and is also an example of the sessile attachment to the stem. Fig. 18 is angular in form, and divided or lobed in regard to its edge. Fig. 19 is elliptical also and entire; it also illustrates *parallel* venation as distinct from net-veining, as seen in the leaves of the Ivy or Wild Rose, etc. Fig. 20 is *hastate* or halbert-shaped, and three-lobed. Fig. 21 is strap-shaped or *ligulate*, and entire. Fig. 22 is an *oblique* heart-shaped leaf, such as the Begonia. Fig. 23 is called *runcinate*, owing to the form and direction of its marginal divisions. Fig. 24 shows a form of attachment to the stem which is called *perfoliate*. Fig. 25 *connate*, as in some varieties of the Honeysuckle. Fig. 26 is *amplexicaul*, the base lobes of the leaf passing round and beyond the stem. EC

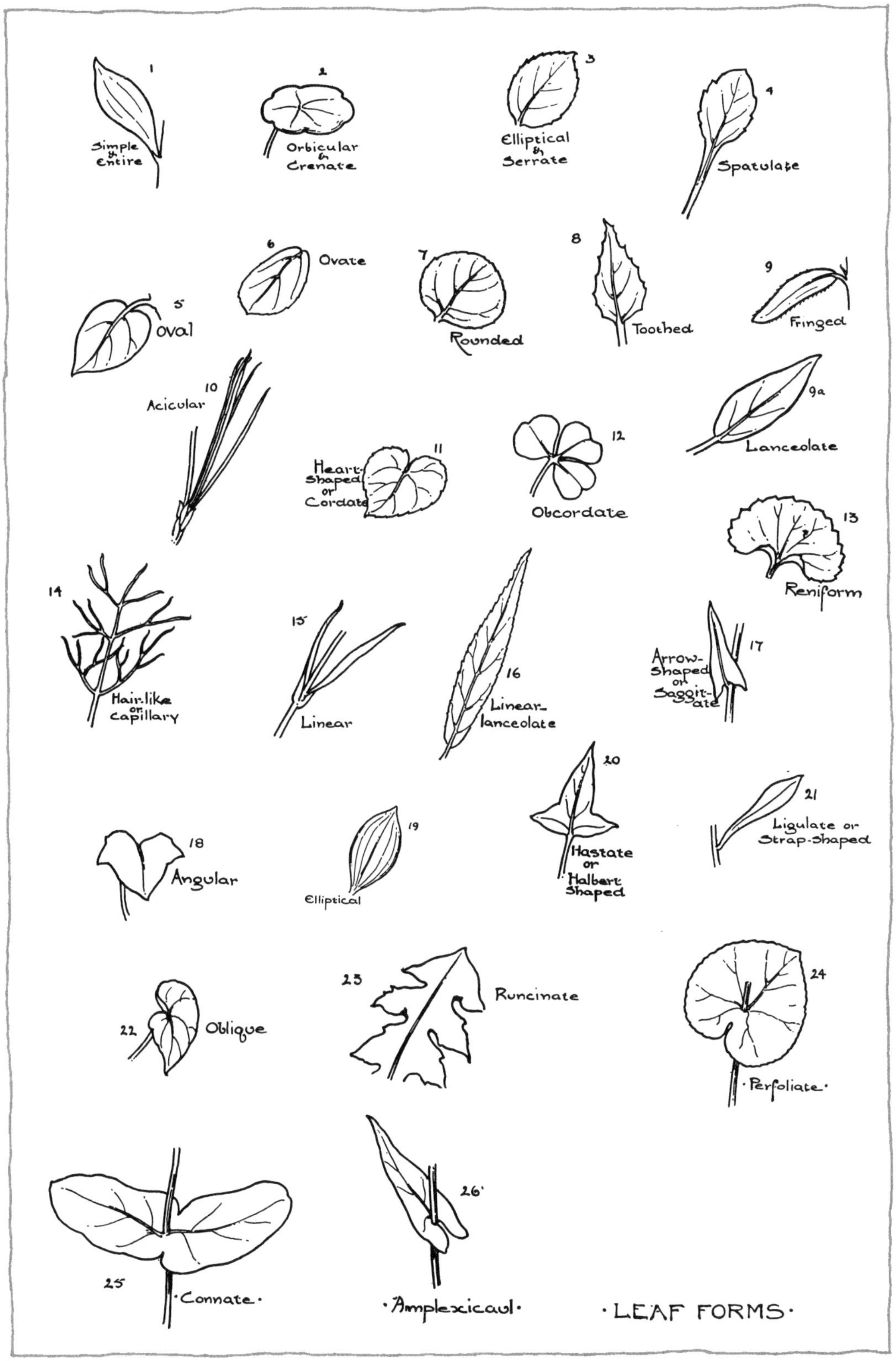
1 Simple & Entire
2 Orbicular & Crenate
3 Elliptical & Serrate
4 Spatulate
5 Oval
6 Ovate
7 Rounded
8 Toothed
9 Fringed
10 Acicular
9a Lanceolate
11 Heart-shaped or Cordate
12 Obcordate
13 Reniform
14 Hair-like or capillary
15 Linear
16 Linear-lanceolate
17 Arrow-Shaped or Saggit-ate
18 Angular
19 Elliptical
20 Hastate or Halbert Shaped
21 Ligulate or Strap-Shaped
22 Oblique
23 Runcinate
24 ·Perfoliate·
25 ·Connate·
26 ·Amplexicaul·

·LEAF FORMS·

MAPLE FAMILY *Aceraceae*

Sycamore

Acer pseudo-platanus

This is not really a native of Britain, but it has been long established here. It is extensively used as an ornamental tree for our streets, parks, and squares. It belongs to the Maple tribe (*Acer*), and is also called the Greater Maple. The leaves are large, five-lobed, and unequally toothed. It flowers in May and June. The English, or Lesser Maple (*Acer campestre*) is very common, and is in our hedgerows. The foliage is very beautiful. EC

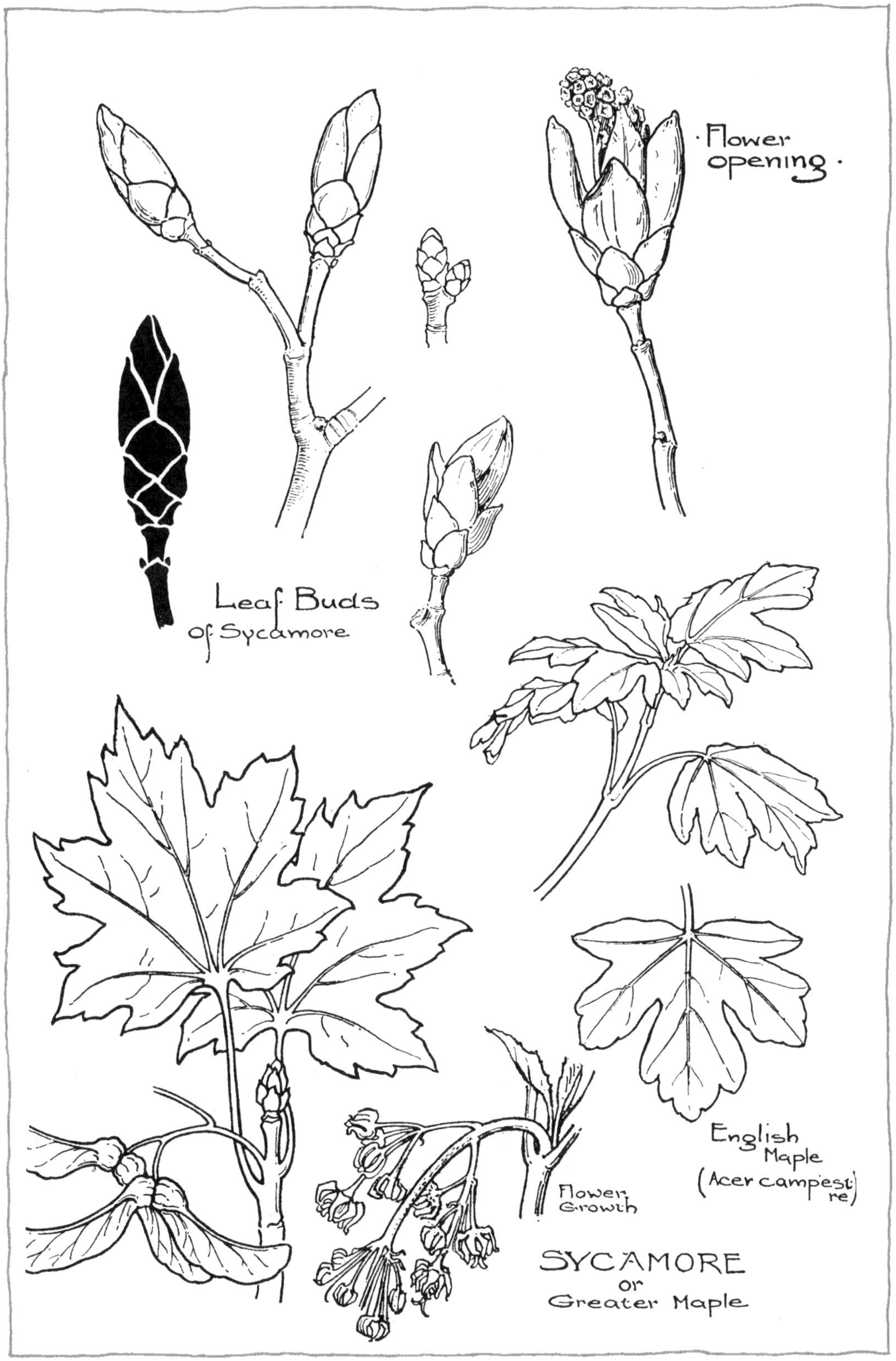
·Flower opening·
Leaf Buds of Sycamore
English Maple (Acer campestre)
Flower Growth
SYCAMORE or Greater Maple

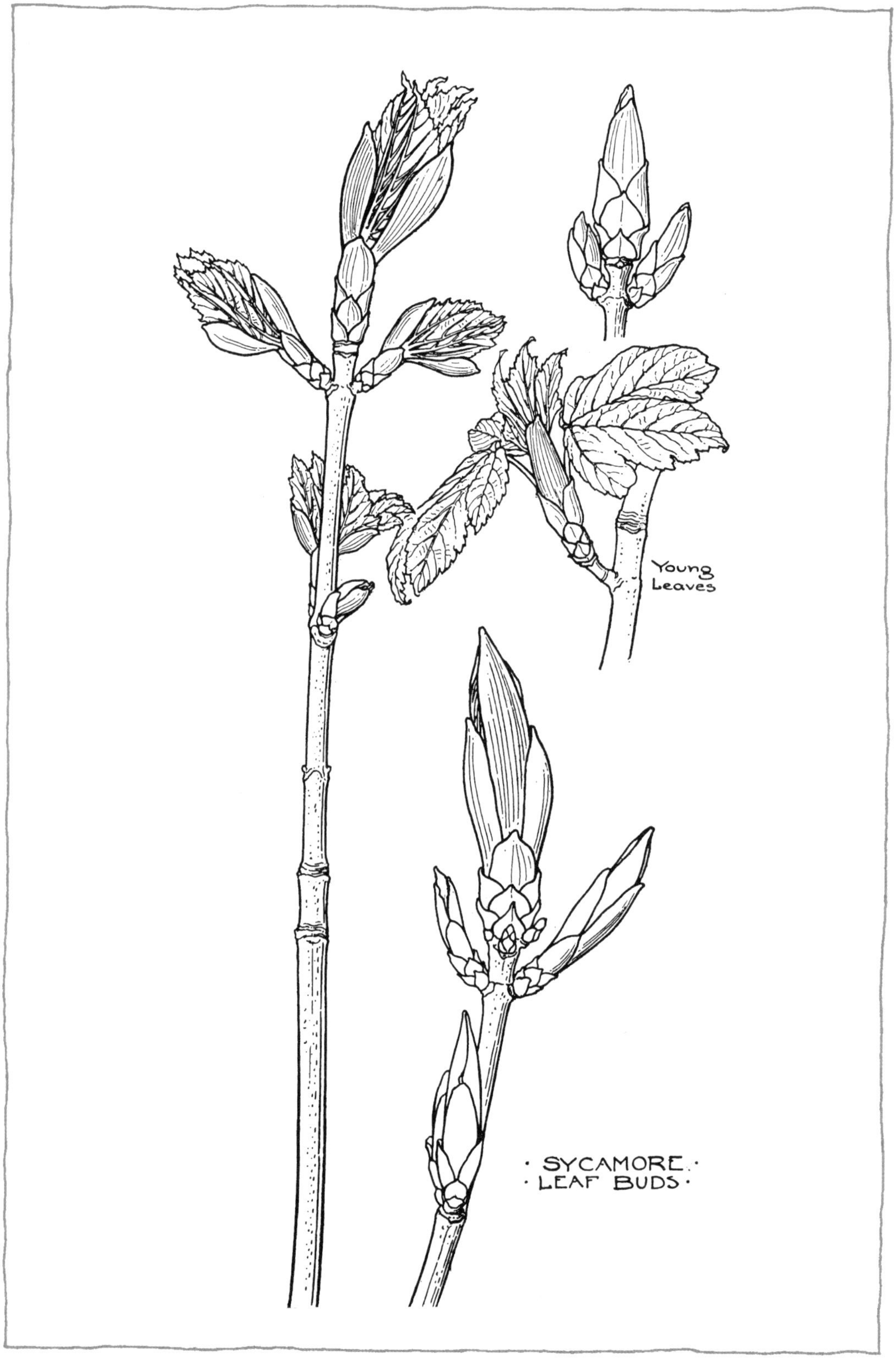
Young
Leaves
· SYCAMORE ·
· LEAF BUDS ·

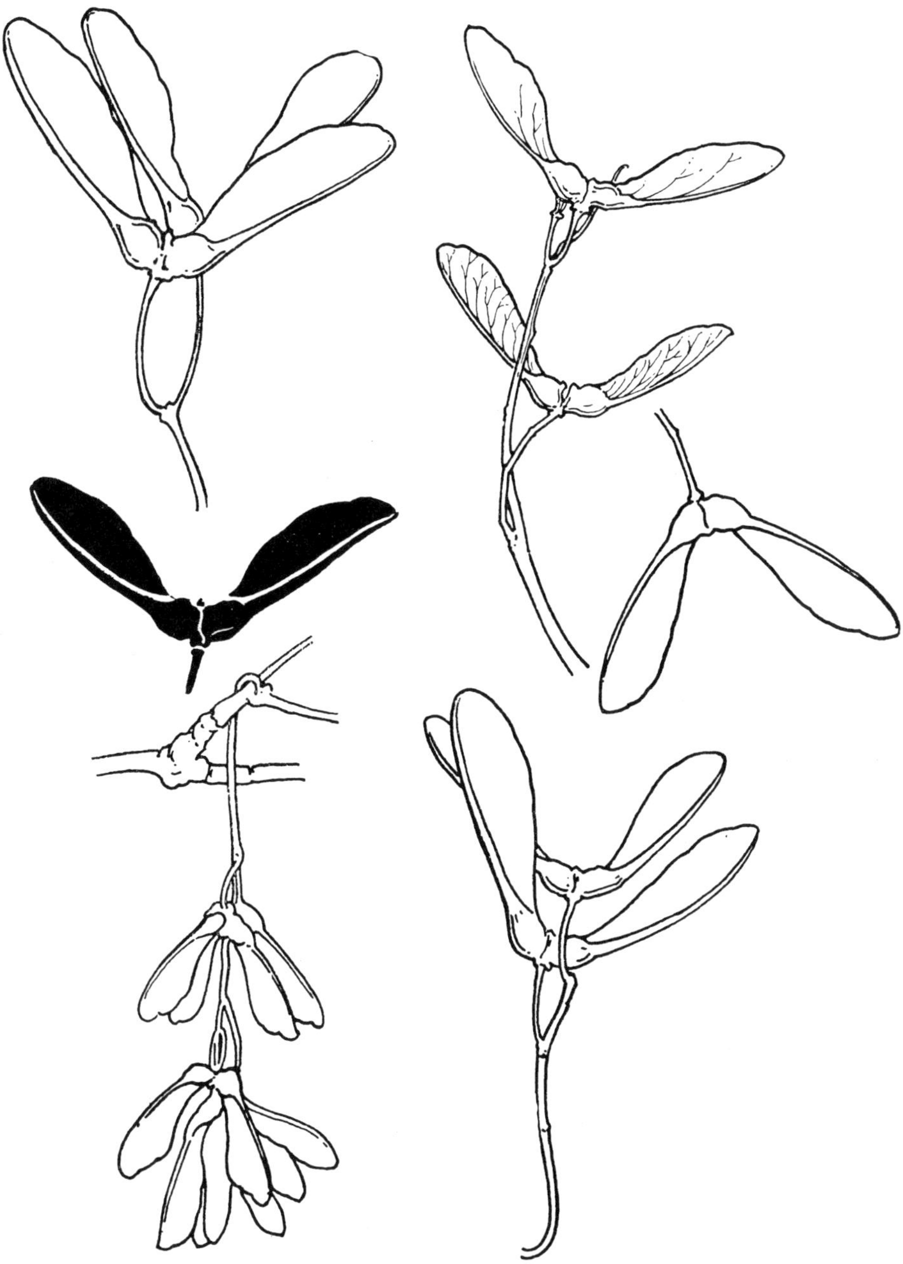

· Winged Seeds of the Sycamore ·

Japanese Maple

Acer palmatum var. *dissectum*

This very old specimen of Japanese Maple (*Acer palmatum* var. *dissectum*) grows in the walled garden at Penrhyn Castle, a National Trust property in North Wales. For over 50 years, from 1862, the gardens were in the care of the famous Walter Speed, one of the earliest recipients of the Royal Horticultural Society Victoria Medal of Honour, and training received at Penrhyn equalled that at Kew.

From the look of the ancient, gnarled trunk, this beautiful acer may well have been known to Walter Speed. I have a soft spot for it, as it helped me to gain an RHS Gold medal some years ago when I decided to record it throughout the year. It presents an interesting face no matter what the season: in winter the serpentine skeleton is laid bare and this is one of the times when graphite best conveys the texture and intricacies of the subject. When snow falls it becomes a stark and beautiful monochrome sculpture, while after a few mild days new shoots break through, followed by the softest lime-green leaves and tiny red-sepalled flowers. In autumn it bursts into flame, its single keys ready to be borne by the wind. So much variety is offered by this one plant and I greatly enjoyed working with it. As this was nearly 20 years ago, I no longer remember details of the materials except that at that time I used nothing but Winsor & Newton Artists' colours.

Keep your eyes open for plants that have year-round in interest, be they shrubs or trees, and patiently record their life cycle; you will find it fascinating. Composition requires thought, but if you have easy access to your chosen subject you could study it throughout the year, making sketches and planning the layout, then work on the finished piece when the seasons come round again. It is always worth asking if you can have access to a particular subject which catches your eye, whether this means an approach to the Head Gardener at a National Trust property or to the owner of a private house. I have found people to be positively delighted when someone shows an interest in their often treasured possession, and the thought of having it painted is as complimentary as if it were a human portrait.

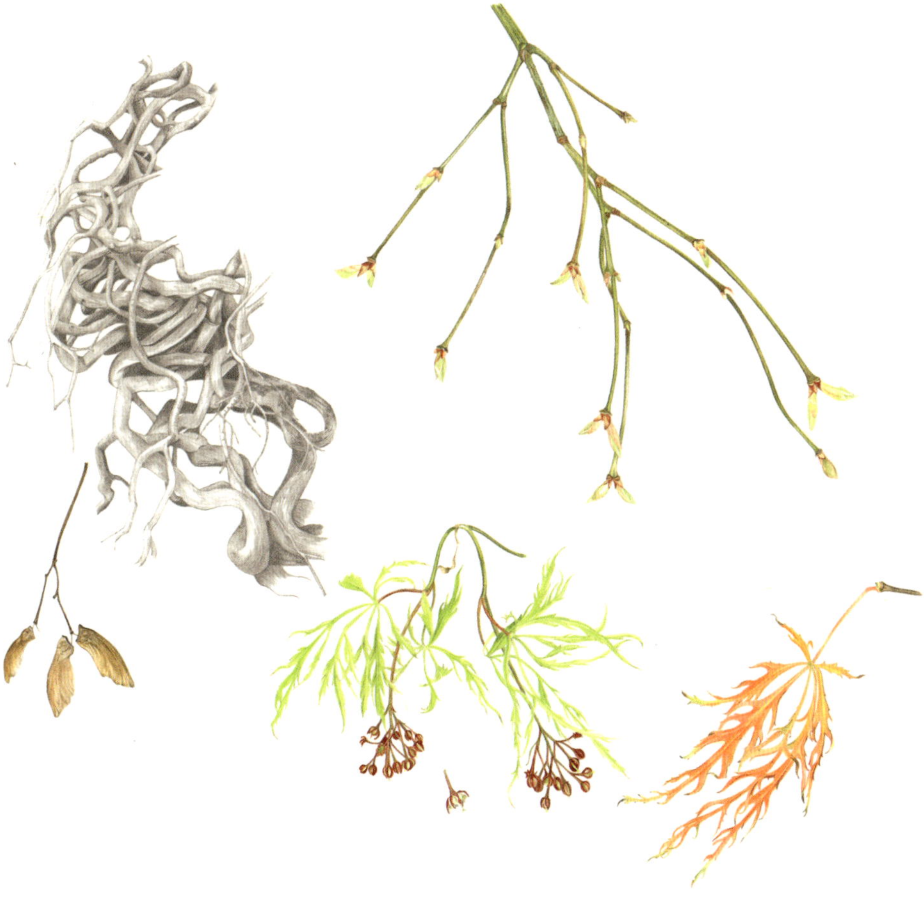

Watercolour and graphite, Margaret Stevens

DAFFODIL FAMILY *Amaryllidaceae*

Daffodil

Narcissus pseudo-narcissus

The daffodil, long a favourite with the poets, has beautiful colour and form. The flower is perianth and tubular, having six segments or sepals and petals oblong, and of a more delicate and paler yellow than the crown or bell, which is usually much more golden in colour, the edge of it being irregularly cut or waved.

The six stamens spring from the sides of the tube. The pedicel or flower-stalk is short, and springs from a membranous sheath or spathe. The flowers are solitary and terminal. It has a style and stigma, which is three-lobed. The fruit is a capsule. The leaves are long and linear, dark green and radical, but a little shorter than the flower-stalks, which are hollow. The root is a bulb. It is to be found in moist woods and copses in March and April. EC

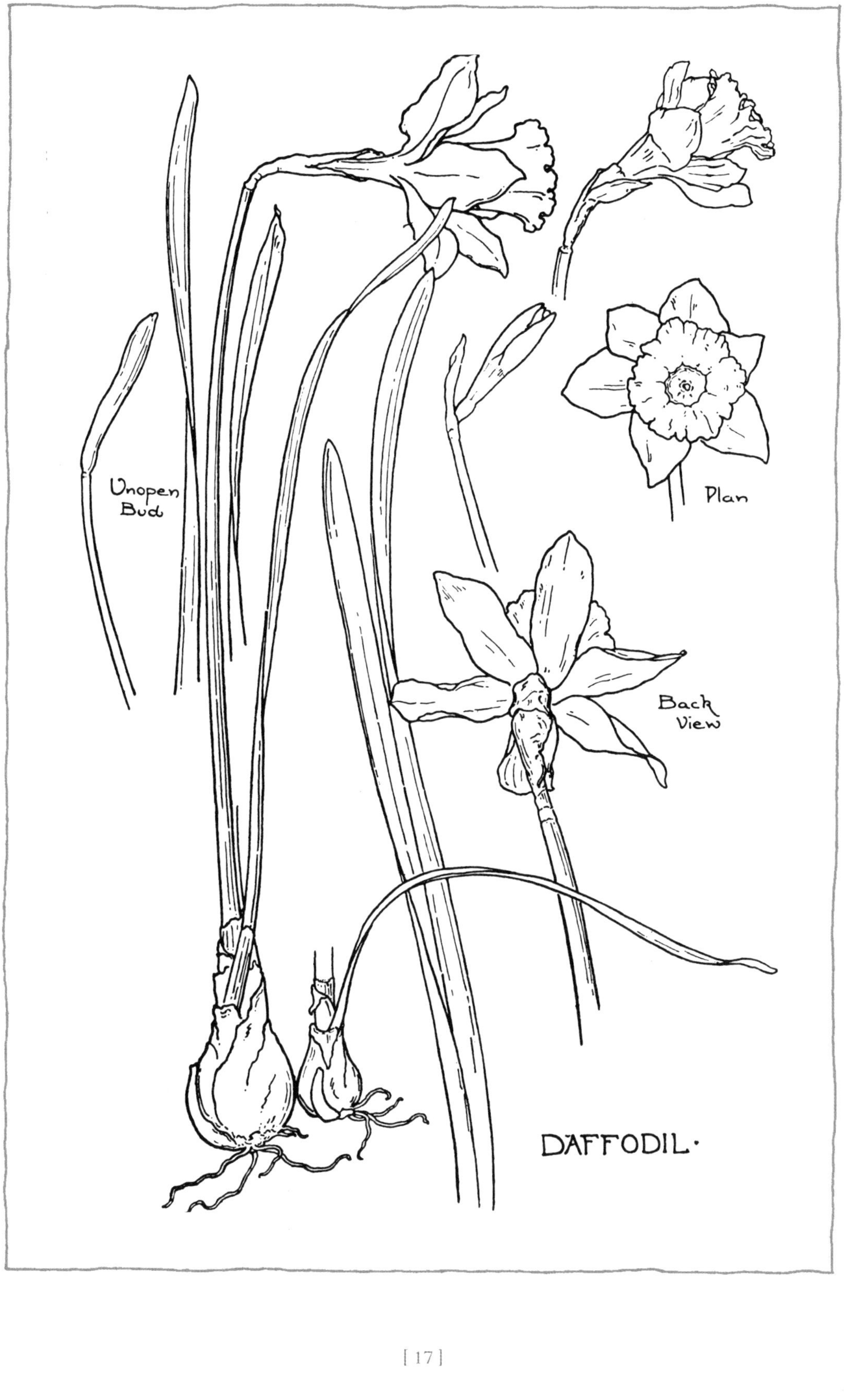
Unopen Bud
Plan
Back View
DAFFODIL·

Daffodil

Narcissus 'Tête-à-tête'

The great artist and lithographer Walter Fitch, writing in the 19th century, said that the daffodil was one of the most difficult flowers to draw correctly. He was right, and anyone choosing this for an examination piece is very brave. Luckily the artist made a good choice, which helped her to gain a Distinction. The flowers were well drawn at various angles with no loss of perspective, which is the most common fault. They are notoriously difficult to shade well, and the artist says she used varying proportions of Perylene Green and Perylene Violet for her shadow mix, laid over Lemon Yellow and Winsor Yellow for the perianth and Cadmium Yellow and Cadmium Orange for the darker corona. Making this distinction between transparent and opaque colours helped the little trumpets to stand out. The judges were also impressed by the attention paid to the fresh green foliage where each leaf clearly received the same care, using a mix of French Ultramarine and Winsor Lemon.

For this assignment the artist needed to fit in detailed dissections as well as bulbs and other parts of the plant, so she made number of thumbnail sketches and used tracing paper to work out her composition in advance. She made an exceptionally good job of her cut-through sections in the style of Arthur Harry Church (see page 162), magnified sufficiently for the viewer to see the detail clearly. The dormant buds within the bulb and the seeds within the ovary were particularly noteworthy. The roots were also very well drawn and painted; too often they are shown hanging off the front of the bulb like a fringe but here they have depth and the shading gives a sense of recession towards the back of the bulb. This attention to the tiniest detail is what makes a true botanical artist.

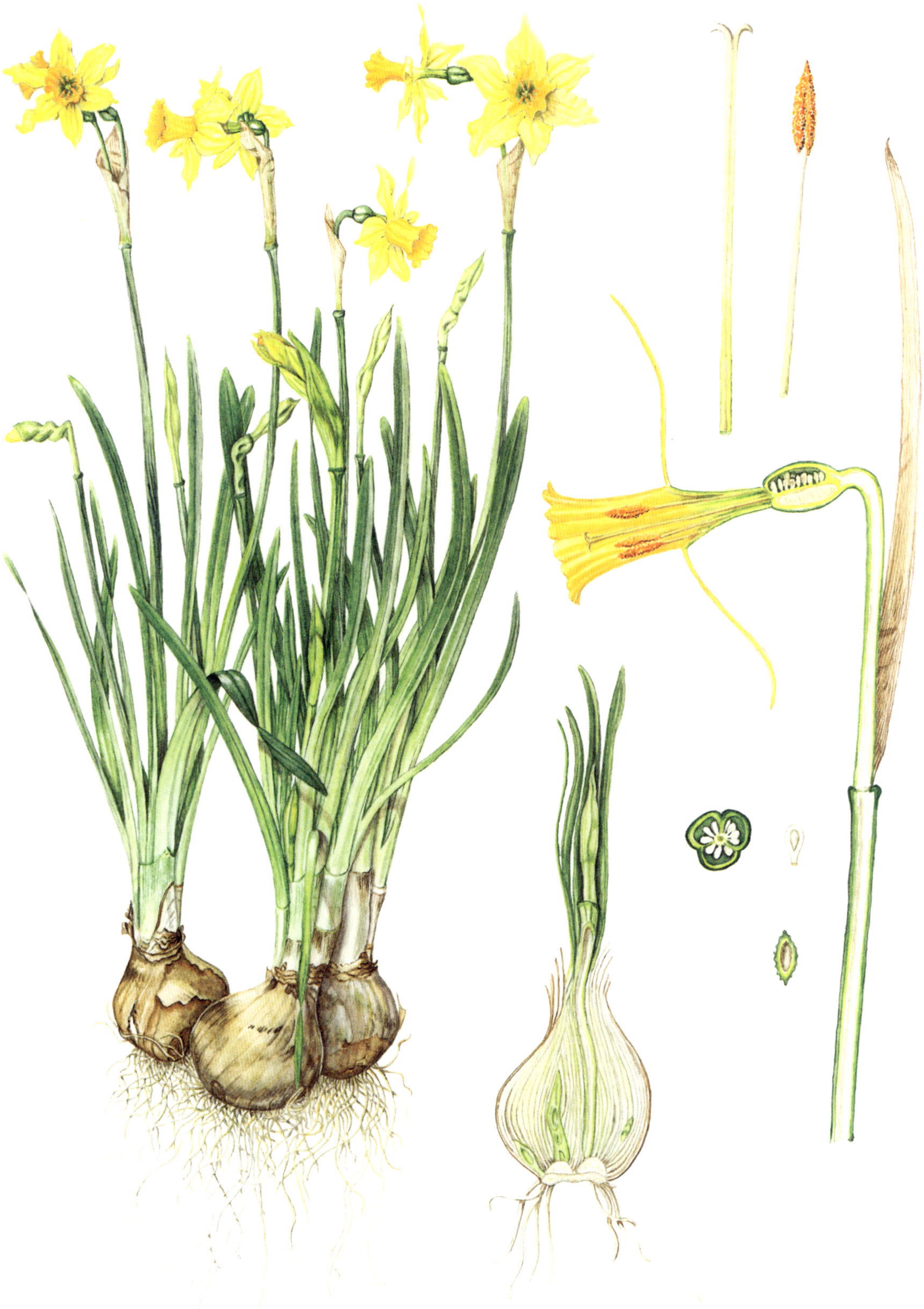

HOLLY FAMILY *Aquifoliaceae*

Common Holly

Ilex aquifolium

Holly is well known as an erect much-branched evergreen shrub, bearing in the spring whitish-green flowers of four petals, and calyx of four divisions, growing in thick clusters in the axils of the leaves. The fruit is the well-known red or yellow berry, giving a vivid touch of colour in contrast to the sombre green of the leaves.

The leaves are shortly stalked, ovate in form, thick and shining; they are sometimes entire, sometimes with wavy outlines and strong, sharply-pointed coarse teeth. The stamens are also four in number, inserted on to the corolla and alternating with the petals. Berries in autumn and winter. The leaves grow spiral-wise on the stem. EC

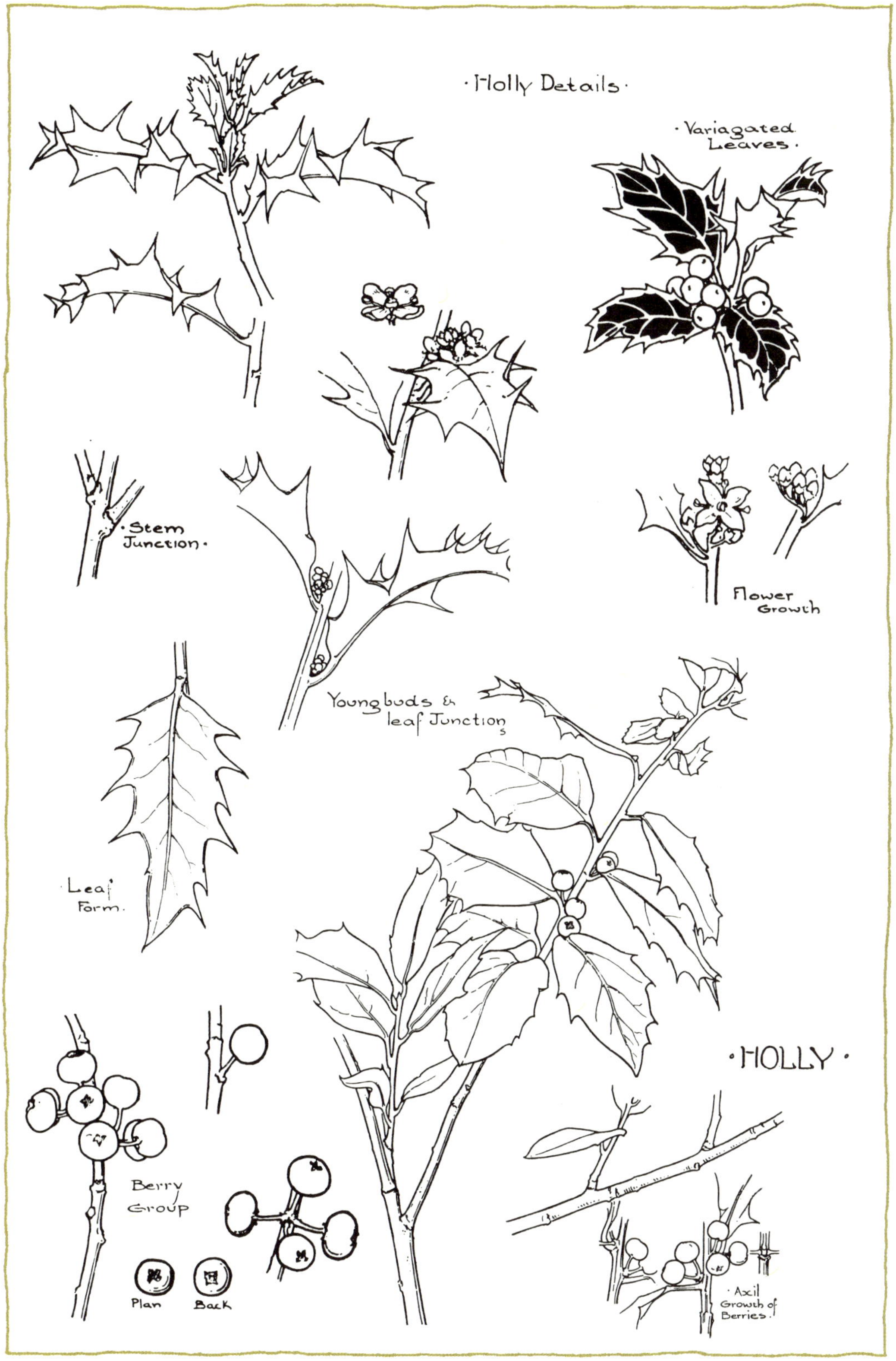
·Holly Details·
·Variagated Leaves·
·Stem Junction·
Flower Growth
Youngbuds & leaf Junctions
·Leaf Form.
·HOLLY·
Berry Group
Plan
Back
·Axil Growth of Berries.

Holly

Ilex aquifolium 'Ferox Argentea'

This variety of holly is known as Hedgehog Holly because of the spines emerging from the top leaf surface as well as around the margin. It pays to observe carefully and make an initial drawing so that the structure is fully understood.

The artist has worked on the buds and flowers, the most transient part of the specimen before tackling the leaves. She used Winsor Lemon for the first wash, the colour of the spines which needed to be retained throughout. Subsequent green washes were applied with care to preserve the spines and highlights and for these she mixed quantities of Rowney Midnight Green, Schmincke May Green and Winsor Perylene Green. In the highlights one sees the stomata, which were delicately stippled in with the point of a brush. A painstaking process demanding time and patience.

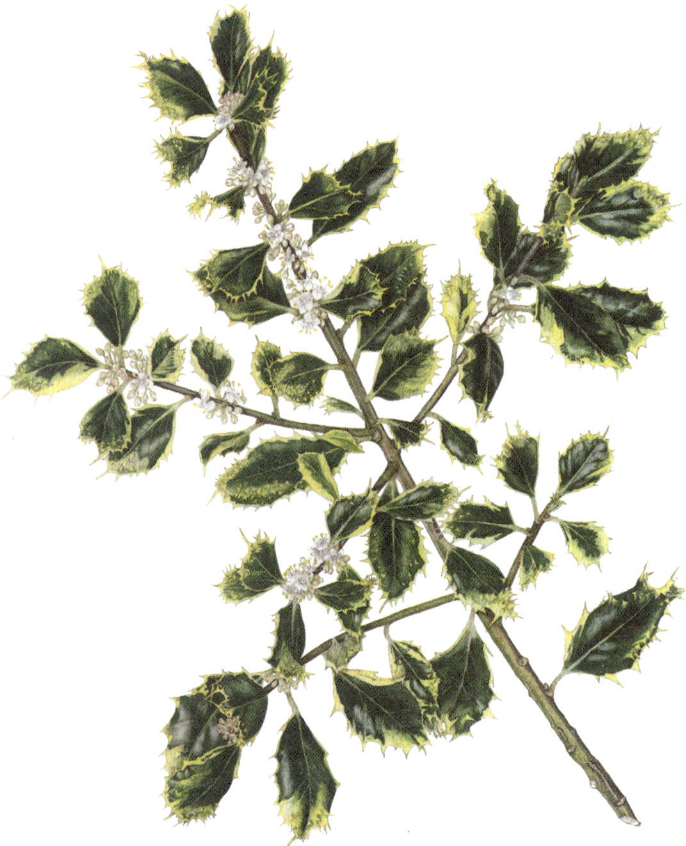

Watercolour, Kay Rees-Davies

Holly

Ilex aquifolium 'Bacciflava'

This is an excellent holly to practice painting glossy dark green foliage. Holly leaves are very thick and leathery, and often the thickness can be seen at the edge which catches the light; the artist must make sure that only one side shows a lighter rim of colour and avoid painting an outline all the way around, which alters the form of the leaf. Stomata show up in the highlights, so these needed to be stippled in with care. Delicate cast shadows and highlights make well-rounded three-dimensional berries. Note the two berries peeping out from behind a leaf; that little touch of yellow breaks up, in a very natural way, what would otherwise be a large expanse of leaves. The hint of Light Red on the new growth is echoed in the green of the reverse leaf colour. The artist has observed every nuance of the plant's character in the search for perfection.

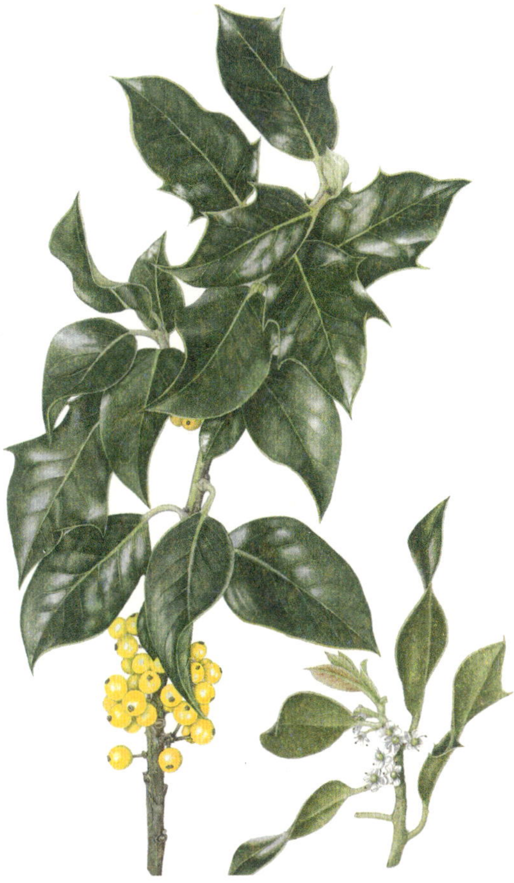

Watercolour, Kay Rees-Davies

ARUM FAMILY *Araceae*

Cuckoo-pint

Arum maculatum

Despite the commonness or profuseness of this plant, which in addition to the above name, bears also the names of Wild Arum, Lords-and-Ladies, and Wake-robin, it is not a very common object during its term of flowering, as it is then hidden by the thick covering and growth of the hedge bottoms where it grows; but when the hedges have thinned down in the autumn you may then see it in its autumn garb – a short thick stem with a group of bright red berries on the top. The leaves are large and glossy, and arrow-head shape or ovate-hastate, sometimes spotted with purple. The inflorescence is insignificant from our point of view, but is nevertheless interesting. The flowers are very small and are borne in rings on a stout column, which is continued upward to some length and terminates in a club-like head; this is called the spadix, near the base of which the large greenish spathe, like a large bract, springs and encloses the greater part of the spadix, growing some distance beyond the top of it, but not completely surrounding it, like a pointed hood. Beneath the ring of florets are a number of sessile ovaries with each a style and stigma. When the berries ripen the spathe and upper portion of the spadix have fallen away, leaving for the winter the aforementioned group of red berries. The root is a tuber, and the leaves are carried on long radical stalks clothed at the base by sheaths. It may be met with in April and May. EC

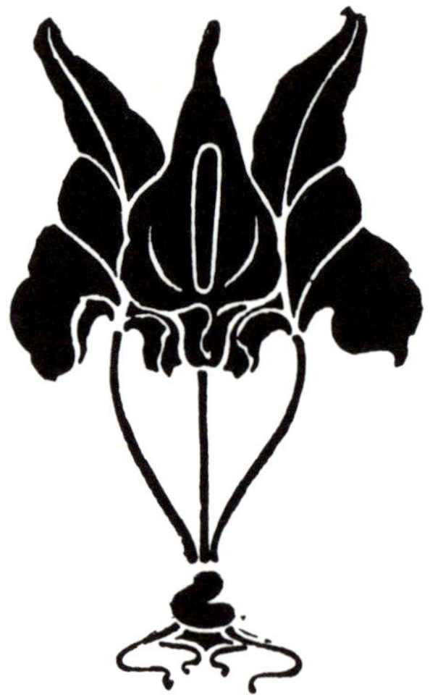

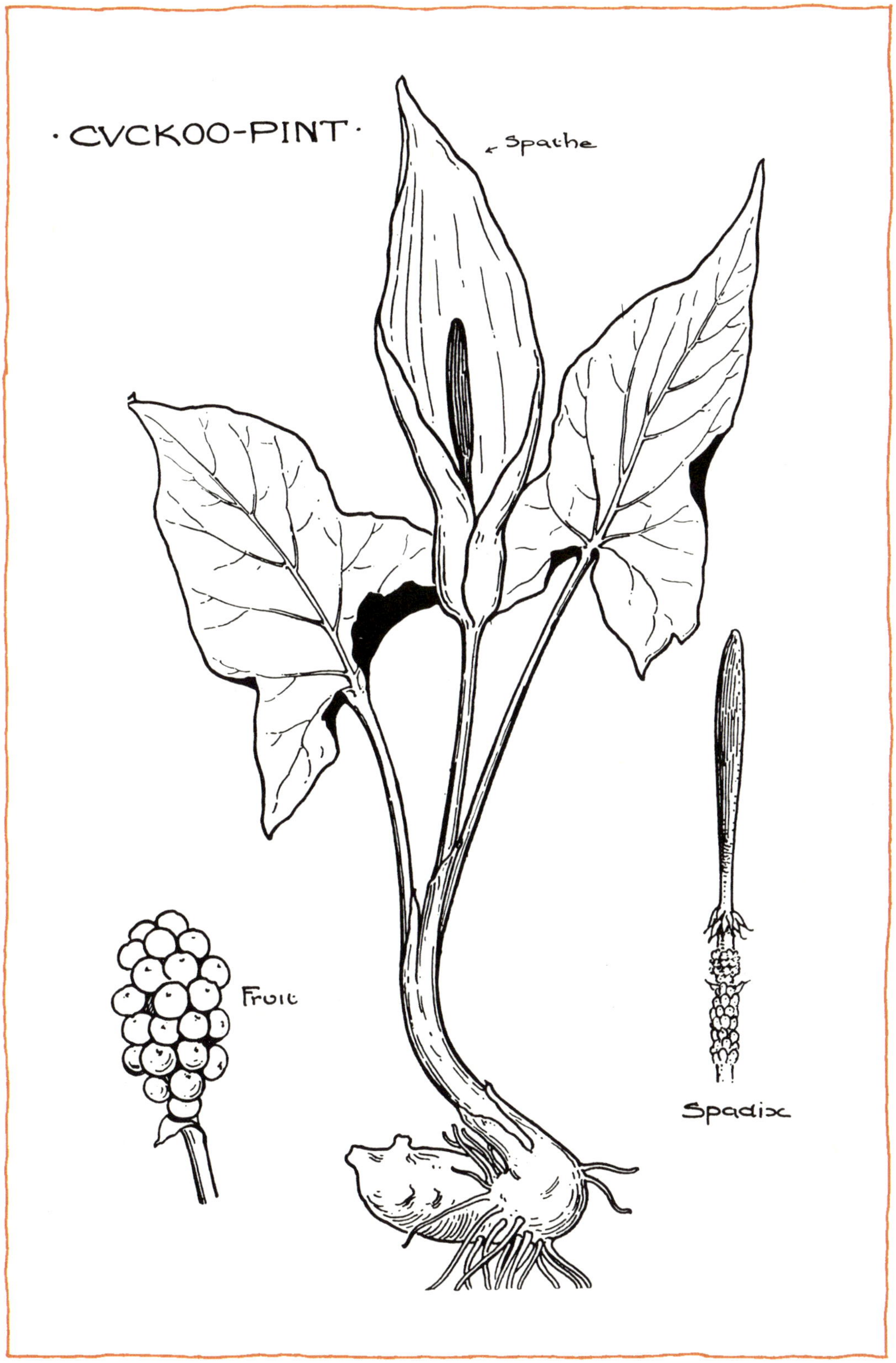
·CVCKOO-PINT·
Spathe
Fruit
Spadix

Calla Lily

Zantedeschia 'Black Star'

Painting this dramatic study of what must be one of the darkest flowers in cultivation gave the artist a lot of pleasure and as always the result is stunning. The sculptural form of the spathes is shown off by the curved leaves, with a shiny texture confirmed by soft highlights. These, combined with the white flecks and colour transference of purple-black from the spathes to the stems and midribs, all create a great deal of visual impact. The artist painted around the white flecks, which provides quite a challenge for even the most experienced painter.

The juvenile leaves are unusual as they start off the same deep purple-black as the flowers and gradually turn green as they mature. The flower stems also have a few white specks at the top end and even the spadex is dotted with white pollen, which can just be seen peeking out from the central spathe.

The artist made the painting especially for this book and in a very short time, so she is to be congratulated at undertaking such a complex work in a hurry. For the flowers she used mixes of Winsor & Newton Perylene Violet, Indigo and Neutral Tint, while for the reverse side of the leaves she used Daniel Smith Deep Sap Green mixed with Daler-Rowney Vivid Green and Midnight Green. The upper leaf surface was painted with Daniel Smith Deep Sap Green with Daler-Rowney Vivid Green and Winsor & Newton Perylene Green and Permanent Sap Green.

Watercolour, Kay Rees-Davies

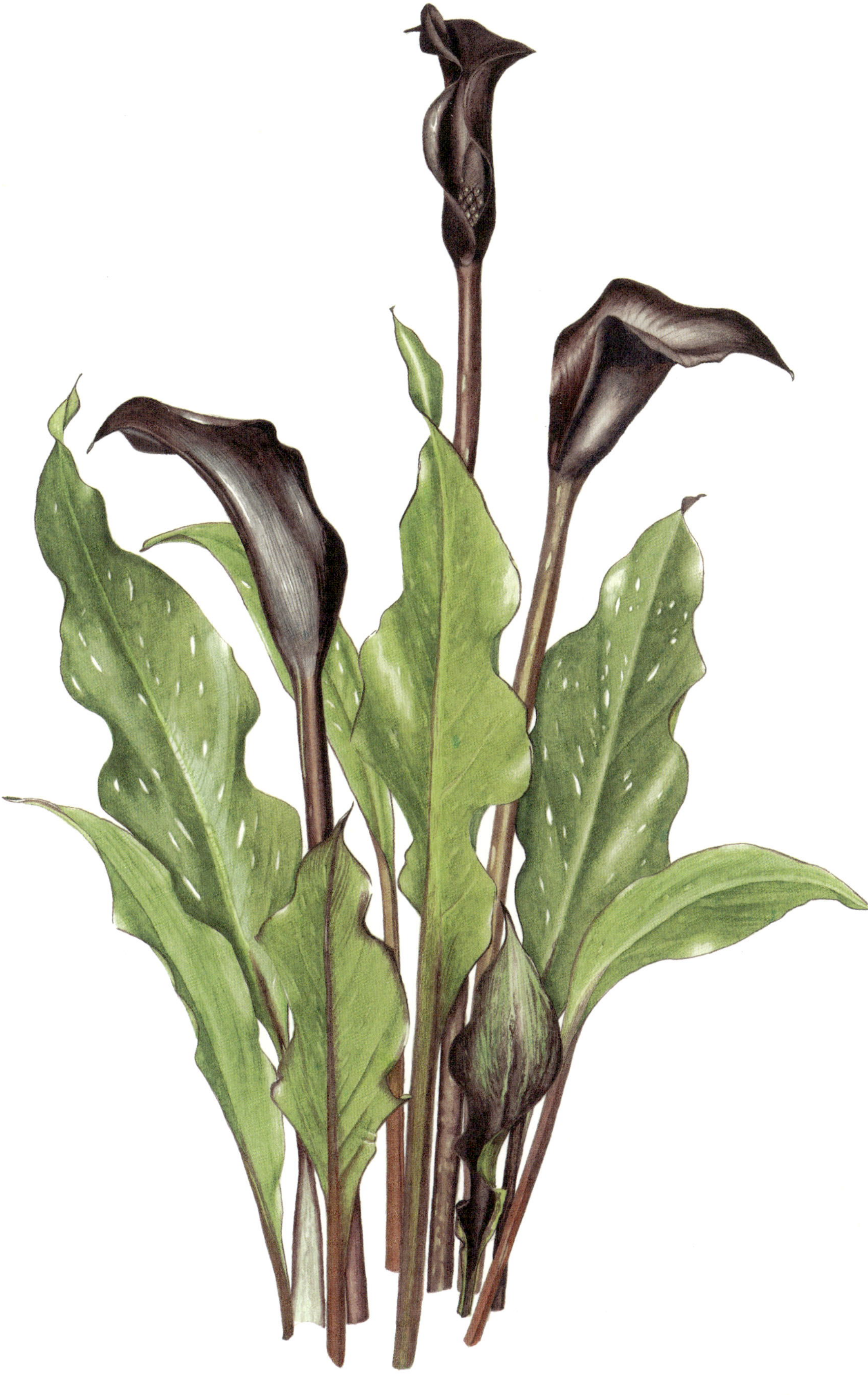

IVY FAMILY *Araliaceae*

Common Ivy

Hedera helix

Of all the climbing plants perhaps the Ivy is the last that could be spared. We are not only bound to it by many ties and associations of a more or less sentimental nature, but it appeals to us also as a great decorator of our ruined shrines. It belongs, of course, to the family of climbers. The flower consists of five petals, and a calyx, of five short teeth. They grow in umbels at the ends of branches; there are five stamens and a short style. Flowers appear in October, but the fruit is not ripe until the following spring. The leaves vary in outline very much, sometimes being deeply lobed or five-pointed, and sometimes simple. The natural order of their growth on the stem is alternate. EC

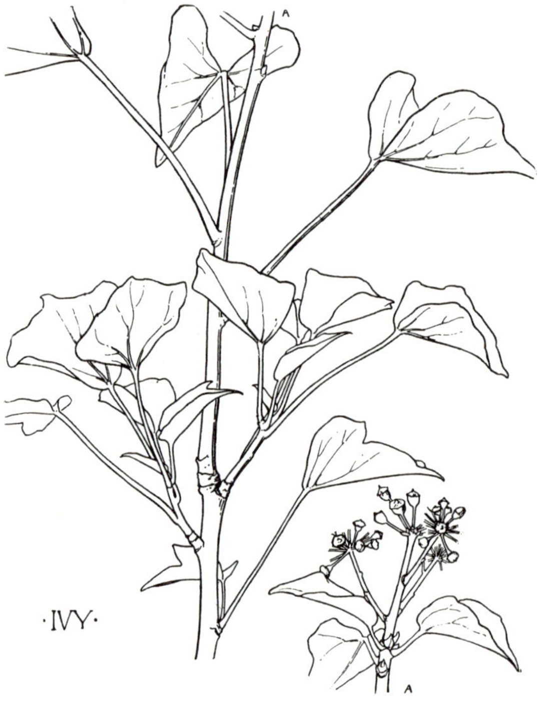

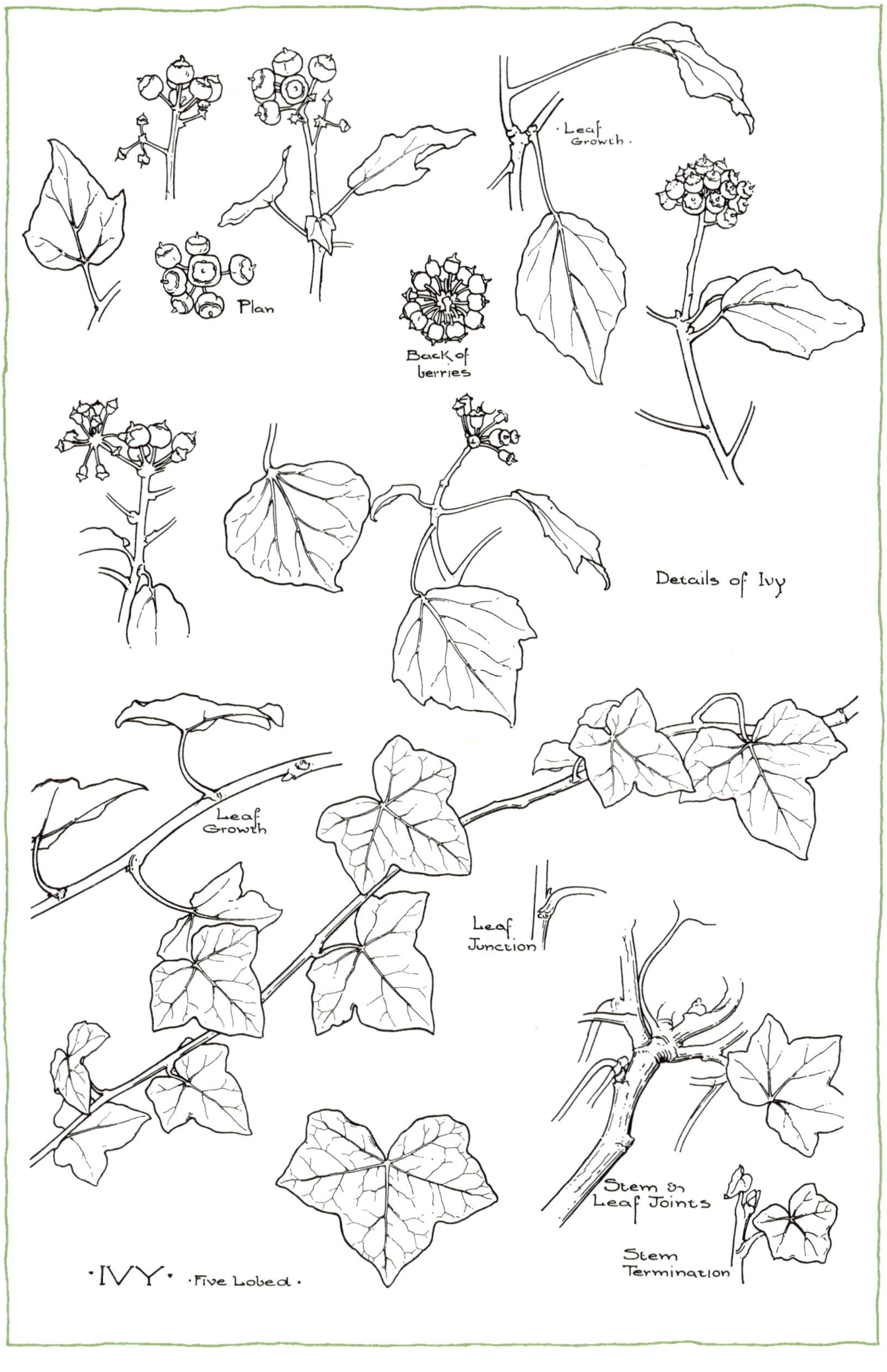
Plan
Back of berries
· Leaf Growth ·
Details of Ivy
Leaf Growth
Leaf Junction
Stem & Leaf Joints
Stem Termination
· IVY · · Five Lobed ·

Ivy

Hedera helix

This composition could so easily be overcrowded because of the numerous and substantial leaves. The artist has used her skills with graphite to create a sense of depth and openness which would otherwise be missing. Ivy flowers were unavailable at the time this was painted, but the fruit is shown from its immature lime-green state through ripening to the mature, almost black berry. The juvenile leaves are also shown.

Note the manner in which the short spray is placed at the bottom left. This enables the tiny young tendril to drop below the level of the two hard woody stems, which breaks up the otherwise rigid bottom line. This painting is one of a series which the artist did at the request of Liverpool University. Core samples taken from the site of the old Senate Building yielded evidence of our truly indigenous plants dating from 2000 years ago.

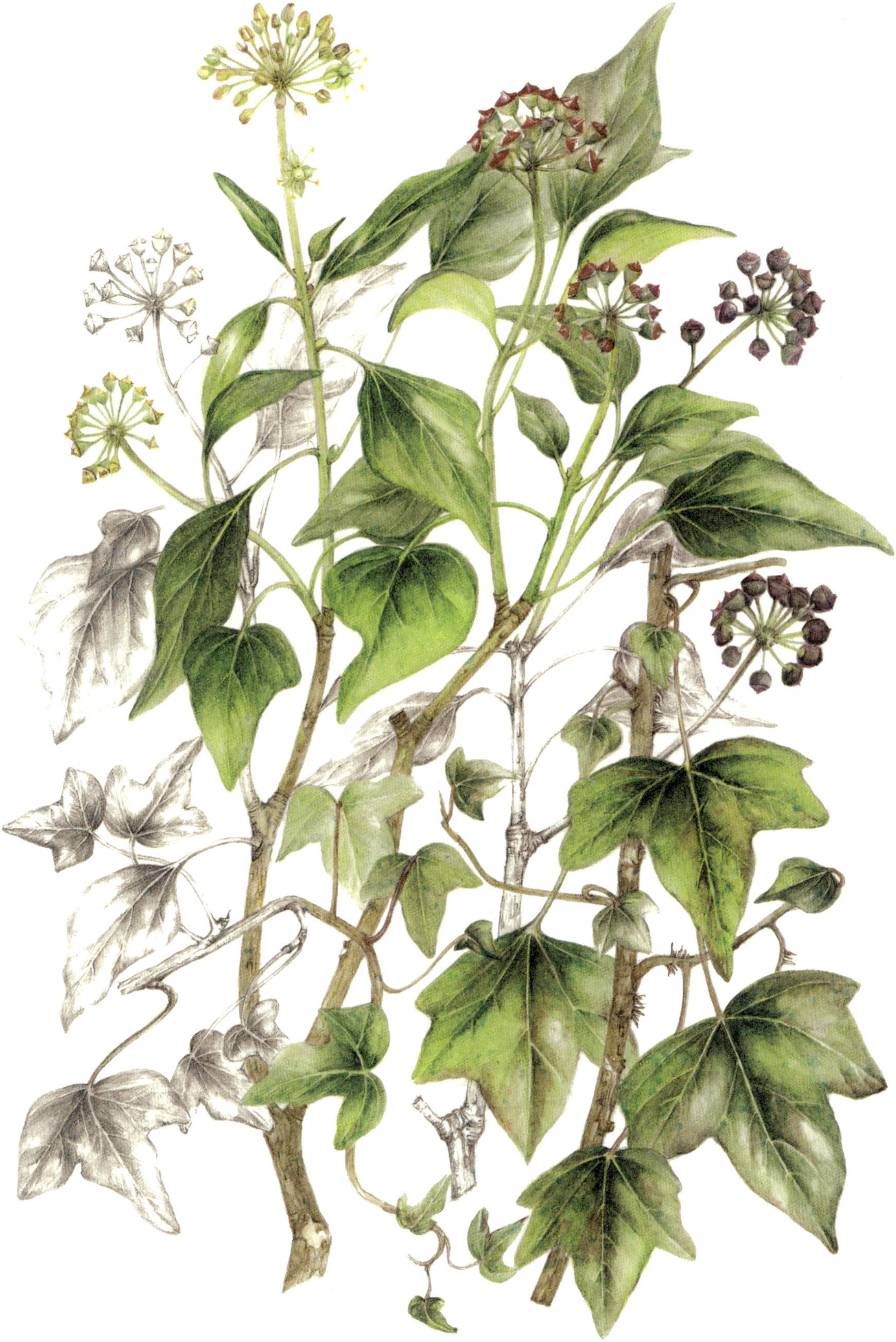

DAISY FAMILY *Asteraceae*

Ox-eye Daisy

Chrysanthemum leucanthemum

This is a member of the large order of composite flowers; it assists greatly in turning our mowing grass fields, where it usually grows in groups, into luxuriant flower gardens. It grows from one to two feet in height. The radical leaves or root leaves are stalked and obovate in form, while those from the long flower stems are stalkless or sessile, thinner and coarsely serrated, alternating up the stem. The flower heads are solitary on terminal stems. Petals long and white, notched at the outer extremity, centre yellow. Stems sometimes branched. The involucre consists of a series of green scales overlapping each other and are membranaceous at their edges. This flower is the original of the Chrysanthemum. EC

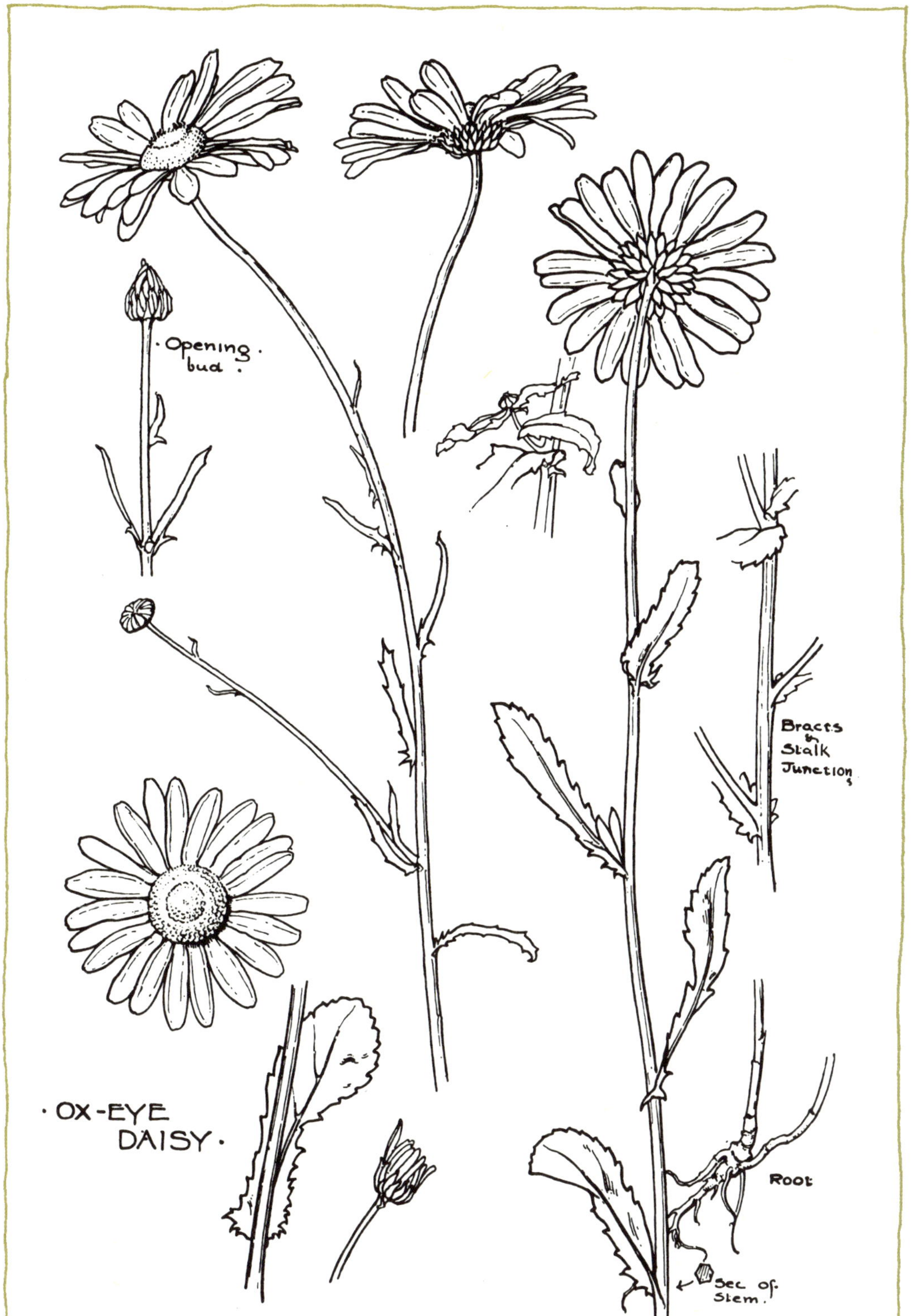
· Opening ·
bud ·
Bracts
&
Stalk
Junctions
· OX-EYE
DAISY ·
Root
Sec of
Stem.

Chrysanthemum

Chrysanthemum

The variety of form and colour to be found in the Chrysanthemum is endless, but the simpler forms are more useful, from the student's point of view, than the more complex ones.

The plant is erect and branching, with single flowers on terminal stems, or it is a shrub with flowers in corymbs. The flower-heads are radiating, consisting of a number of long florets, tube-like for a portion of their length, the outer ones being the largest, diminishing in size towards the centre, which is a compact mass of small florets. The calyx is formed of close scaly bracts, and thin pointed bracts occur on and at the base of the flower-stalks. The bud forms are very decorative features, and frequently grow from the axils of the leaves, or are surrounded by a leafy whorl.

The leaves vary a good deal on different plants, but all have the same broad characteristics; they are mostly lobed, some of them almost to the midrib, and deeply serrated, with broad and narrow stipules at their junctions, some of which take the form of separate small leaves, and others are wing-like appendages to the petiole. The growth up the stem is in this case a spiral. Varieties of the plant may be found from May to December; the example here given is an autumn-flowering variety. EC

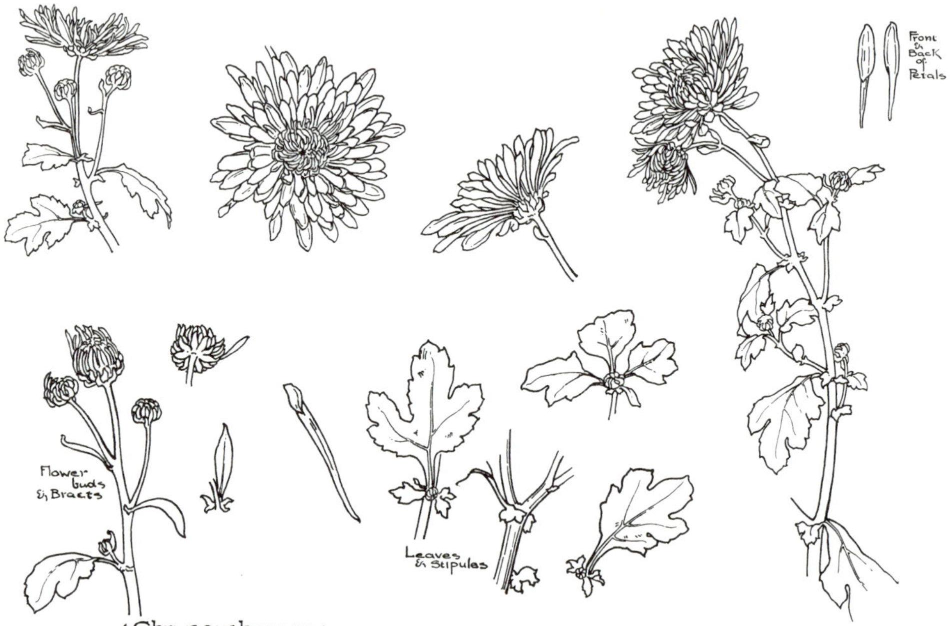

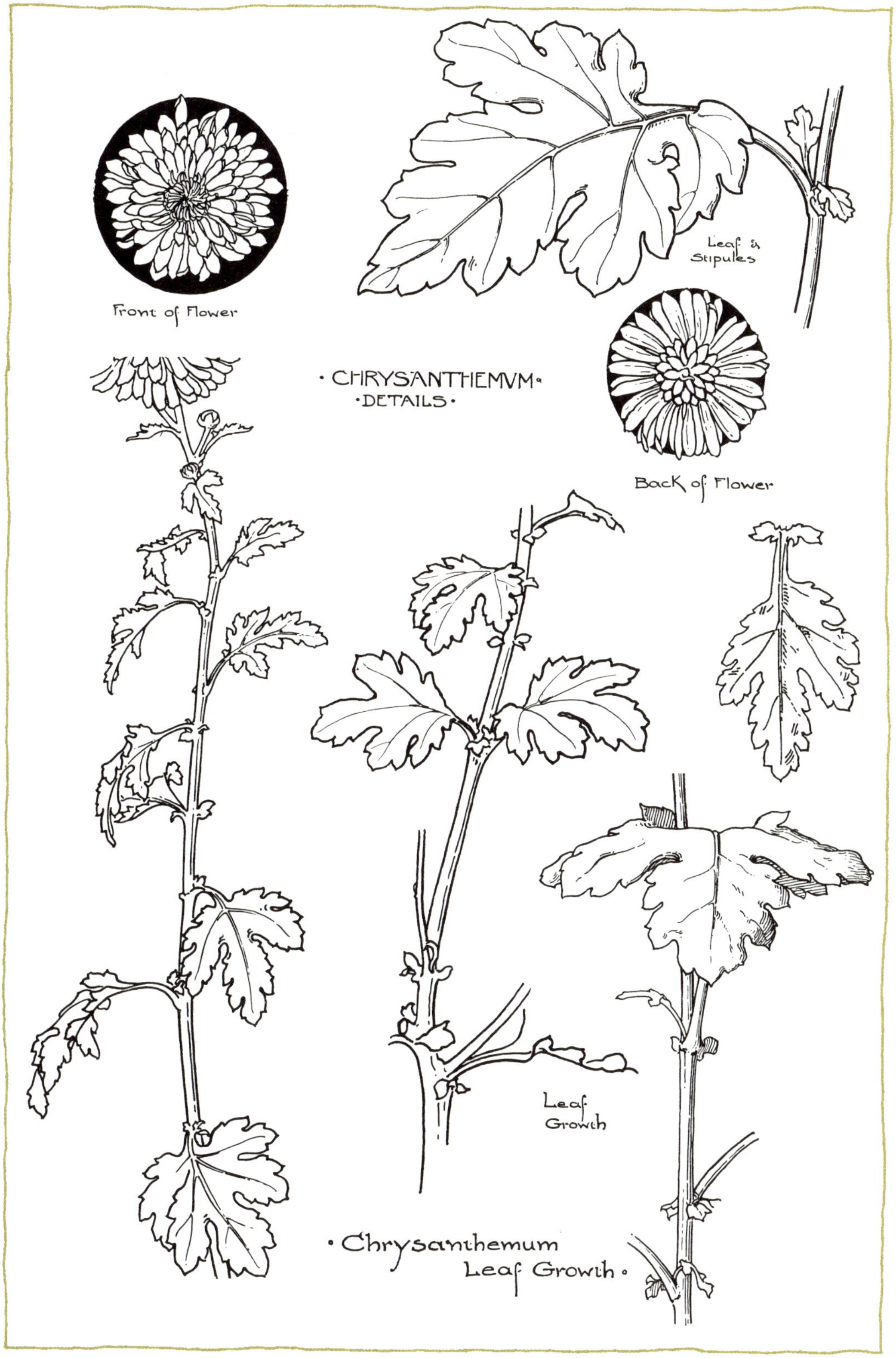
Front of Flower
Leaf & Stipules
· CHRYSANTHEMUM ·
· DETAILS ·
Back of Flower
Leaf Growth
· Chrysanthemum Leaf Growth ·

Chrysanthemum

Chrysanthemum 'Anastasia'

This very striking bloom has a surprising hint of turquoise in the petals and the artist supplied a comprehensive explanation of the method she used to capture its brilliance. She painted the shadows first, using a technique which she refers to as harmonic shadows. This consists of mixing a grey from the three primary colours which will appear later in the painting to ensure that the shadows are in harmony with the subject's true colour. In this case she used Winsor & Newton Blue (Green Shade) for the turquoise hint, plus Lemon Yellow with a touch of Permanent Alizarin Crimson to slightly mute the resulting green. This shadow colour was used for the petals and the foliage, though the washes were less diluted on the foliage so that they would show through the final glaze of dark green. This was made by adding French Ultramarine to the green mix, its granulating quality giving texture to the leaves.

The artist worked her way around the flower-head a few petals at a time, first with one or two washes of shadow colour and then with up to four washes of true colour. This process takes time, but with a long-lasting flower such as 'Anastasia' this is not a problem. In fact, as the petal arrangement remains consistent in the flowers, another can be substituted if the first dies before the painting is finished.

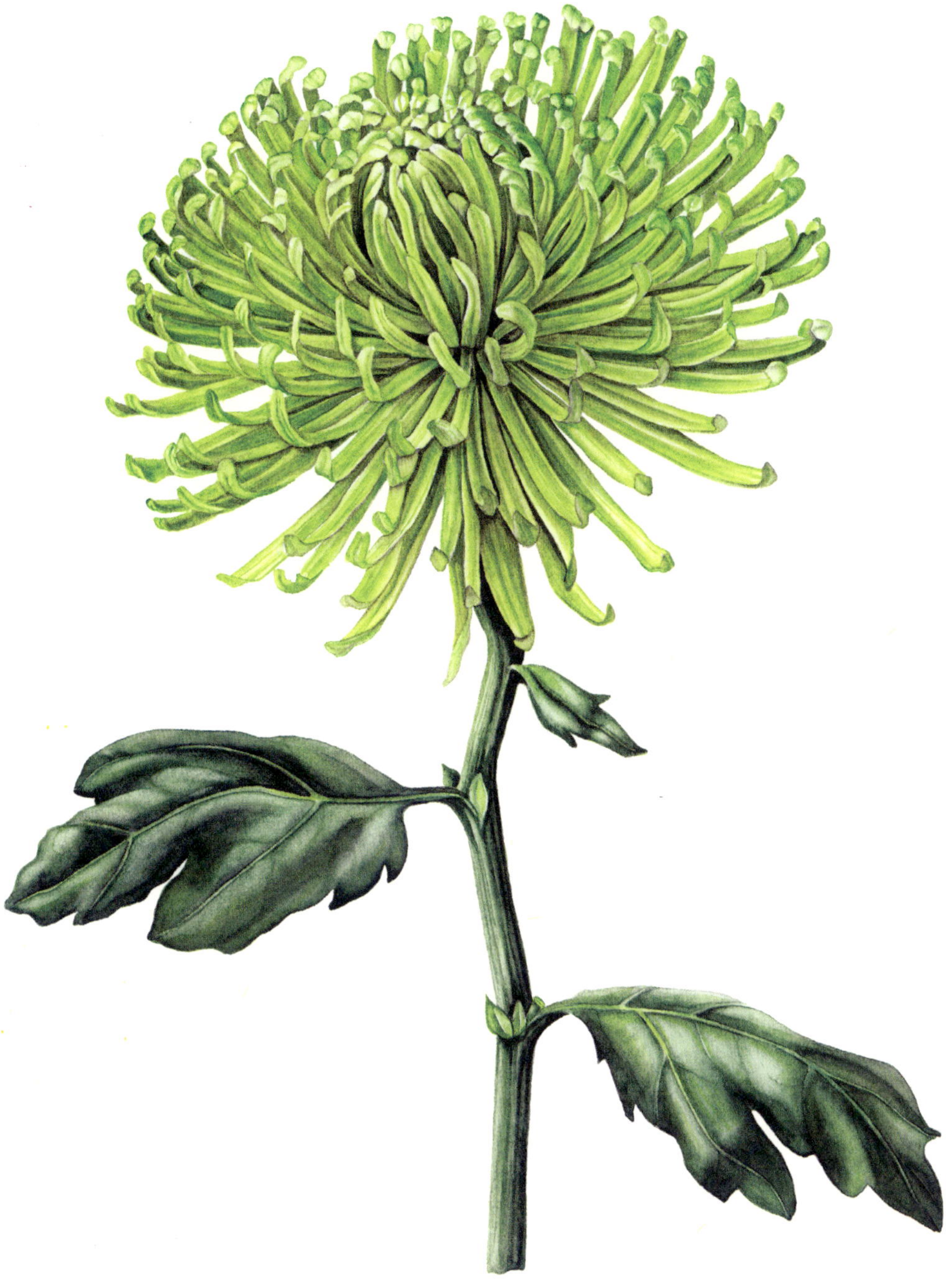

Watercolour, Sandrine Maugy

Dahlia

Dahlia

The example here given is one or the single varieties, which offer greater facilities to the artist than the complex double ones.

It is a vigorous-looking, shrub-like plant, bearing a dark-green foliage and rich, variously coloured blooms, making a good show of colour in any garden during August and September.

The flowers are of the composite order, consisting of an outer ring of petals, six or eight in number, the centre being formed of closely packed yellow florets. The calyx is of green sepals, and there is also an epi-calyx. The plant is much branched, and the flowers are borne singly on long stalks. The leaves are opposite, the lower ones consisting of three or more segments or leaflets, the upper ones are simple, and all are serrated. The fruit forms a conspicuous and interesting feature. The natural size of the flower is from two to three inches across.

EC

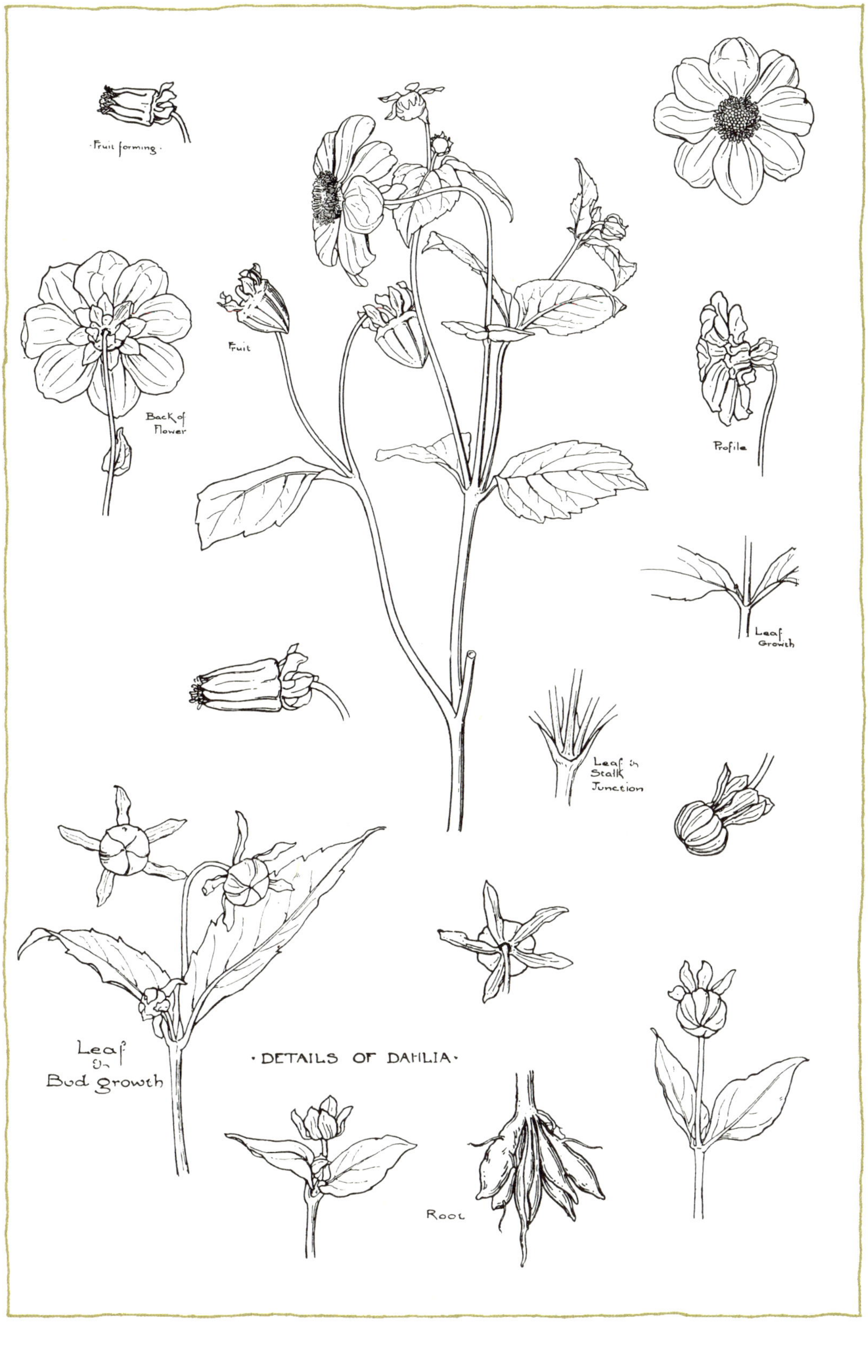
·Fruit forming·
Fruit
Back of Flower
Profile
Leaf Growth
Leaf in Stalk Junction
Leaf & Bud growth
·DETAILS OF DAHLIA·
Root

Pink Dahlias

The ability to tackle a large and complex painting of this nature comes after many years of practice coupled with a hefty dose of natural talent, which sadly no one can teach. In the case of 'Pink Dahlias', one of the first things to impress the viewer is the complexity of the stems and leaves, showing that this artist is not afraid of massed foliage. So many promising paintings are ruined by unnatural, badly mixed greens, which is why it is so important for a student to spend time preparing green colour charts. These are invaluable for future colour reference and save much time in the long run.

Colour transference of deep magenta into some of the stems helps to merge the upper and lower areas of the painting, while the light underside of the leaf in the bottom left quadrant adds an additional note of interest, breaking up what would otherwise have been a density of dark leaves. It is the stem to which this leaf is attached that carries the foremost flower, the central one of the three single dahlias, identified as 'Roxy'. All the other foliage has been built up around this, gradually placing stems to achieve a sense of depth and making sure they disappear and re-emerge from behind the leaves correctly. My maxim for students is 'Don't block your options' and it is particularly apt for paintings of this kind, as a badly placed stem can totally ruin a composition. Rescue is rarely possible and any attempt to fudge things will always be detected by the discerning eye.

The paler pink decorative dahlias help to lighten the overall study and numerous buds create a truly life-like arrangement. The simpler tones of these flowers were built up using washes of Permanent Rose, while the 'Roxy' dahlias were painted using Quinacridone Magenta with Holbein Bright Rose, which added translucency to some petals. Perylene Maroon mixed with Winsor Purple captured the deep burgundy centres, with the addition of a little Payne's Grey giving more depth to the shadows.

The leaf colours were similar for both varieties; the artist used a base of Oxide of Chromium with Perylene Green added to capture the blue tones, while Hooker's Green gave vibrancy to the lighter areas. Pale washes of Oxide of Chromium covered the leaf undersurfaces, with a touch of Perylene Green or Payne's Grey for the shadows. The stems required Perylene Red with washes of Olive Green, while the buds were painted with washes of Green Gold over Permanent Sap Green. The aritst used Winsor & Newton Artists' colours unless otherwise stated.

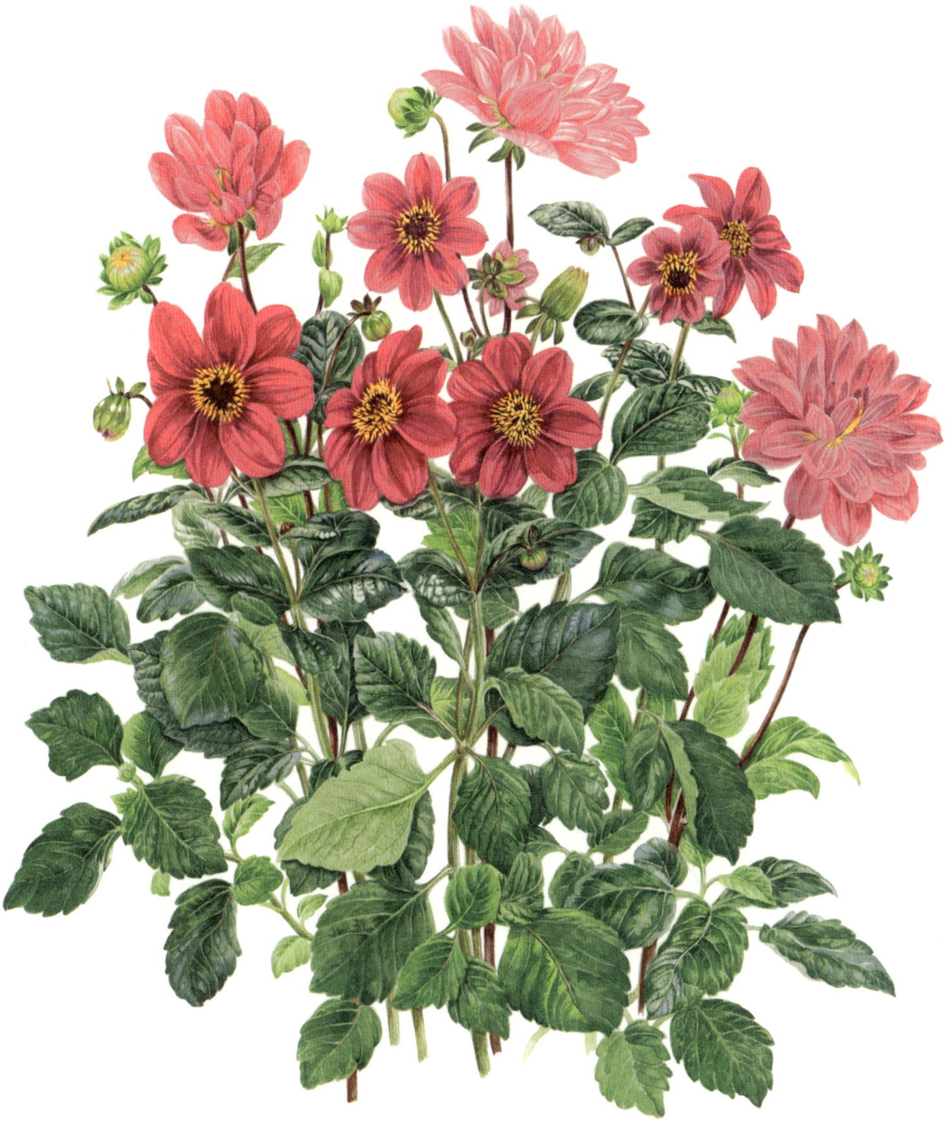

Watercolour, Sandra Wall Armitage

Globe artichoke

Cynara scolymus

The globe artichoke is a versatile plant, at home in the herbaceous border or the vegetable garden and interesting to paint whether in bloom or earlier, at the edible stage. There are one or two cultivars suitable for cool climates, allowing British artists the pleasure of painting the magnificent purple flowers, which are also very attractive to bees.

Here we see a typical greengrocer's specimen, which the artist chose to paint for one of his course assignments. This is the immature flower bud which, dissected laterally, shows the layers of edible scales, the pale edible heart at the top of the stem and, above that, the prickly and inedible choke, which is composed of numerous florets.

Careful observation and some excellent variation in tone have produced a very life-like study which has certainly worked well from the dissection point of view. The outer scales could have retained a few lighter tones as one gets the impression here of an ageing specimen, which perhaps it was. However, the ribbed stems are very well painted and the cut ends give us some idea of the texture.

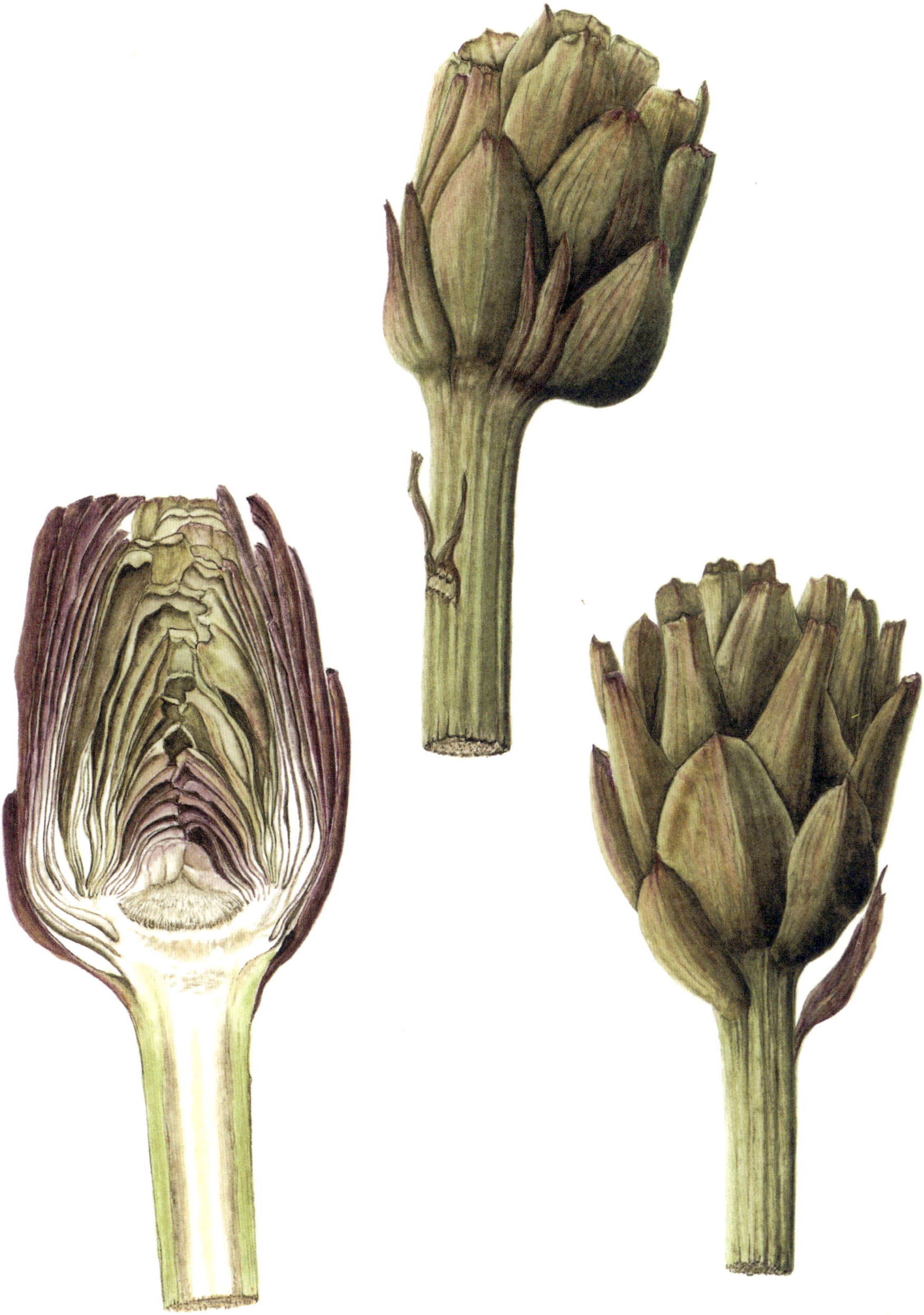

Watercolour, Peter Gravett

Sunflower
Helianthus

Occasionally a truly natural talent comes to light. The artist says that she didn't know that she had the ability, yet within ten months this was an example of her work, a single-species study required for her fifth assignment. No photograph can do justice to the fine pencil work and exquisite detail; this is as close to perfection as I have ever seen in 30 years of teaching botanical art.

The colours and tones of the sunflower are seamlessly merged, particularly on the leaves where the variation in the veins, following the contours and reflecting the light, makes them glow with life. The ribbed stems are dense with tiny hairs, light against dark or dark against light, both in paint and pencil, so that one can sense the rough, slightly sticky texture which extends to the mass of sepals in the graphite rear view of the plant.

There is little any tutor can say when this level of expertise is encountered, except to encourage the student and pray that botanical art will always play a part in his or her life. Lucky will be the owner of any painting or drawing which bears this artist's signature.

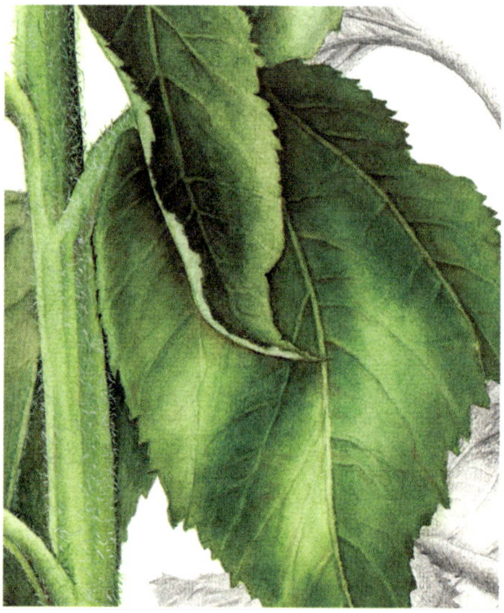

This enlarged section shows the extent of the fine detail that the artist has achieved. Most artwork will be made to appear sharper with crisp outlines when the size is reduced. The test of a true botanical illustration, or a miniature, is the quality displayed when the subject is enlarged. This example speaks for itself.

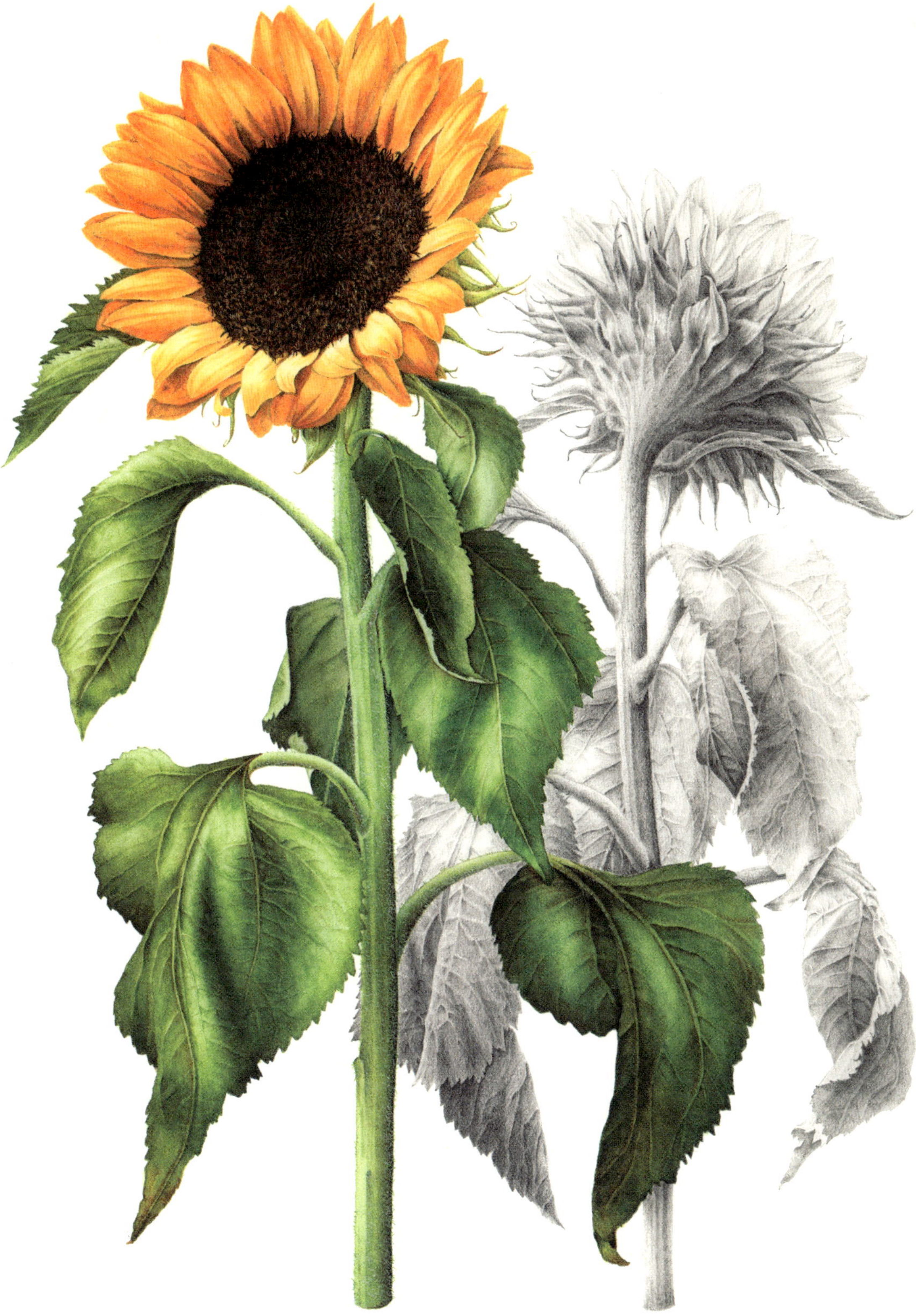

Dandelion

Leontodon taraxacum

Few flowers offer more material for decorative purposes than 'this vulgar herb', the homely Dandelion. The bright yellow flowers may be found the greater part of the year round along the roadside and on waste land, as well as in more cultivated spots. It is a composite flower, with long, narrow, strap-shaped petals, toothed. When these decay the inner scales of the involucre close and the seed ripens, opening out again into the well-known fairy-like seed-head, which is scattered by the wind broadcast. The leaves and flower-stalks grow straight from the root, the flower-stems being from six to eight inches long. There is considerable difference in the form of the leaf, some being much more deeply lobed and notched than others. Stalks hollow. Stamens five, one style, stigma cleft in two, to each floret. The leaf is, with regard to the way in which the margin is divided, an example of the *runcinate* form. The root-stock terminates in a long tap-root.

EC

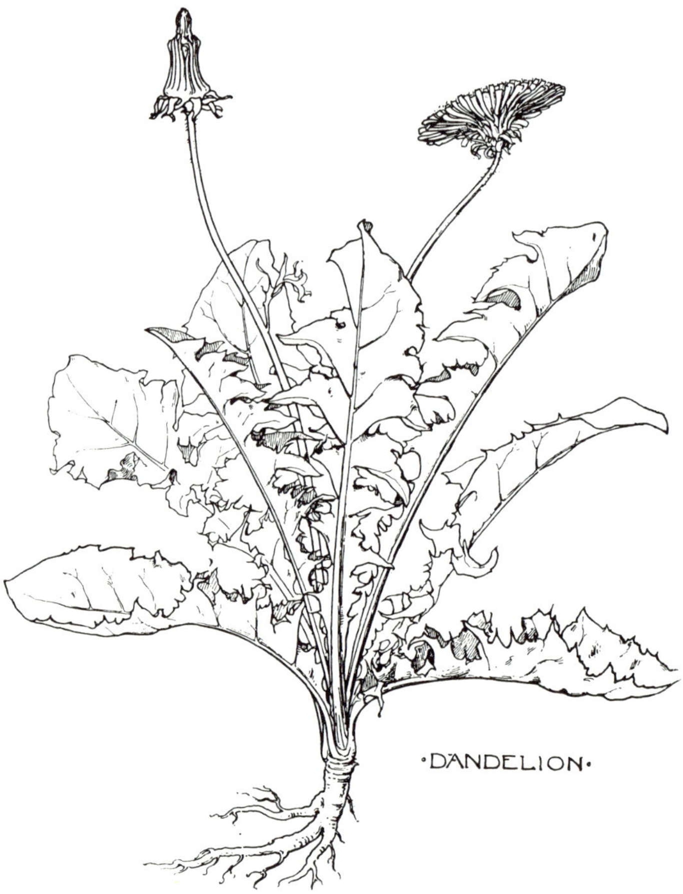

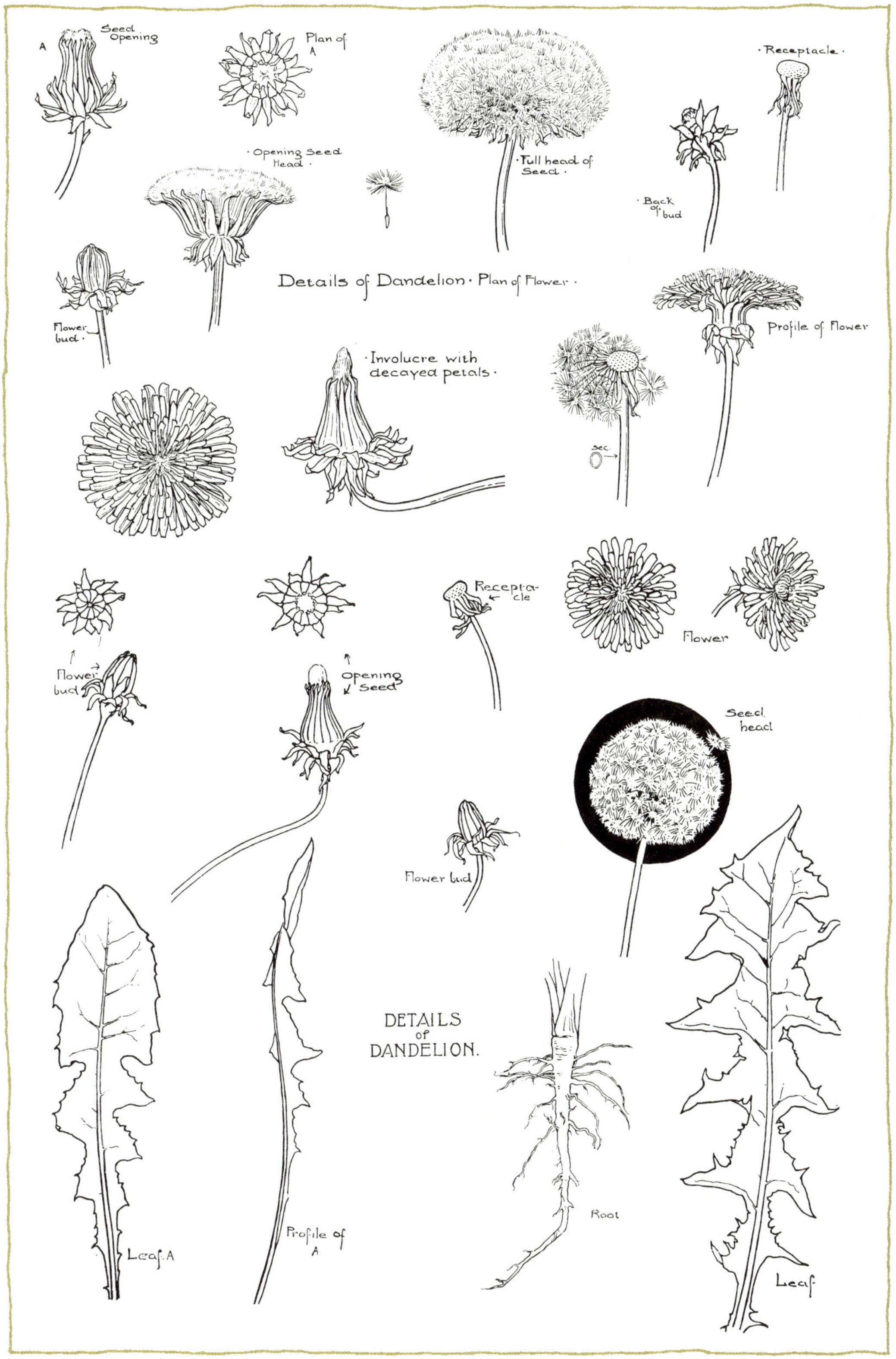
Seed Opening
A
Plan of A
Full head of Seed
Receptacle
Back of bud
Opening Seed Head
Details of Dandelion · Plan of Flower ·
Flower bud
Profile of Flower
Involucre with decayed petals
sec.
Flower bud
Opening Seed
Receptacle
Flower
Seed head
Flower bud
DETAILS of DANDELION.
Leaf. A
Profile of A
Root
Leaf

Dandelion

Taraxacum officinale

Separated by more than 100 years, this modern study of a Dandelion closely resembles the original drawing in the *Handbook* but with the added interest of seed heads both emerging or dehiscing and dispersing. the artist made good use of graphite for this purpose and tells me that she used five grades of pencil: H, HB, 2H, B and 2B. With the graphite leaves in the background, this helps to keep the whole study from becoming too dense, which can so easily happen when many leaves emerge from a central rosette.

One might of course paint the furthest leaves with paler washes of colour to create recession; this is certainly acceptable for the flower painter, but can be frowned upon by some professional bodies who expect a botanical illustration to be given the same weight throughout. For artists who are not seeking a medal for their work a balance can be struck by taking a certain amount of artistic licence, or if the nerve fails, falling back on graphite.

Finally, the tap-root helps to anchor the composition, while the introduction of the brown shades brings warmth to the painting.

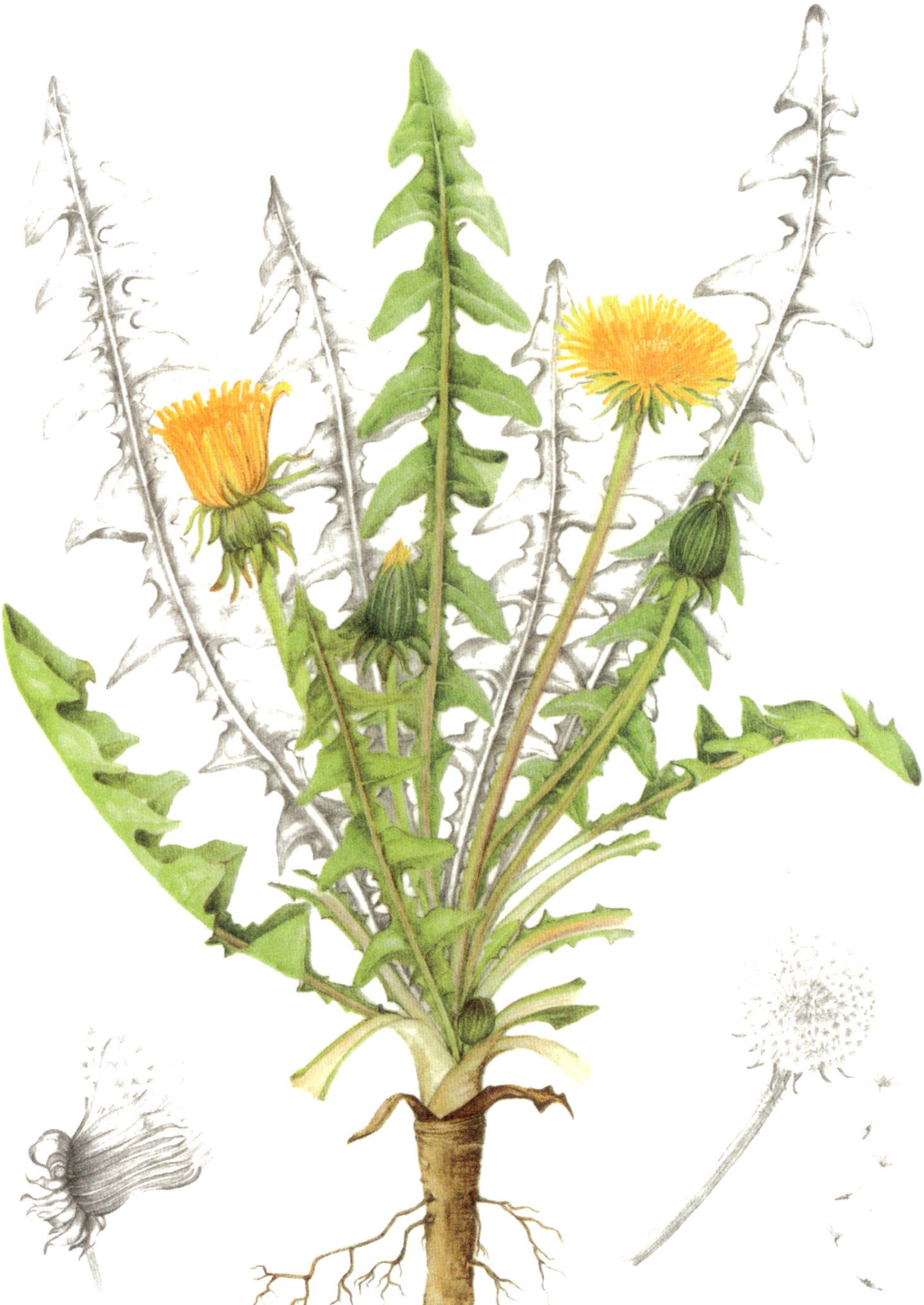

MUSTARD FAMILY *Brassicaceae*

Red cabbage

Brassica oleracea, Capitata group

As the artist grows his own vegetables, he was able to choose a more interesting specimen to paint than the neatly trimmed cabbages available in the supermarkets. Discoloured or caterpillar-nibbled outer leaves are worth seeking out when the purpose is art rather than food.

He used all Winsor and Newton paints, Indanthrene Blue with Perylene Maroon and a touch of Raw Sienna to create a delicate violet-grey mix for the first pale wash. He was careful not to paint over the holes in the leaves where a less experienced artist might have used masking fluid to block them out. His method of adding another pigment while the previous wash is still wet, allowing them to mix, is also a mark of his ability to handle colour and ensures that neither the colour or tone is too uniform.

With very pale and very dark areas quickly established, the artist produced a fairly loose image with some degree of form which was retained and worked up in the finished painting, particularly the light undulating edges of the leaves. It is easier to darken later on, whereas lightening a dark surface can result in overworking. He used a stronger mix of colour to darken tones and also to build up veins, some of which stood proud while others were recessed. He also noted that some shadows were warm, others cool. The initial mix of pigment was used with less water to create a dark dull violet. The central glossy red leaves were painted with Perylene Maroon and a touch of Transparent Yellow. The latter was also used to create the fairly bright green patches on some leaves. The dead leaves at the base of the cabbage required Raw Sienna varied with Indanthrene Blue and Perylene Maroon. This area acts as a foil to the rest of the plant in terms of colour, texture and a sense of decay. Details such as fine veins, thin shadows on the edges of holes, and crinkling of leaf edges were left until last, as were the very darkest tones which are adjacent or very close to the lightest tones. It is this that creates the three-dimensional image.

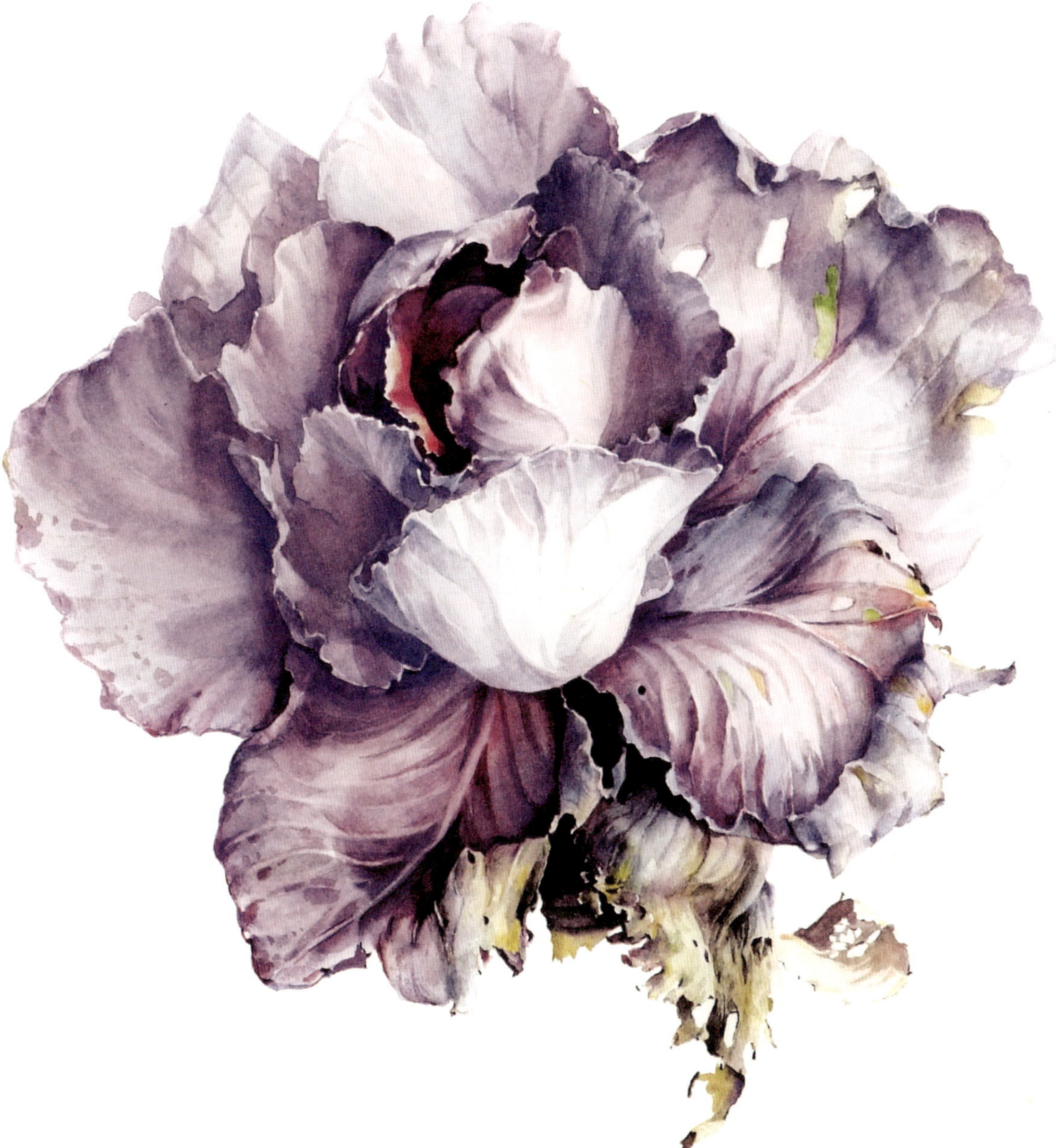

Watercolour, Paul Fennel

Brussels Sprouts

Brassica oleracea, Gemnifera group

This exemplary study of a humble stalk of Brussels sprouts forces one to look into it deeply and marvel at the beauty displayed, not least in the finely wrought veins. From the prominent midribs to the most delicate tracery, the artist has shaded with care so that the difference between upper and lower leaf surfaces are clearly displayed. Shading has also been used to capture the curl of the leaves on the side furthest from the light source, with a disappearing edge in two places, all of which adds to the realism.

Note also how the top leaves have been delicately shaded with pale mauve, a colour which often shows up in members of the brassica family. This attention to detail has been extended to each individual sprout, and not content with that, the artist has given us something of interest right at the bottom of the painting by cutting a sprout in half and the stalk on the diagonal so that we see the inner structure.

The artist did her usual careful sketchbook preparation by painting two of the top leaves. Her greens throughout were mixed from Winsor and Newton paints French Ultramarine with Cadmium Yellow in varying quantities, to which she added Cadmium Lemon, Cadmium Red Deep, Winsor Violet and Winsor Blue (Green Shade) as required.

Watercolour, Minna Keeler

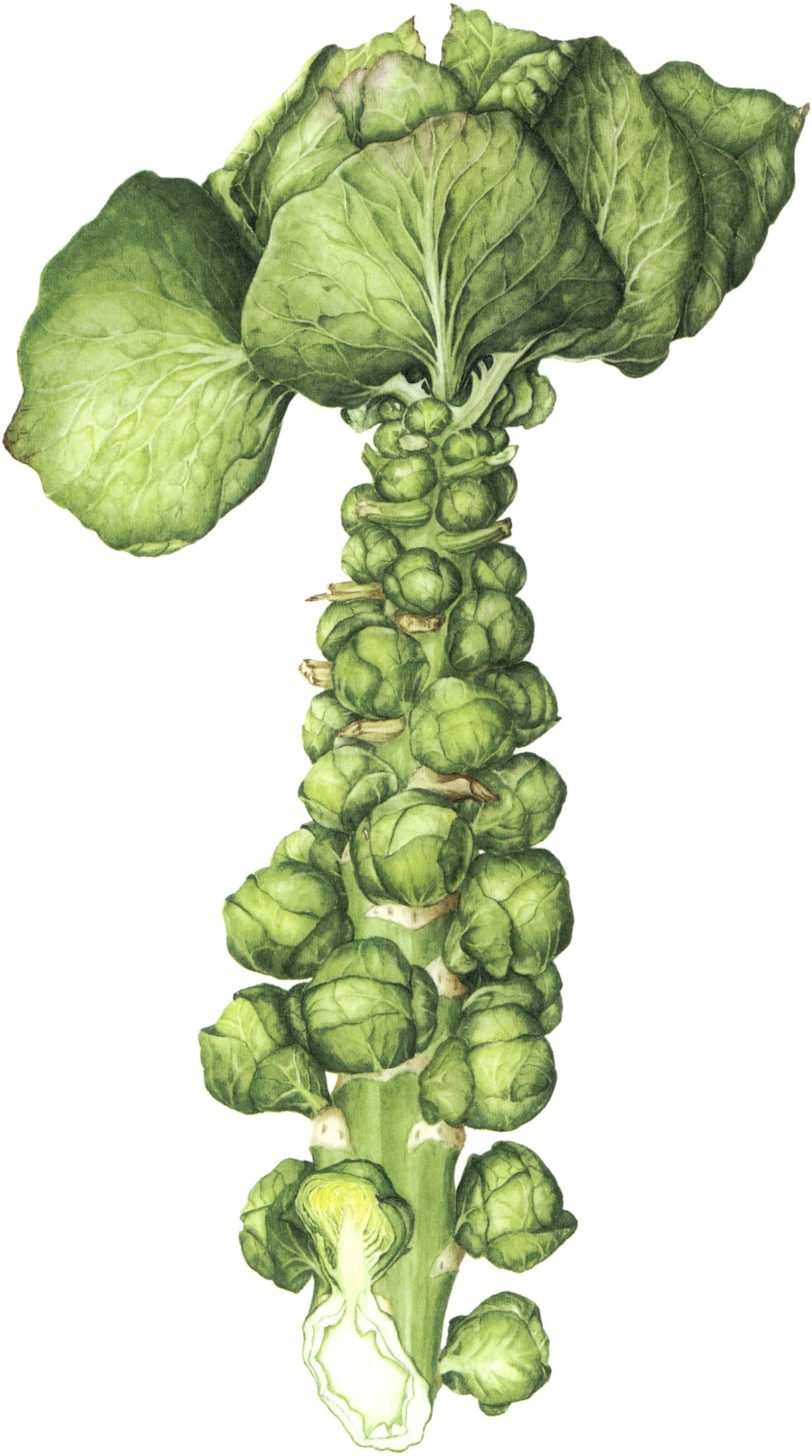

Nasturtium

Tropaeolum majus

The common Nasturtium of our gardens is sometimes called the Indian Cress; its flowers, leaves, and fruit, combined with its trailing growth, offer plenty of material for the artist.

The flowers, which run from a bright yellow to a deep red, have five petals, the two upper ones being slightly larger than the rest, and as a rule are patched and streaked by deep rich markings running from the base upwards; the three lower are fringed near their bases by a hair-like growth. The calyx is one of five divisions terminating in a long spur, from the underside of which the long flower-stalk grows. The colour of the calyx is a pale yellow generally, sometimes tinged with red; these form the outer covering of the flower-buds, and at this stage take the same pale green colour as the stems.

The leaves are orbicular in form and flat, with a broadly scolloped edge, the stalk is attached near the middle of the leaf on the under side, forming a centre from which the veins radiate to the margin of the leaf. Both leaves and flowers grow from the same junction on both sides of the twisting stalks. The main stem is round and branched. The flowers have eight stamens and a pistil. The fruit which succeeds the flower usually consists of three lobes, which are grooved or channelled.

Flowers, buds, and leaves may all be found growing on the same plant together. The *Tropaeolum claratum*, which is figured opposite, is another variety of the same genus. The main difference will be seen in the leaves, which in *T. claratum* have a lobed character. EC

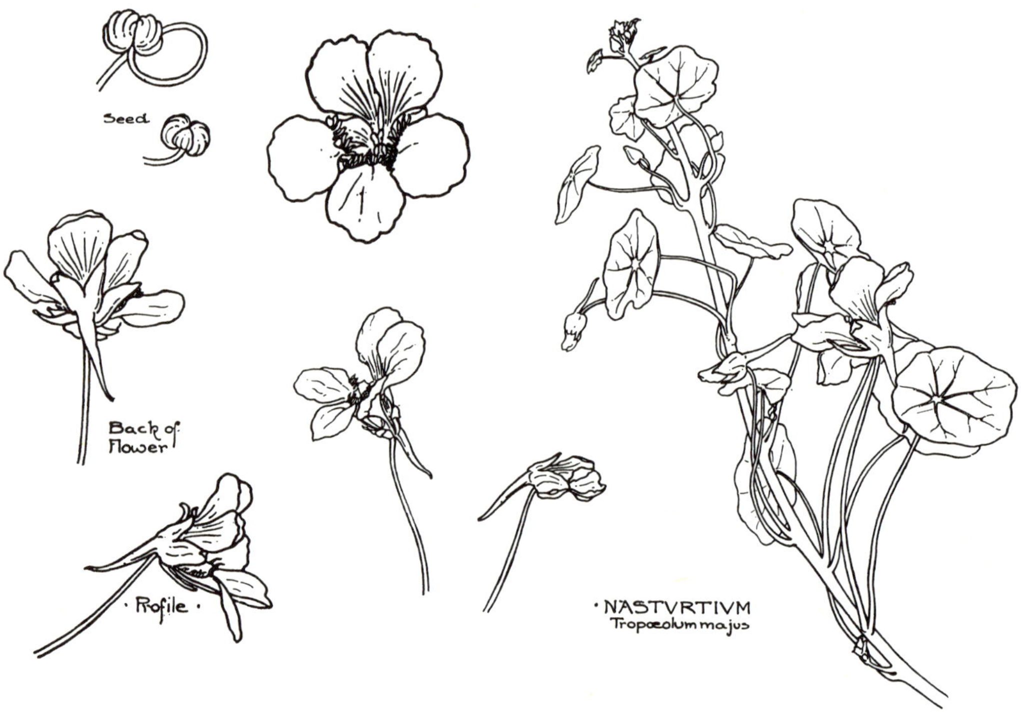

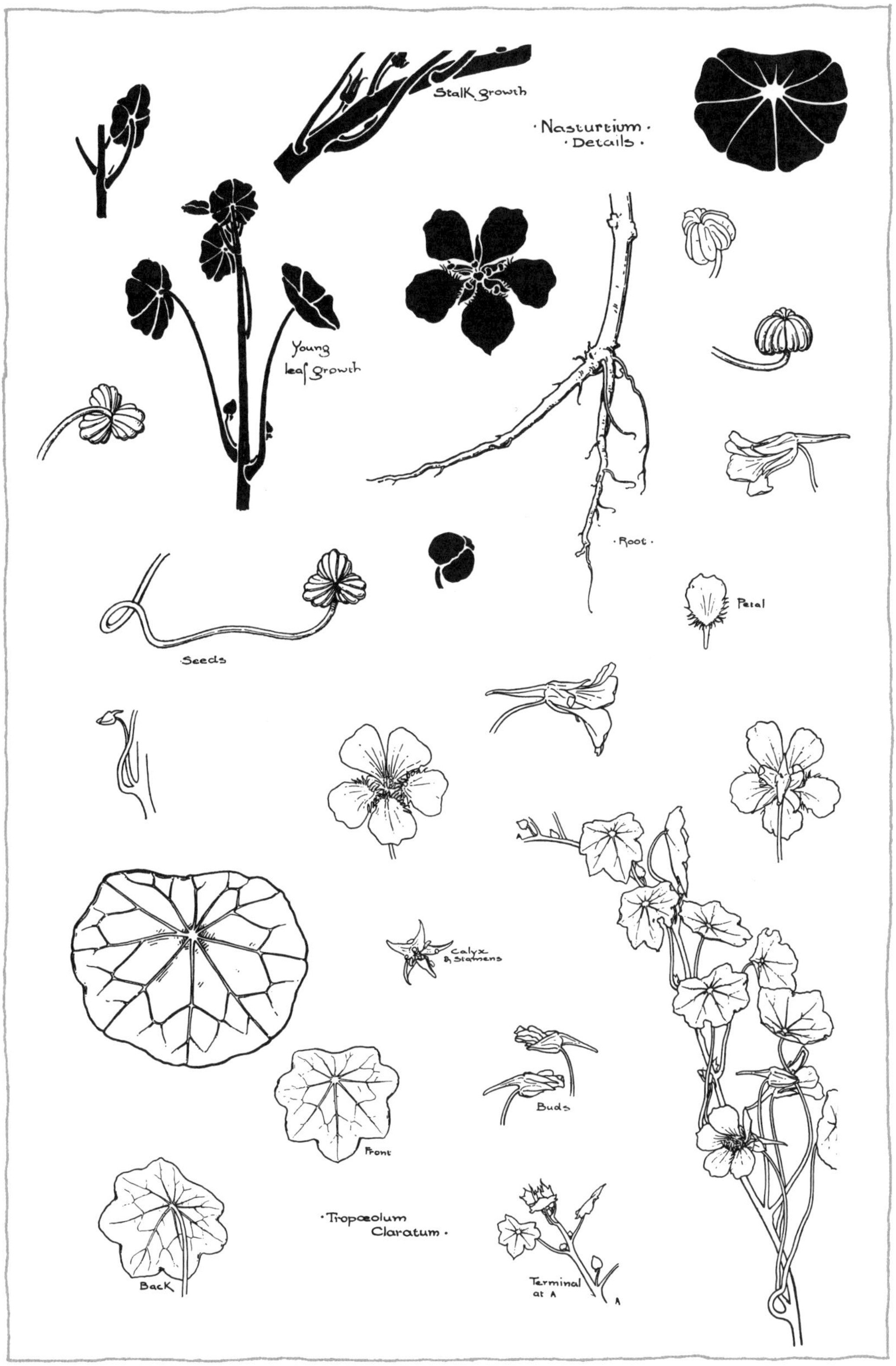
Stalk growth
· Nasturtium ·
· Details ·
Young
leaf growth
· Root ·
Petal
Seeds
A
Calyx
& Stamens
Buds
Front
· Tropæolum
Claratum ·
Back
Terminal
at A
A

Nasturtium

Tropaeolum majus

The artist prefers to use gouache for his illustrations as it allows for bold imagery which can still be delicate. The humble climbing Nasturtium lends itself well to this medium and here the colours sing against the light background.

He worked on Daler-Rowney Hot Pressed watercolour board for this study, using a limited palette of Marigold Yellow and Spectrum Yellow, with a small amount of Naples Yellow where a more creamy shade was called for. A mix of Spectrum Yellow with Cerulean Blue provided the leaf colour, with the addition of Indigo for the darker green areas. All these paints were from the Winsor & Newton Designer Gouache range.

The way in which the flower centres appear to glow is not an easy effect to achieve, yet it is essential when painting certain flowers, such as *Ipomea purpurea* (Morning Glory), or some of the hardy geraniums – *Geranium* 'Johnson's Blue' springs to mind. It would be interesting to experiment with watercolour and gouache for both of these flowers to see which medium gives the best, most luminous result.

The artist kept the colours light in the early stages to avoid the flowers becoming dull or thick with pigment, and also took care that no white pigment got into the mix on the palette otherwise vibrancy would be lost. As with watercolour, he worked from light to dark throughout, only allowing the paint to build up more opaquely in the latter stages.

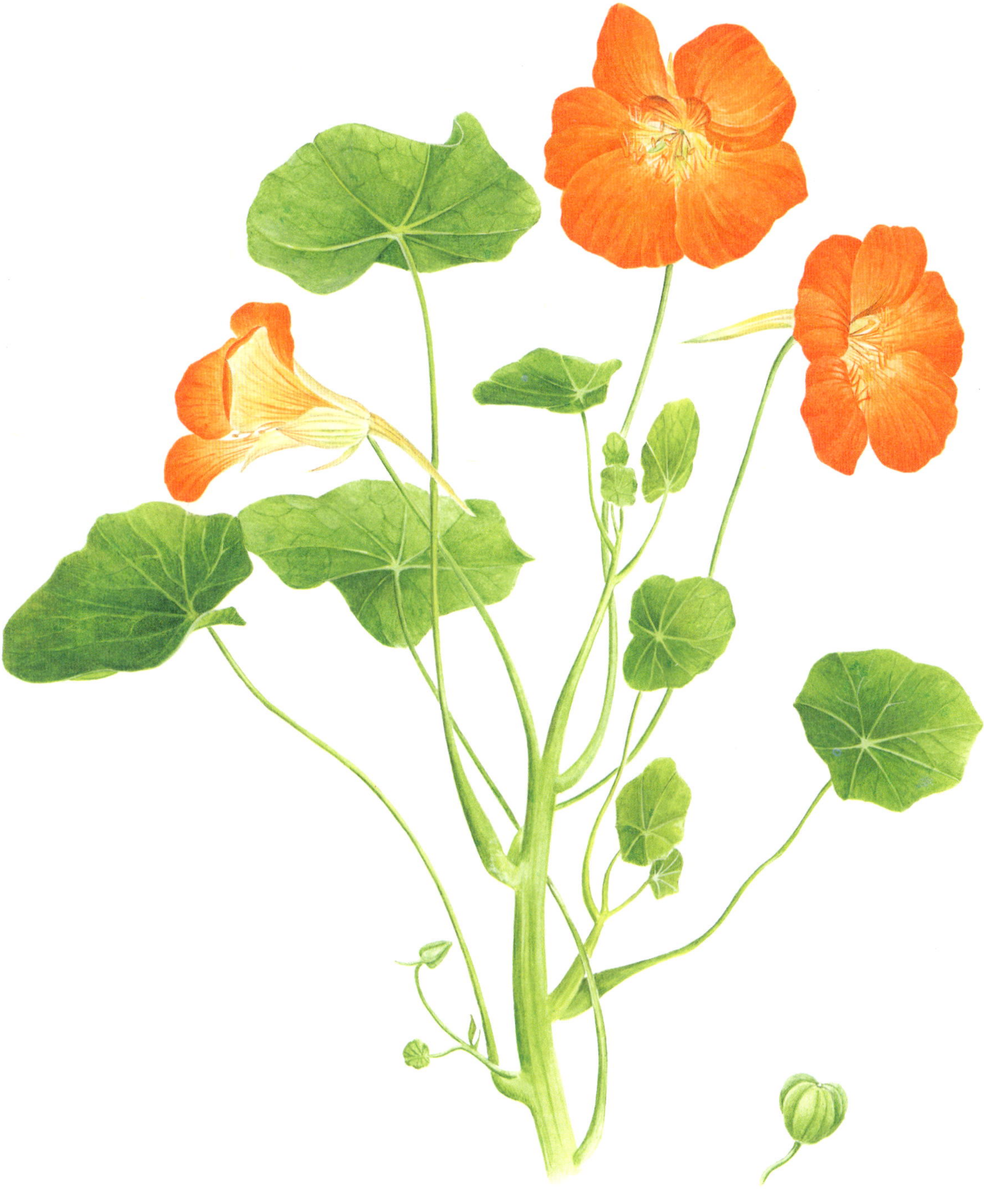

BELLFLOWER FAMILY

Campanulaceae

Harebell

Campanula rotundifolia

To be found in pastures and moorland, or in the grassy banks of the roadside, from July to September. The flowers grow on very delicate stems, gracefully hanging their heads and nodding to every breeze. Several blossoms usually grow at different angles from the main stem, which reaches from an inch or two to about a foot in height. A pale purplish blue is the colour of the flowers. The lowest leaves near the ground are very round in form and serrated, getting long and narrow or linear the higher they reach up the stem. The stem is very often branched, terminating in one or more flowers. The segments of the calyx are long and pointed. The flower, as its name implies, is bell-shaped, divided into five lobes. It has five stamens, a style with three to five stigmas. EC

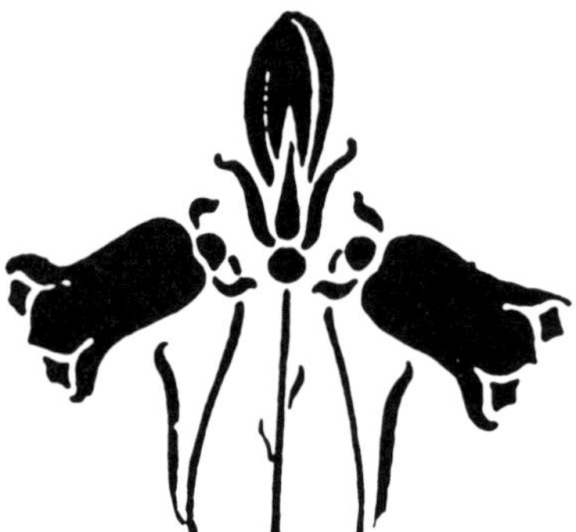

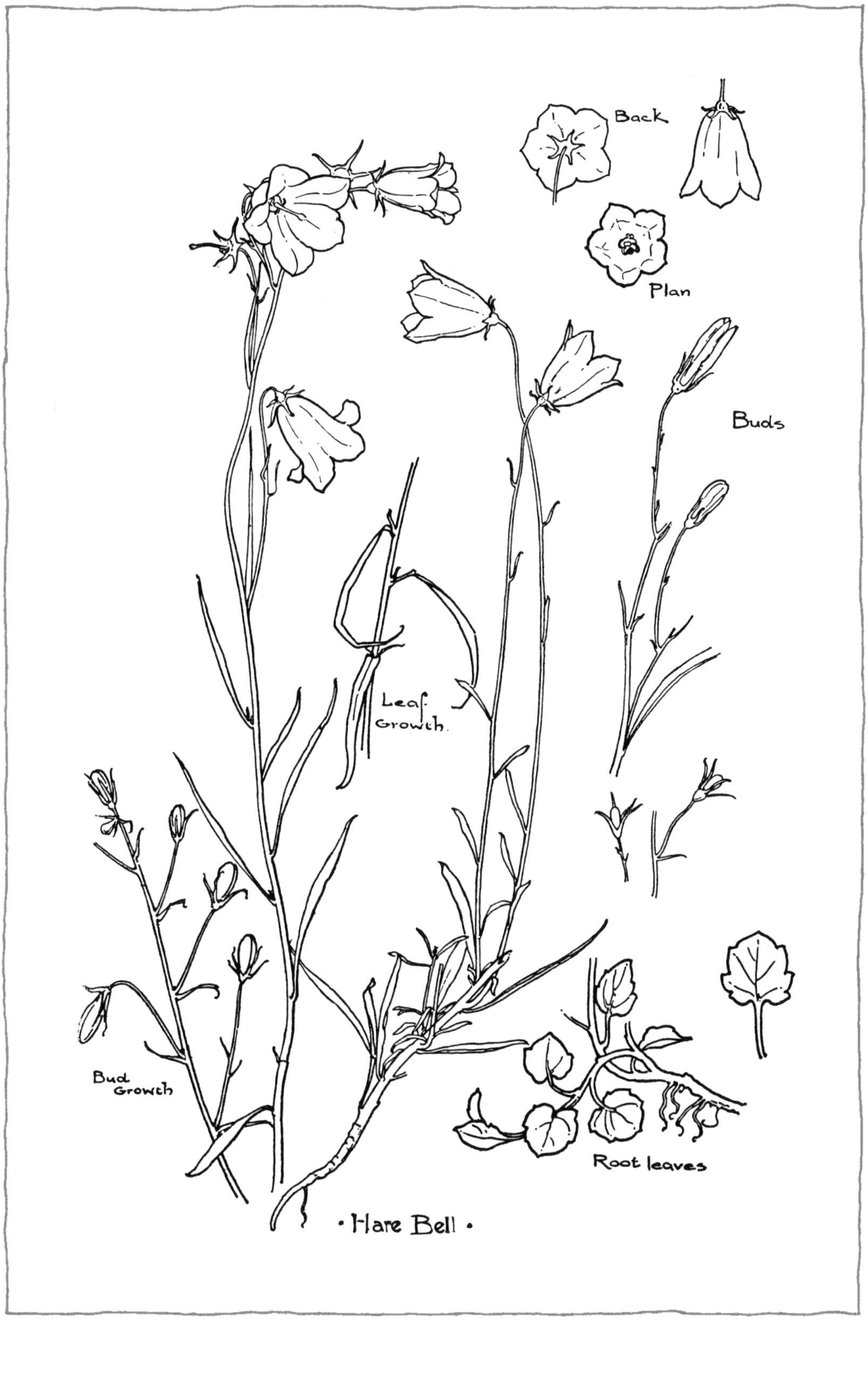
Back
Plan
Buds
Leaf Growth
Bud Growth
Root leaves
· Hare Bell ·

Harebell

Campanula rotundifolia

This campanula – England's Harebell and Scotland's luebell – grows all around the northern hemisphere from Europe and Asia to North America and is a lot tougher than might be supposed from its fragile appearance. The wiry stems support it very well so that it easily withstands the strong winds that blow across the high ground near my home on the edge of Snowdonia. The name *rotundifolia* refers to the rounded leaves of the basal rosettes, which tend to disappear before flowering, leaving just the narrow stem leaves seen here.

The artist enjoys the challenge of working on site and this was drawn in the Swiss Alps as part of her project recording alpine campanula species. When working outdoors she makes a very detailed drawing, together with some colour notes. The drawing is then transferred onto watercolour paper using a light box so that it may be completed in the studio. For this study she used Winsor & Newton Winsor Violet, French Ultramarine, Winsor Lemon and Burnt Sienna.

Watercolour, Reinhild Raistrick

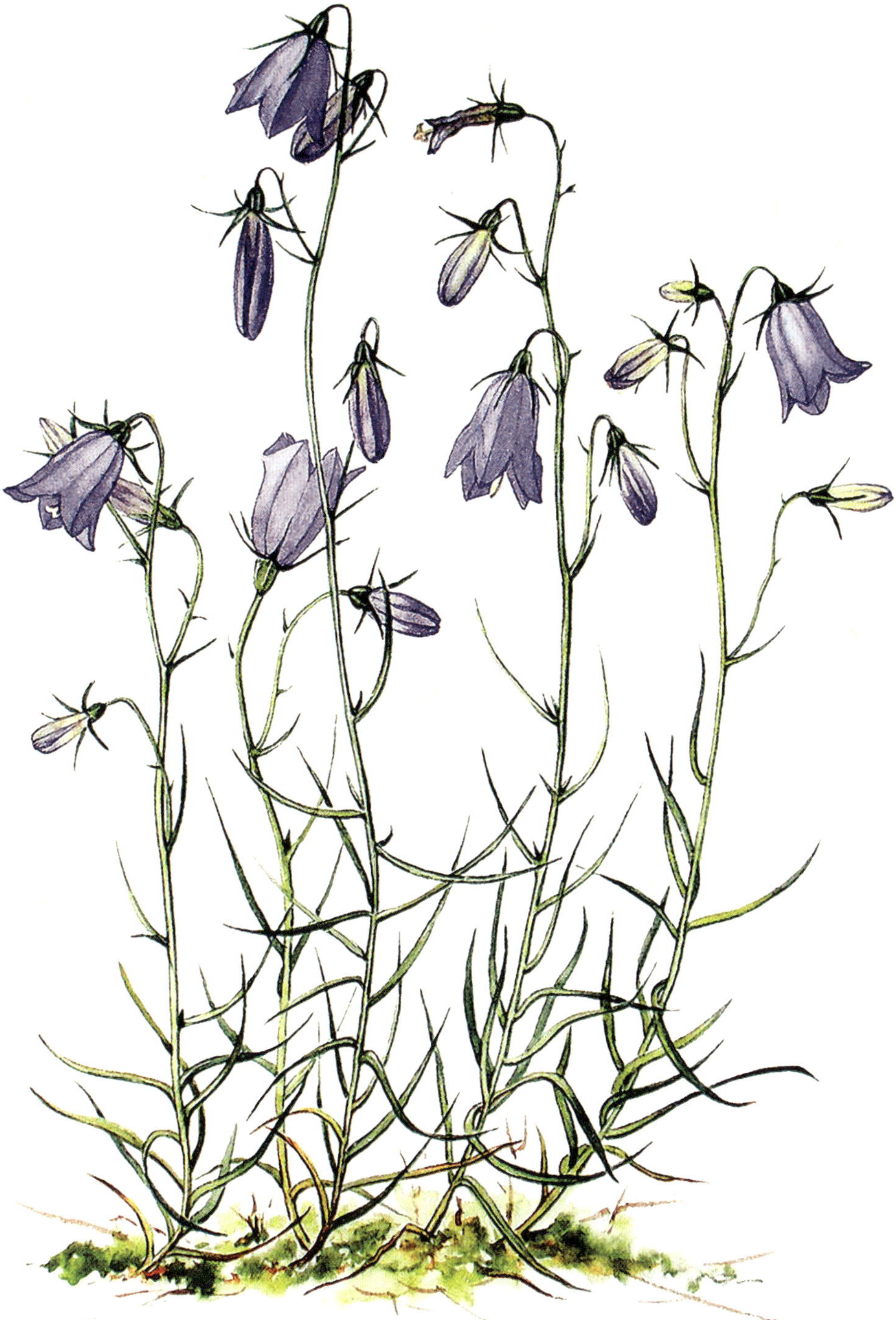

Bellflower

Campanula incurva

This beautiful example of *Campanula incurva* was painted as part of a project recording alpine campanula species from the National Plant Collection held by Sue Wooster near Bury St Edmunds in Suffolk. It was a very large plant and the challenge was how to show it life size. The artist therefore painted one flower spray life size (upper image) but also added a detailed reduced drawing on site, illustrating the whole plant. The pencil background was added to give an indication of the rocky habitat on which this species grows in Eastern Greece. It is a stunningly beautiful plant with large pale blue flowers opening from rosy-tipped buds. For this painting thea artist used a limited palette of Old Holland Dioxazine Mauve with Winsor & Newton French Ultramarine, Winsor Lemon and Permanent Rose.

Watercolour and graphite, Reinhild Raistrick

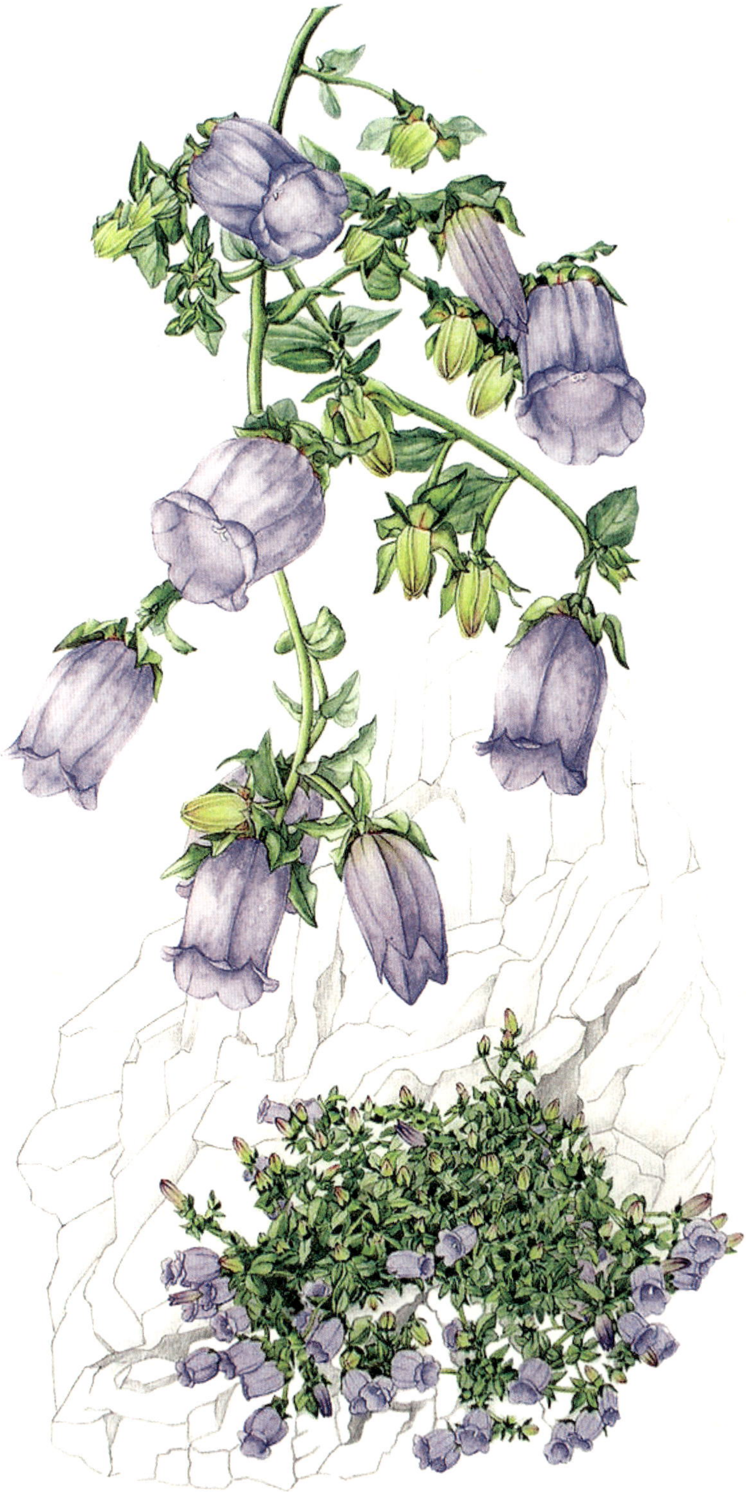

HONEYSUCKLE FAMILY

Caprifoliaceae

Honeysuckle

Lonicera periclymenum

Woodbine, as it is frequently called, forms a prominent feature along British country lanes and hedgerows; and in some of the southern counties may be found from June to September. It is one of our favourite climbers, not only on account of its beautiful flower forms, but also by reason of its strong, sweet odour. Its flowers grow in terminal heads; each one consists of a long tube, from one to two inches in length, splitting into two petals, the larger one being divided into several lobes.

The calices are small and have fine teeth. The leaves grow in pairs, and the upper ones, as a rule, have no stalks. The main stem grows to a great length, and twines from left to right round any obstacle in its path. Its flowers are succeeded by a group of green berries, gradually turning to a deep red. The stamens are five, and the stigma knobbed. EC

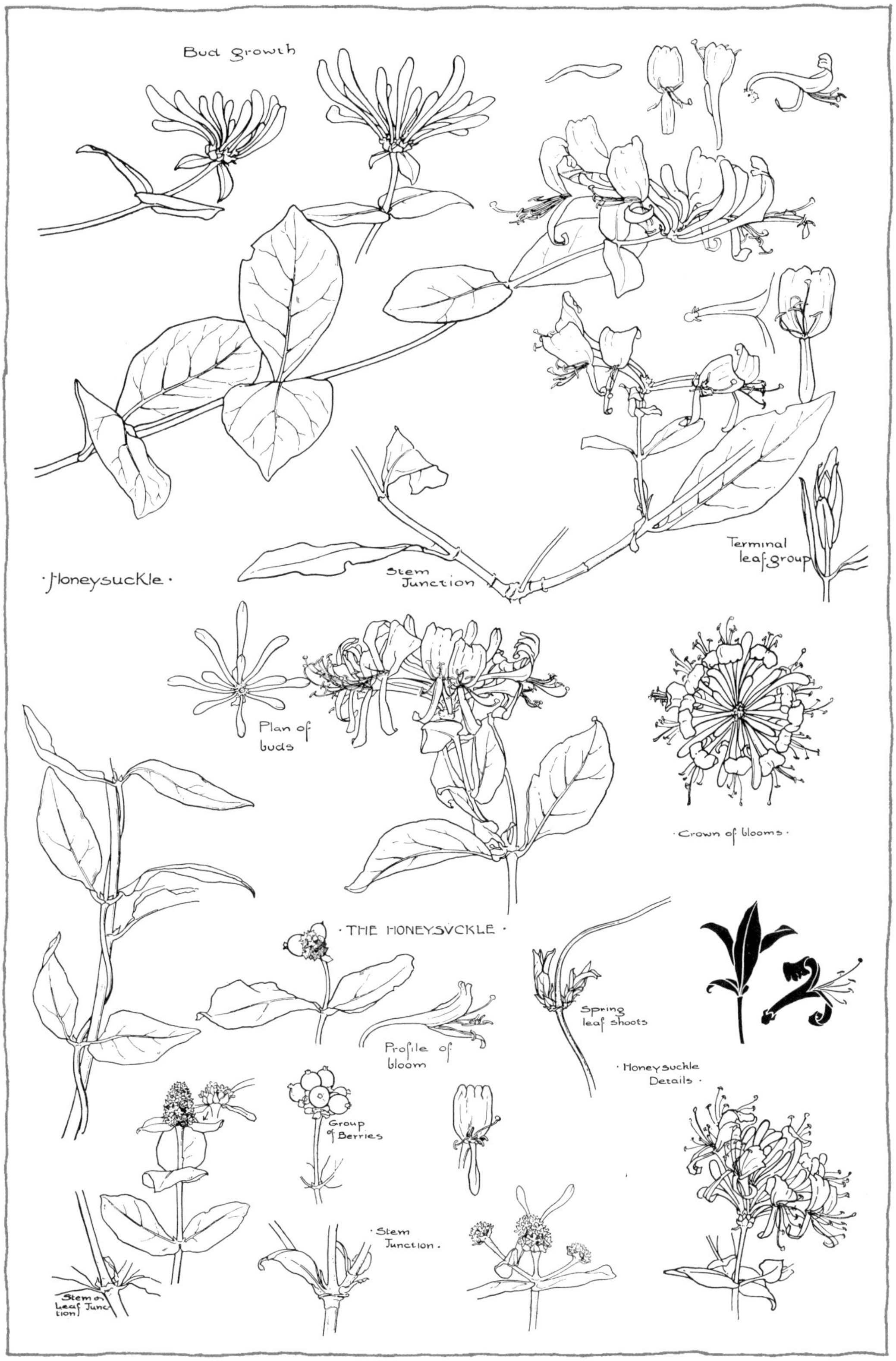

Bud growth
·Honeysuckle·
Stem Junction
Terminal leaf group
Plan of buds
·Crown of blooms·
·THE HONEYSVCKLE·
Spring leaf shoots
Profile of bloom
·Honeysuckle Details·
Group of Berries
·Stem Junction.
Stem or Leaf Junction

Woodbine

Lonicera periclymenum

In the manner of a true botanical illustrator, the artist started with a thumbnail sketch of this honeysuckle to work out the key features – growth habit, flower-heads, leaf junctures, stems and berries. She then colour-matched her specimen, thus ensuring that if the flowers died, as they surely would before she had finished, the colours would remain true.

For the flowers she used Winsor & Newton Naples Yellow, Indian Yellow, Rose Madder and Brown Madder, with final glazes of Schmincke Transparent Yellow and Transparent Orange to unify the overall colour. The leaves were painted with a base of Winsor & Newton Olive Green, with Schmincke May Green or Cadmium Yellow Lemon added as required. For the darker leaves, the artist added a touch of Schmincke Indigo to the basic Olive Green. Woody stems were painted with Winsor & Newton Burnt and Raw Umber, to which Schmincke Vandyke Brown and Sepia Brown were added for the darker areas.

As always, the artist finished off by going over her work with a magnifying glass, checking that details such as smooth edges and accurate leaf joints were correct.

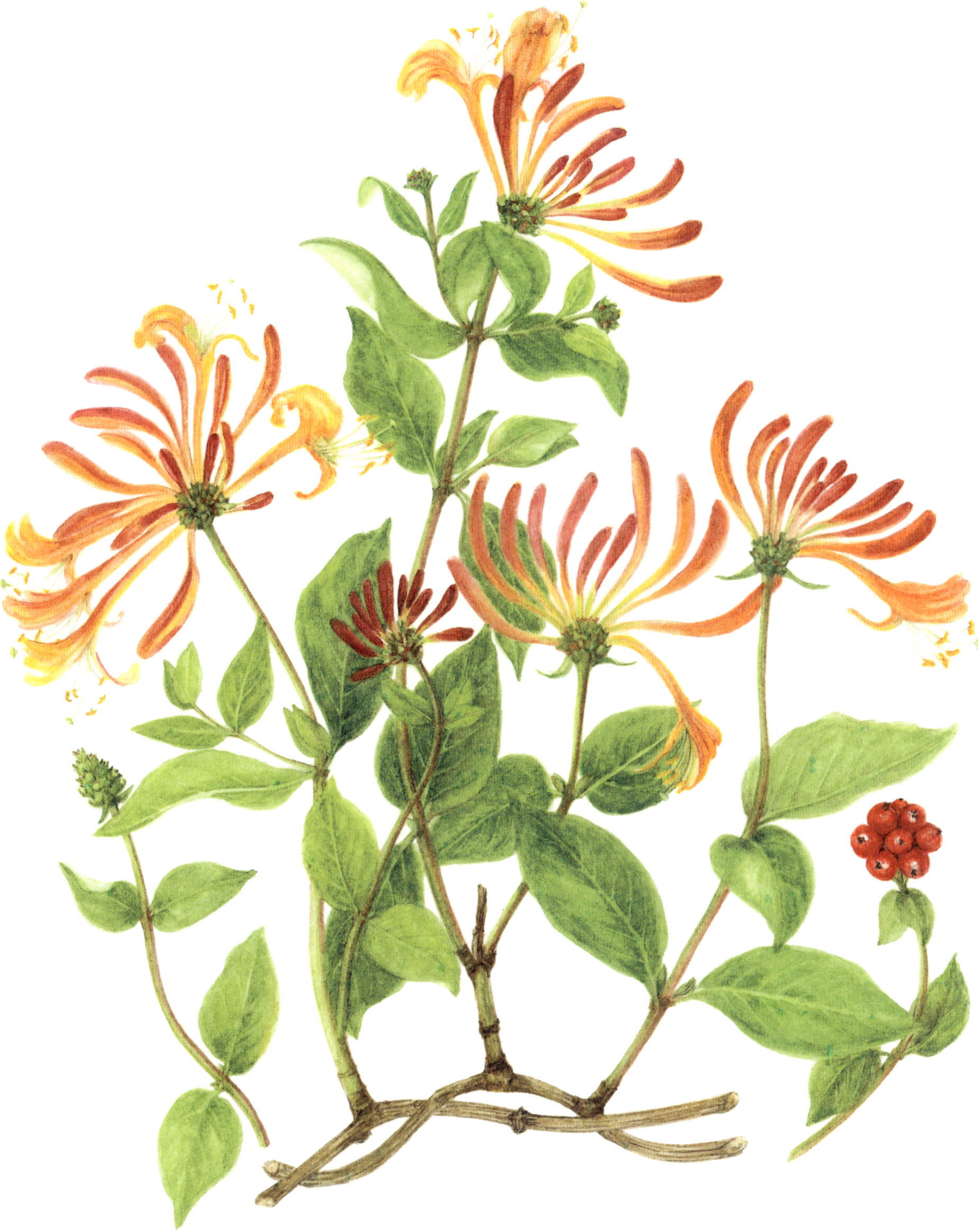

CARNATION FAMILY *Caryphyllaceae*

Red Campion

Lychnis diurna

Found plentifully in hedge-bottoms and copses from June to September. Commonly known as the Cuckoo. Colour of flowers is from a light to deep pink; five petals, each of which is cleft; the calyx is purplish and hairy, with five angular divisions, connected into a tube; stamens ten. The leaves are pointedly oval, grow in pairs opposite, upper ones are sessile, lower ones stalked, entire. White Campion is another variety, the flowers being larger, and the plant generally coarser in growth. The calyx is also larger and rounder. The White Campion opens its blossoms in the evening air, and is slightly scented; the Red blossoms all the day, and is scentless.

EC

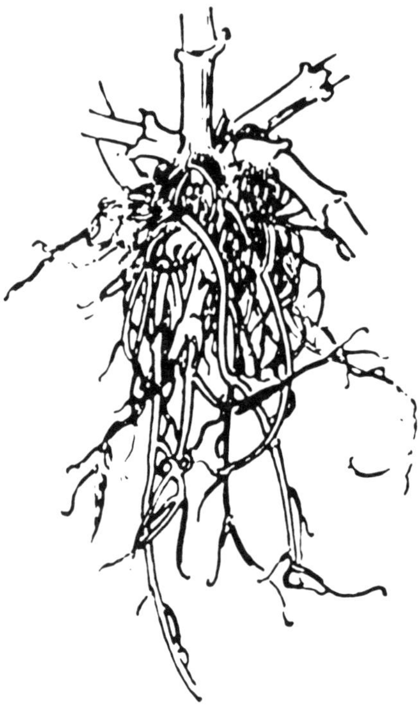

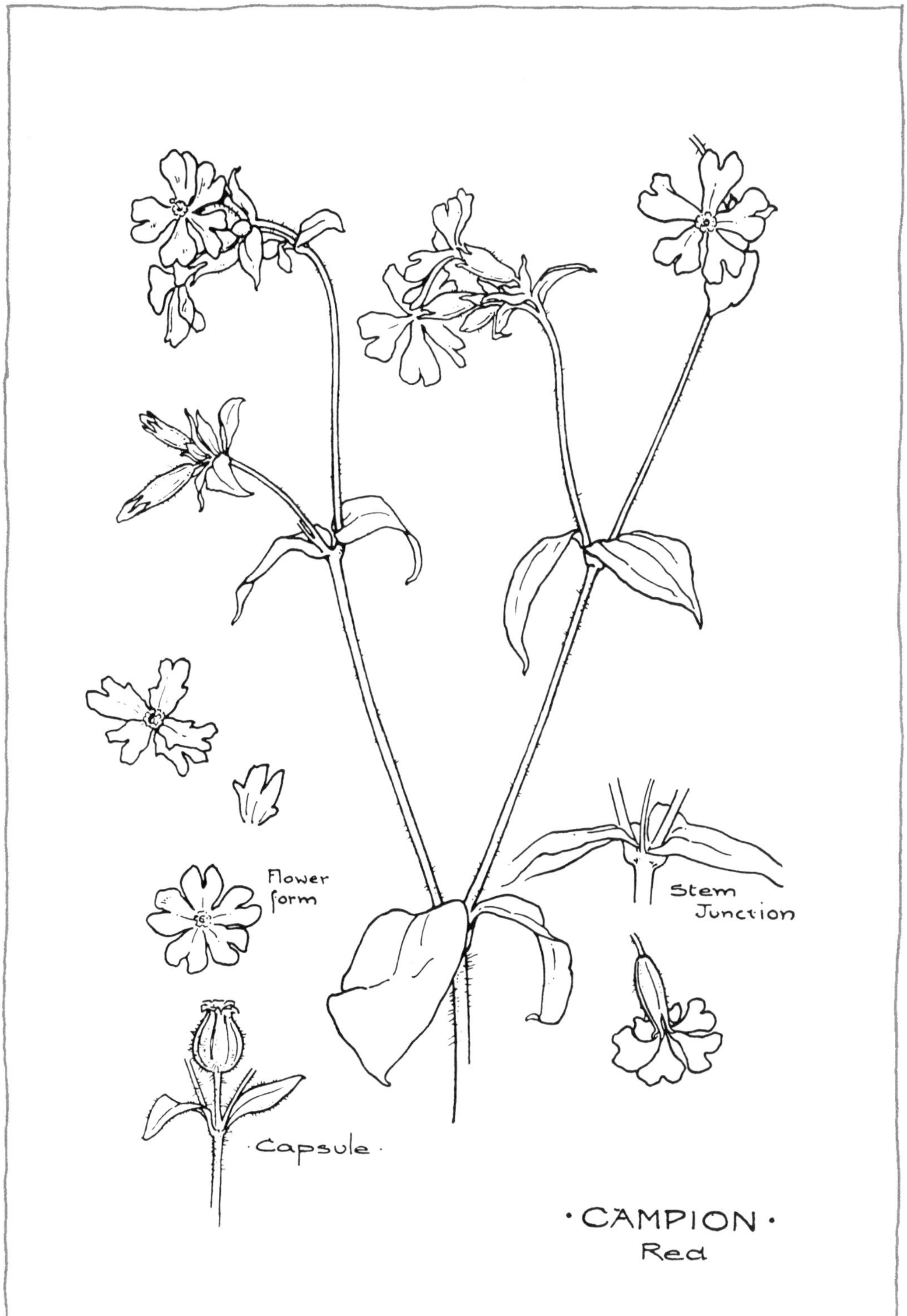
Flower form
Stem Junction
Capsule
· CAMPION ·
Red

Dianthus

Dianthus 'Romance'

This simple study uses an elongated diamond-shaped composition to show off the complex flowers and their elegantly scrolled leaves. Generally speaking, an odd number of flowers makes the best composition; an even number usually results in a square, awkward arrangement, but sometimes the difficulty can be overcome by the addition of a simple bud, which adds the fifth feature and in this case does not detract from the double-triangle layout. These stems were isolated from a very busy plant as I prefer to show individual beauty rather than massed blooms.

Winsor & Newton Quinacridone Red provided the initial wash for the flowers, with Scarlet Lake and Permanent Carmine used for the deeper shades. Winsor Violet mixed with Schmincke Olive Green captured the steely blue foliage.

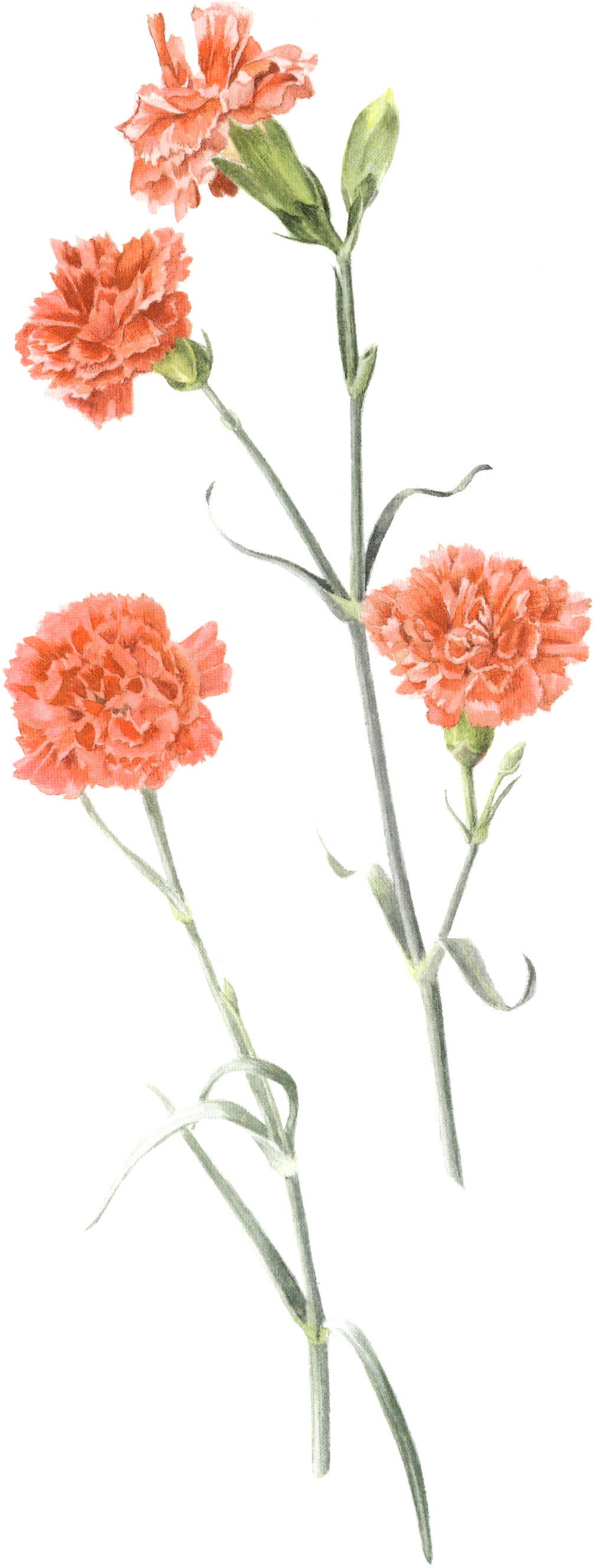

BINDWEED FAMILY *Convolvulaceae*

Hedge Bindweed

Calystegia sepium

Although this is of the same family as the small Field Bindweed (*C. arvensis*) it is a much more important-looking member, and, instead of trailing along the ground, climbs up the hedges and thickets to a height of six or seven feet. Its flowers are large and pure white, having a trumpet-shaped corolla of five lobes or petals, each decorated by a broad plait. They are solitary at the end of their long stems; at the base of the tube are two large heart-shaped bracts, which form the hood, completely hiding the calyx of five sepals. The petals in the bud form are twisted.

There are five stamens, one style, and two oblong stigmas. The leaves are broad spear-head forms with angular lobes at the base, growing, alternately up the stem and from the same junction as the flowers. It may be found from June to August or September in the hedgerows and bushy places. The bindweeds are no friends of the gardeners, who look upon them as troublesome weeds.

EC

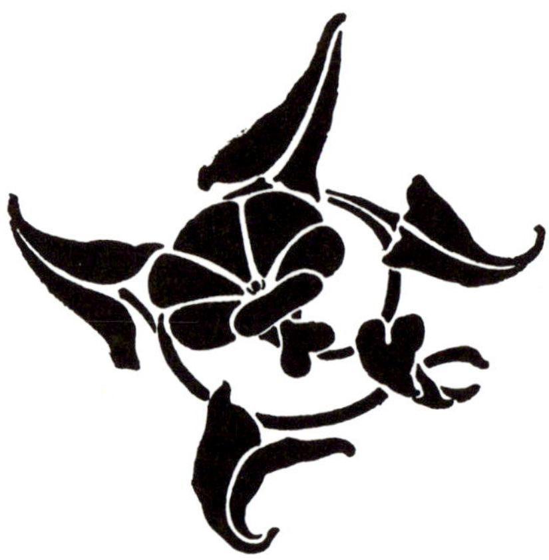

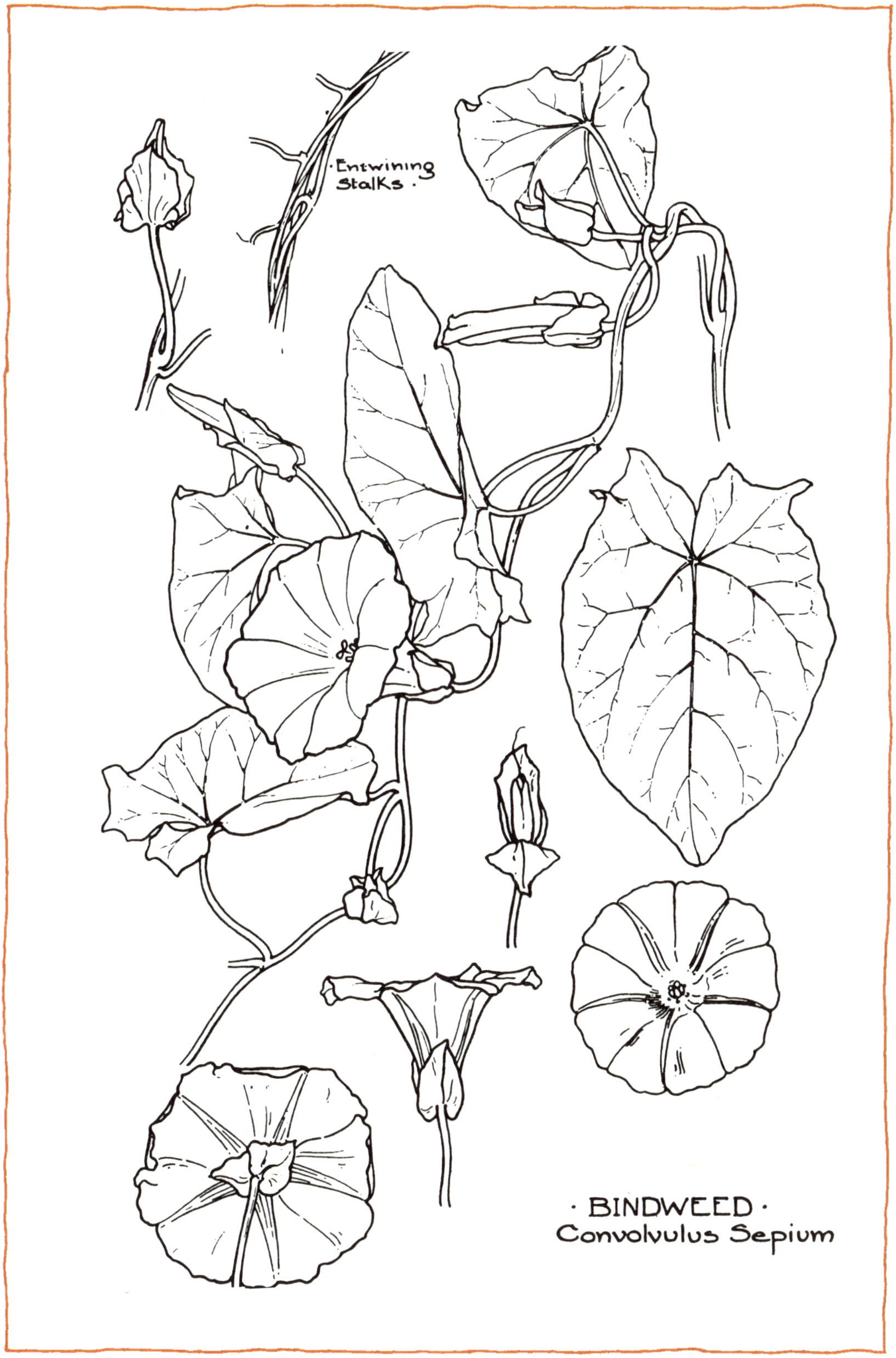
·Entwining Stalks·
·BINDWEED·
Convolvulus Sepium

Hedge Bindweed

Calystegia sepium

Using gouache enables the artist to work from dark to light, giving the same advantage as that enjoyed by the oil painter only with the fast-drying quality of watercolours. Some might say it offers the best of both worlds. Here the artist has used mount board as the support, in this case black although dark green is also popular for creating maximum impact. Here the hedge bindweed flower positively glows, reminiscent of how one sees pale flowers in the garden at dusk, attracting moths for pollination purposes.

Artists such as the late, revered Sally Keir kept the flag flying for gouache until Simon Williams took up the medium. My hope is that it will increase in popularity and take its rightful place as an equal to transparent watercolour. The artist has used a base of Titanium White Acrylic as an alternative to Winsor & Newton Bleedproof White; he says he needs to apply the colour delicately and without too much water, otherwise the opaque layers might lift off. For the flowers, he used Permanent White gouache on top of the acrylic base.

No matter which medium is used, cultivating a light touch should be the aim of all botanical artists. Imagine you are painting a butterfly's wing where one rough move would rip it to shreds; relax your grip on the brush and keep this thought in mind as you work.

Gouache, Simon Williams

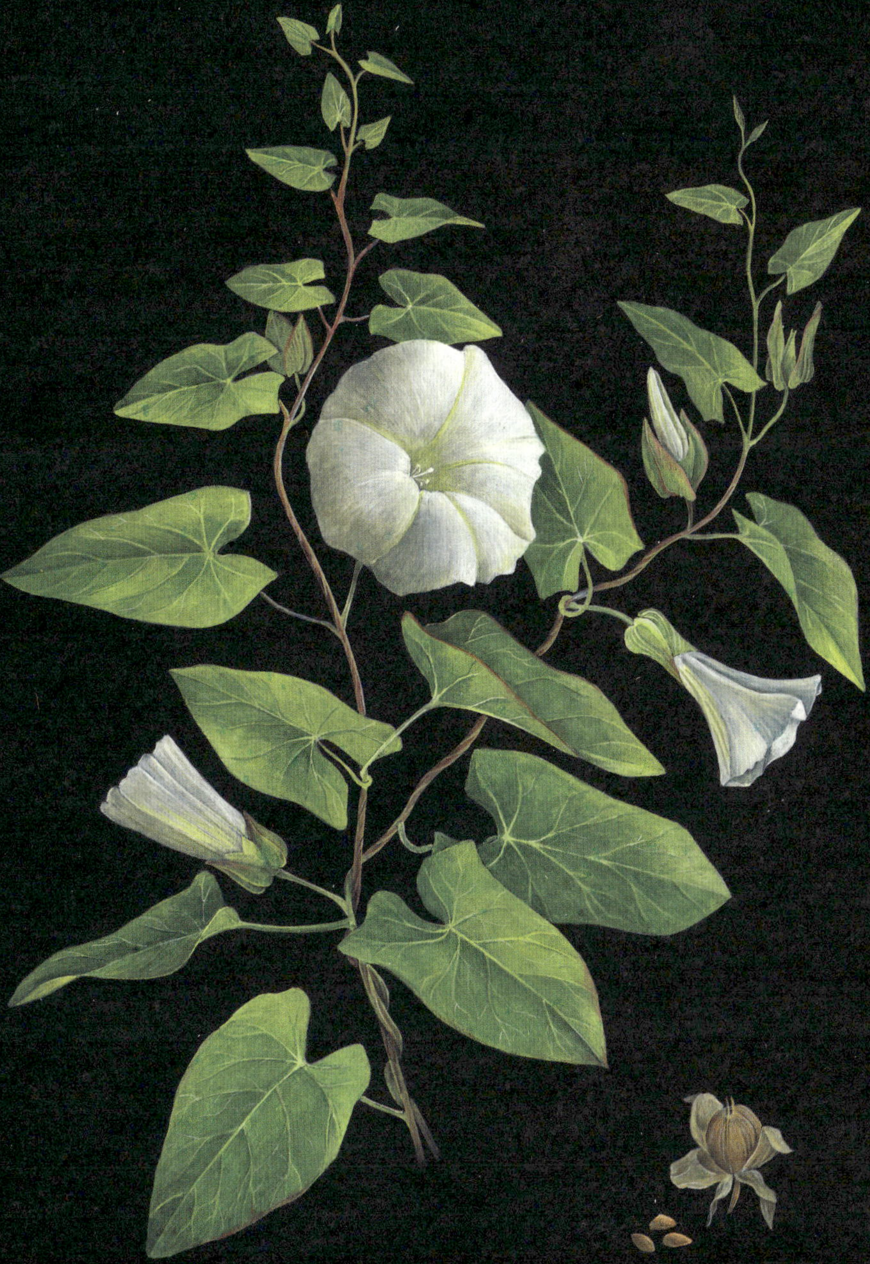

GOURD FAMILY *Cucurbitaceae*

White Bryony

Bryonia dioica

One of the trailing plants which makes such a beautiful feature in some of the British hedgerows in July and August, forming a thick curtain-like mantle wherever it grows, climbing by the aid of its beautiful tendrils from one object to another until it reaches a height of 6 or 7 feet. Its flowers are small, and of a pale greenish-yellow tint, bearing five petals, five stamens, and a calyx which is five toothed. The flowers are followed by round berries changing from green to red, with a dry surface. The blossoms grow in stalked racemes from the same attachment as each leaf and tendril. The leaves are lobed and angular, and coarsely toothed. The root-stock is thick and tuberous, sometimes branched. It must not be confounded with the Black Bryony, with which it has no relationship. EC

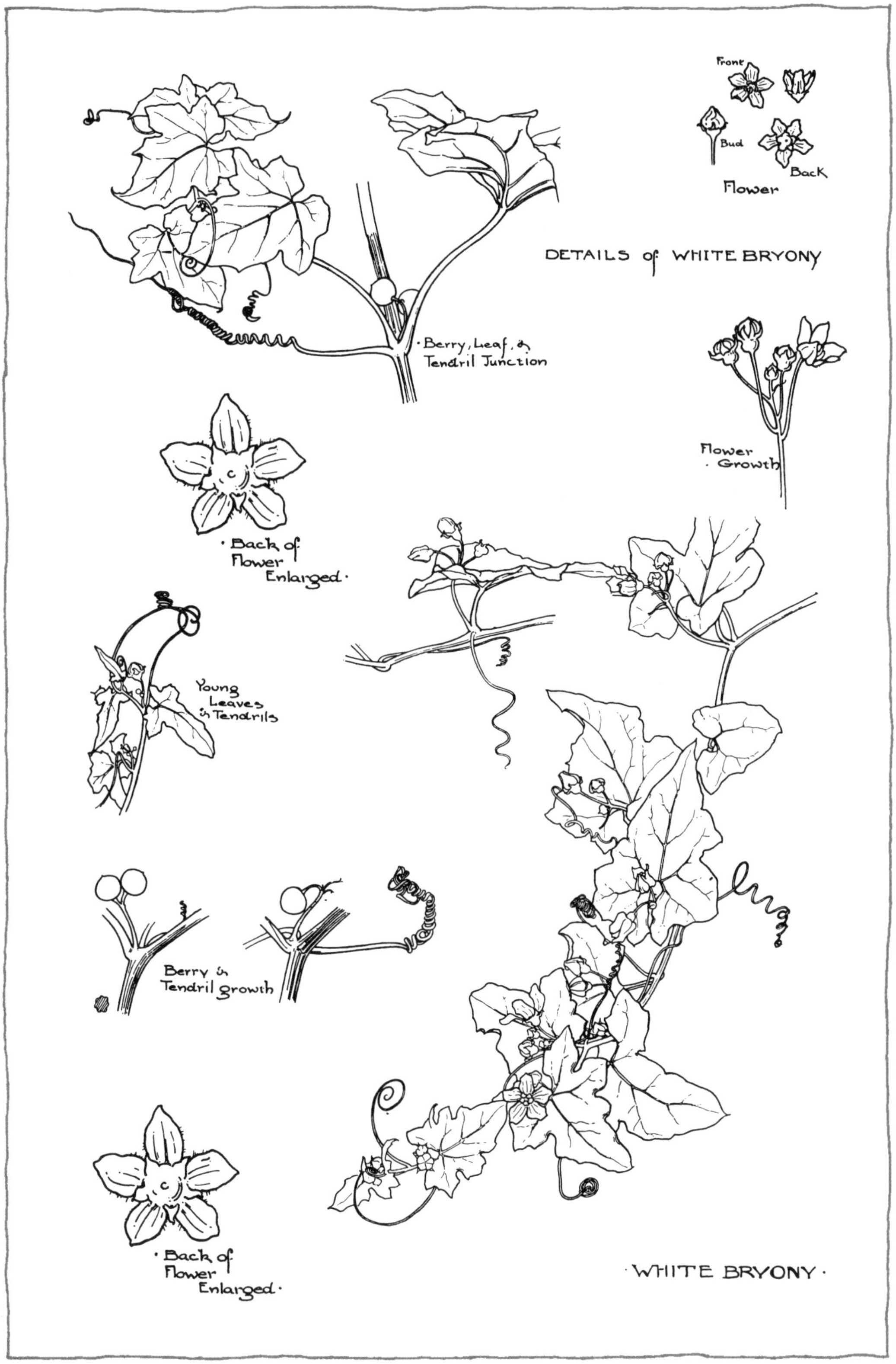
DETAILS of WHITE BRYONY
Front
Bud
Back
Flower
· Berry, Leaf, &
Tendril Junction
Flower
· Growth
· Back of
Flower
Enlarged ·
Young
Leaves
& Tendrils
Berry &
Tendril growth
· Back of
Flower
Enlarged ·
· WHITE BRYONY ·

Vegetable Marrow

Cucurbita pepo ovifera

Creeping along the ground, this fine plant ties itself by the aid of its tendrils to any other plant in its path, and climbs by the same means up anything strong enough to support it. Its stalks are thick, hollow, and hairy, throwing off, on either side alternately; broad heart-shaped leaves, slightly lobed and serrated. The flowers are yellow, and about three inches across, having the stamens and pistils in separate flowers. The stamens are five, and the anthers are twisted. The style is short and thick, the stigma lobed. EC

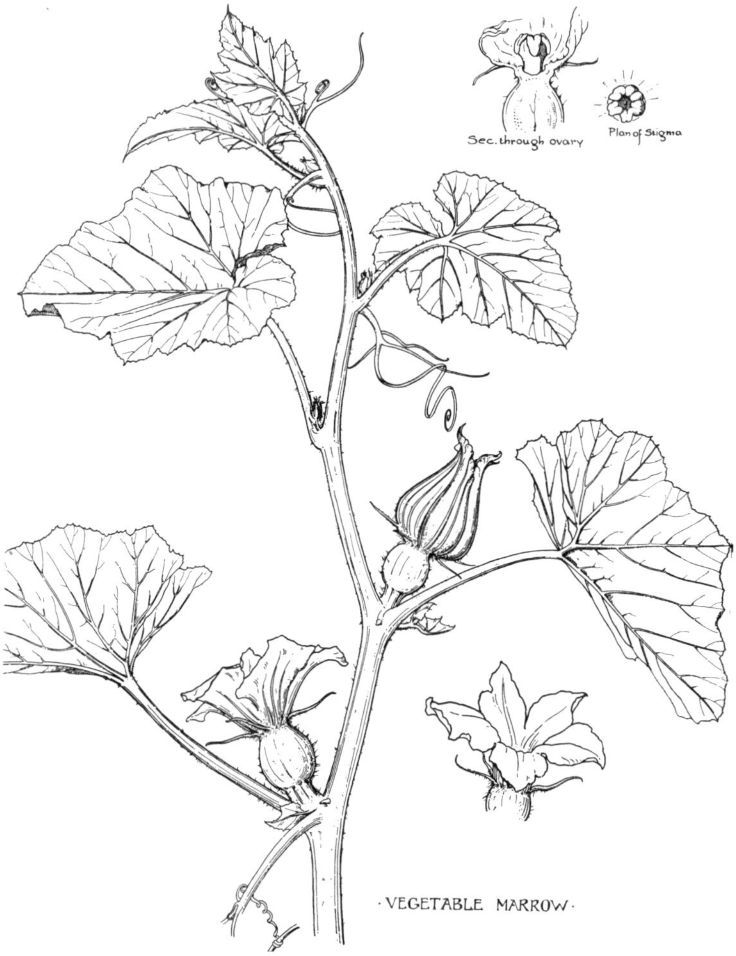

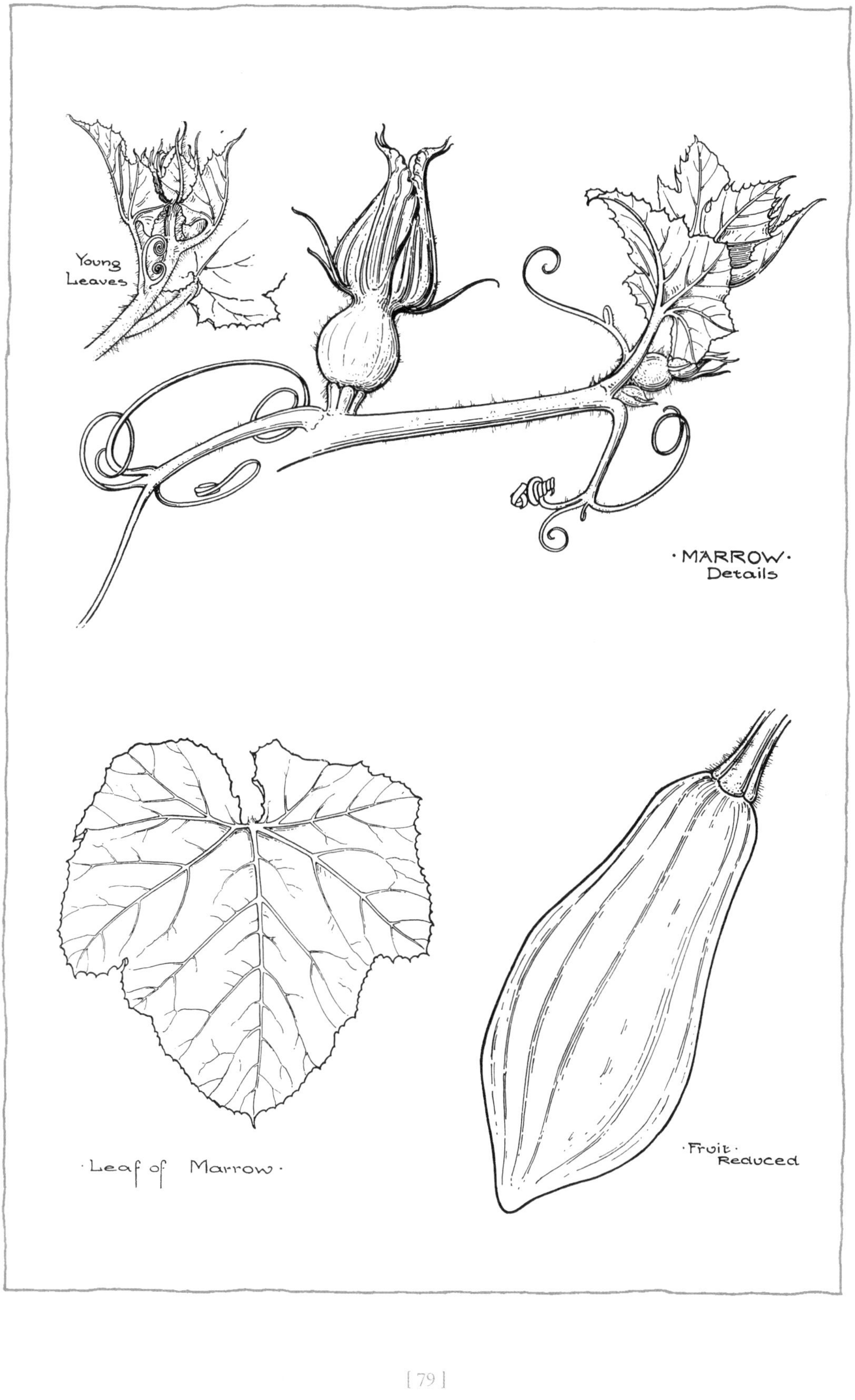
Young Leaves
·MARROW·
Details
·Leaf of Marrow·
·Fruit·
Reduced

Three Squashes

Cucurbita pepo

At the time this painting was done, the artist was working through her botanical course and these three squashes of unknown variety were her choice for the fruit assignment. This always comes as a relief to students because fruit and vegetables tend to last longer than flowers, so a more relaxed approach is taken and marks are usually higher as a result.

From a compositional point of view, one large fruit and two small ones is not ideal, although the odd number is commendable. However, the composition would have been better balanced had one fruit been of medium size. Large, medium and three small would have been perfect, but time constraints would not have allowed the artist to do this and meet her deadline.

She overcame the compositional problem by her choice of colours, which blend together perfectly. Her use of opaque Cadmium Orange for the central squash helped to create a more solid impression of texture, while the transparent Lemon Yellow wash on the large squash was the perfect foundation on which to work the more solid green markings, which are handled very well, with pleasing soft highlights. Shading away from the light gives a real sense of form and solidity, and the artist realized that a little orange reflected light onto this squash would have given an added touch of authenticity.

The small green fruit started to ripen and turn orange while she was working on it, so Cadmium Orange came to the rescue. This is a shiny little squash which gives a really tactile impression – another of the illusions the botanical artist hopes to achieve.

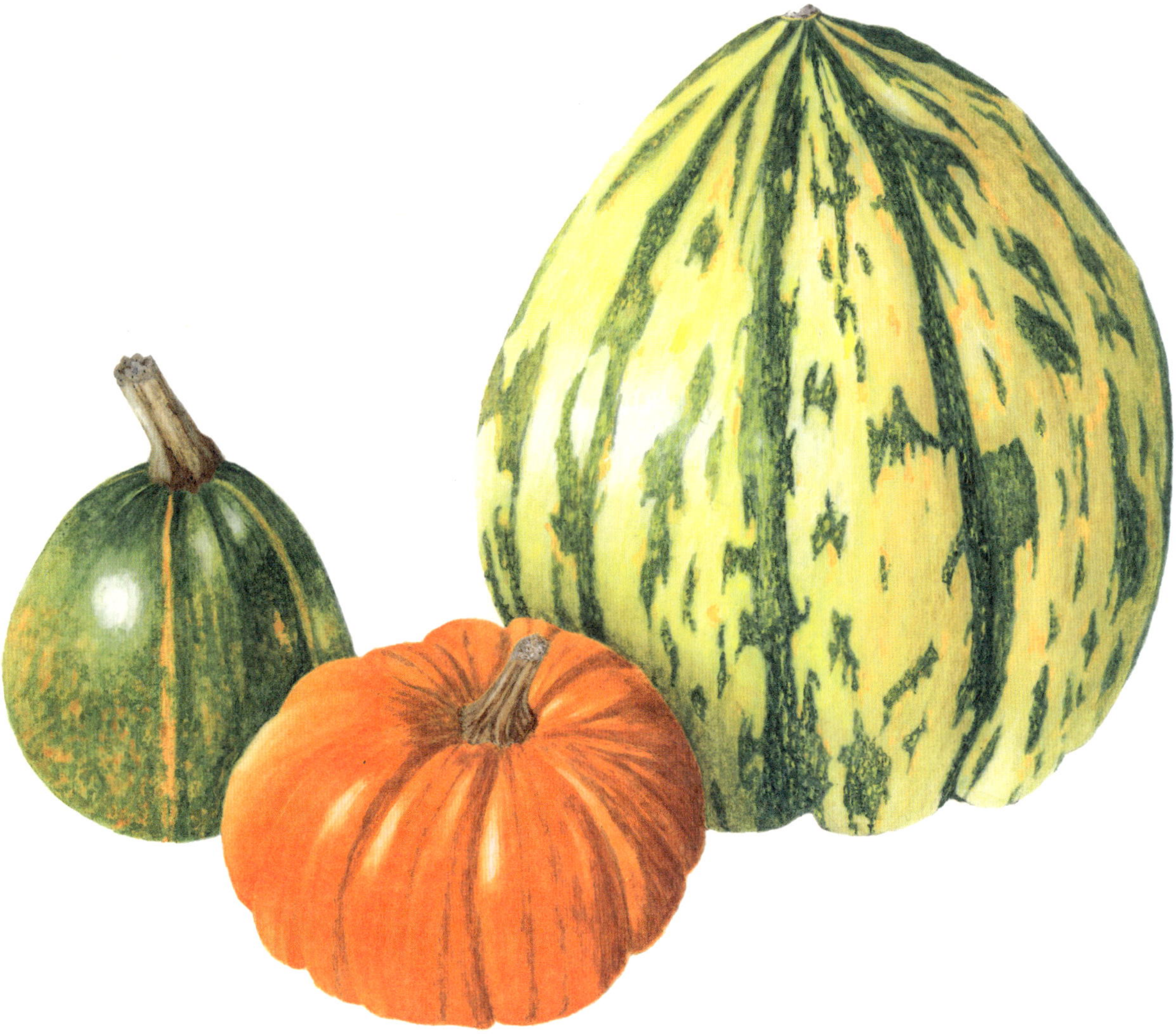

YAM FAMILY *Dioscoreaceae*

Black Bryony

Tamus communis

Although this is a trailing or climbing plant it bears no relationship to the White Bryony (*Bryonia dioica*), which belongs to the gourd tribe. The Black Bryony forms a conspicuous feature in Southern Britain where it is common, when its clusters of large bright green and red berries in the autumn give patches of brilliant colour to the hedgerows. It climbs to some considerable height up the hedges and thickets, draping them with a thick covering of dark-green glossy leaves, growing alternately up the stem, cordate and pointed in form, sometimes lobed at the base, but otherwise entire, gradating from the lowest, which are very large, sometimes measuring six inches across, to the upper ones, which are less than an inch. The flowers, which appear in the spring and early summer, are small, and grow in slender racemes from the junctions of the leaves, and are yellowish-green in colour, each consisting of six segments, the flower being a perianth. The males have six stamens, and the females the pistil with three stigmas, but grow on separate plants.

The one figured here is the male-bearing plant. The fruit or berries, of course, only succeed to the pistillate or female flowers. The roots are large and fleshy, black externally.

EC

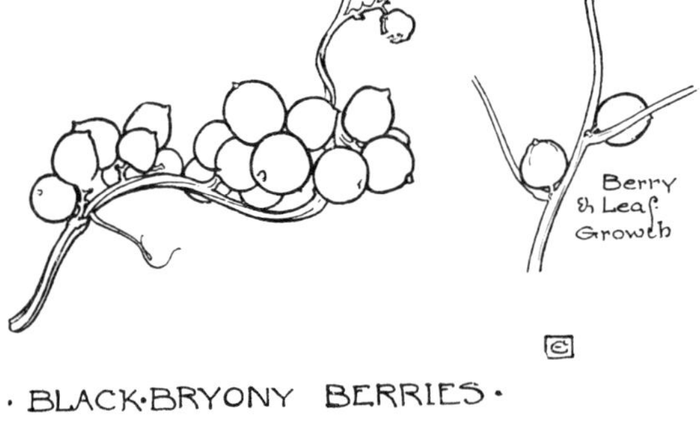

· BLACK·BRYONY BERRIES ·

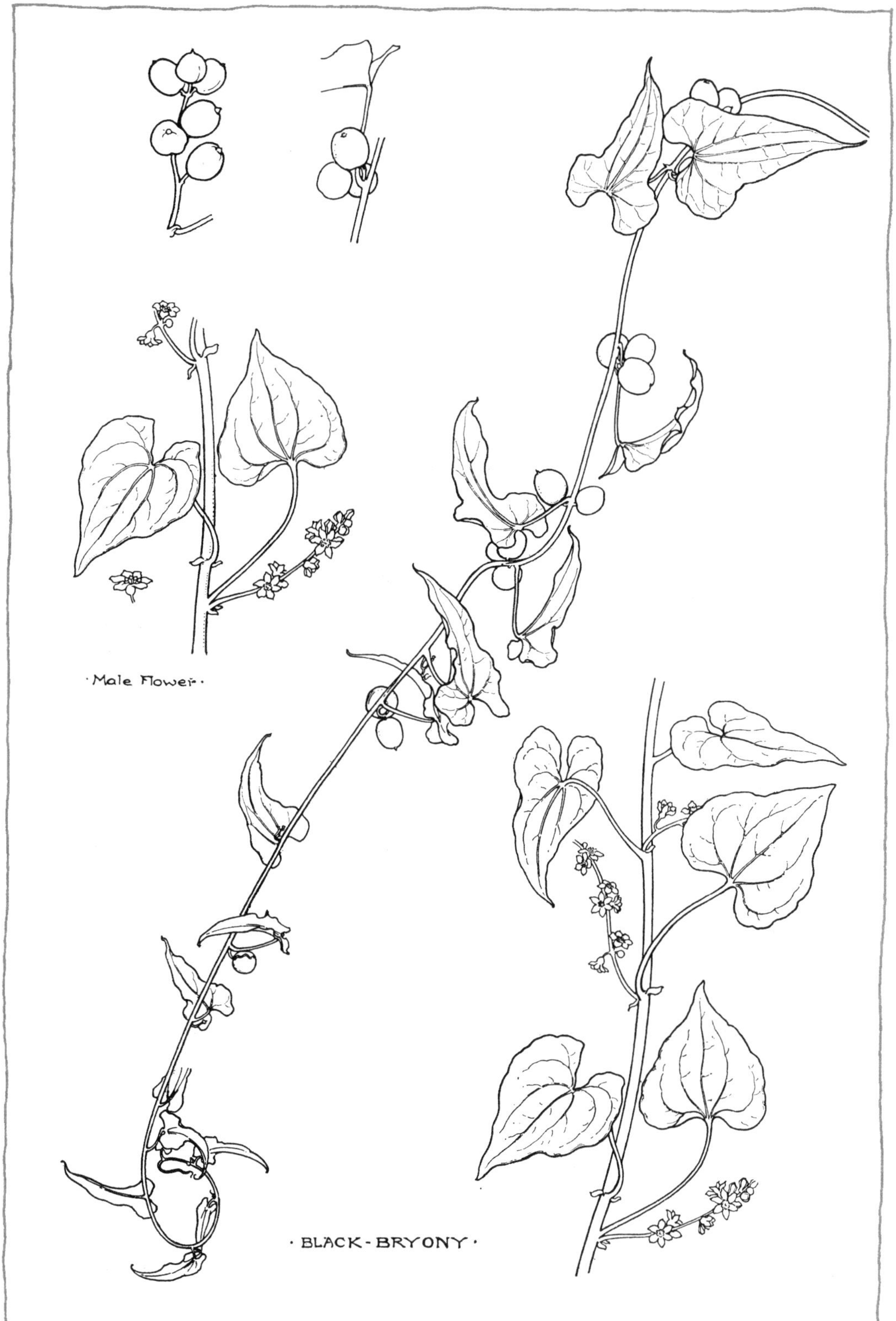
·Male Flower·
·BLACK-BRYONY·

Black Bryony Berries

Tamus communis

Commonly known as Black Bryony, this plant is unrelated to White Bryony, which is a member of the Cucurbitaceae (gourd) family. Its colourful berries are a familiar sight in hedgerows, often persisting throughout the winter months. It is poisonous, although the young shoots are said to be eaten in Greece and it was doubtless known to Dioscorides, the Greek compiler of *De Materia Medica*, whose name is reflected in the family classification.

As with the *Solanum dulcamara* on page 214, the artist has allowed the natural trail of the plant to dictate the composition and she has also adopted a similar illustrative style. Here she has combined crisp, dark outlines with white spaces around the glowing fruit, as a formal hint at a disappearing edge. This works well when so many small fruits are on display and it prevents the study from looking fussy or muddled.

Fine brush drawing is a predominant feature on this painting – note the twisted string-like texture of the vine, particularly at the top. It is also worth noting that however fine the stems and tendrils may be they are still shaded with care. Highlights too are dealt with individually, each one reflecting light differently. Too often a student will adopt a regimented method and make the reflections similar, so that the end result is unreal. Such careful observation and execution takes time but it is the only way to achieve a life-like depiction of what at first may seem a simple subject. These are often the ones that take hours to complete.

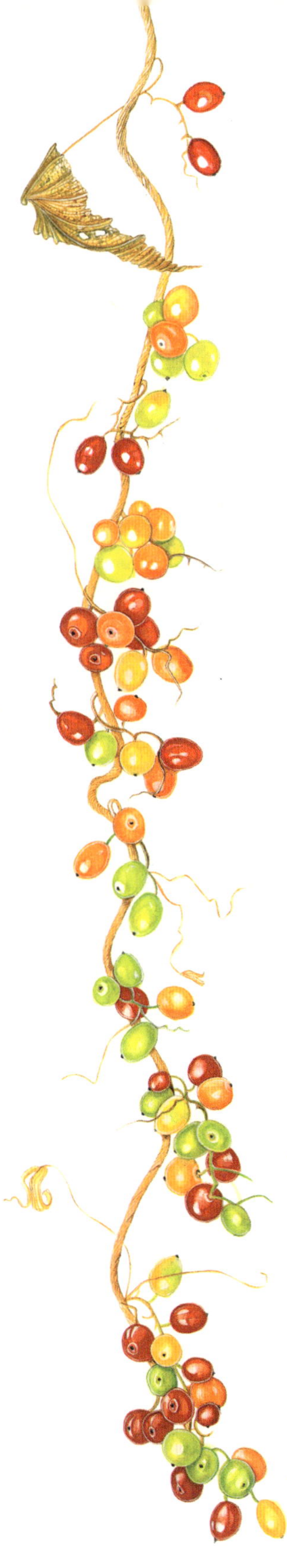

Watercolour, Linda Dearden

TEASEL FAMILY *Dipsacaceae*

Wild Teasel

Dipsacus sylvestris

The heads have numerous slender spiny bracts, from eight to twelve forming an involucre at base; they are curved upwards, ending in a sharp point. The flowers are purple and expand in irregular patches on the head; the corolla is tubular and consists of four unequal lobes. The stem leaves are opposite and not stalked; the lower couples are joined together by their bases, i.e. connate, forming a cup in which the water collects. They grow from three to six feet high. The stems are angular and spiny. To be found on the roadsides and waste places. Flowers in the late summer and autumn. EC

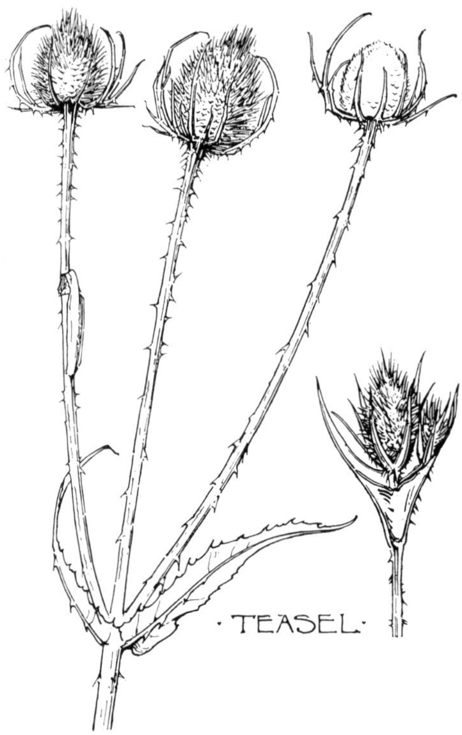

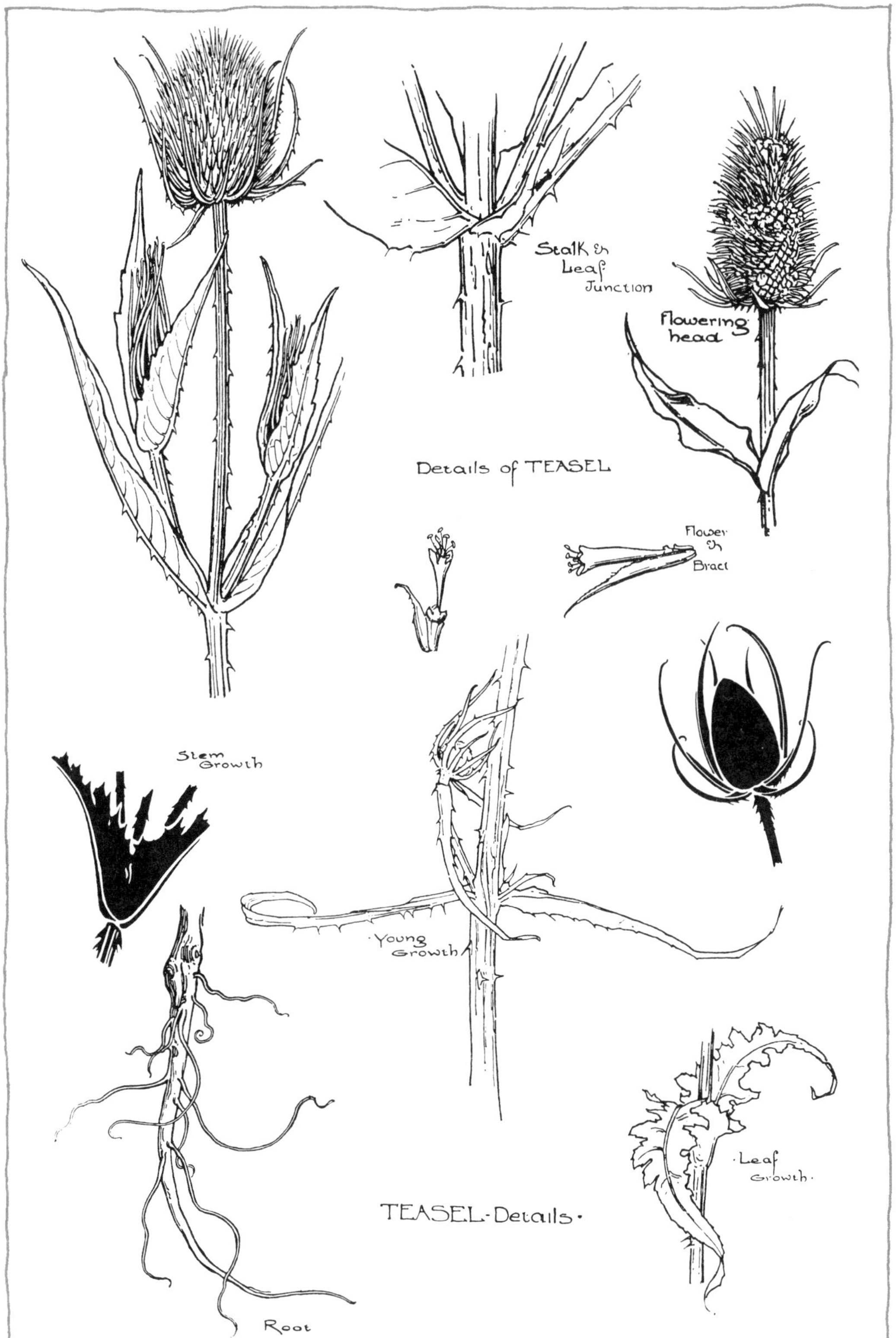
Stalk & Leaf Junction
Flowering head
Details of TEASEL
Flower & Bract
Stem Growth
Young Growth
Leaf Growth
TEASEL-Details
Root

Teasels with Poppy Seedheads

Dipsacus sylvestris with *Papaver orientalis*

An artist needs to be in the right frame of mind when settling down to paint anything as intricately formed as a teasel as it will require concentration and observation in equal measure. For the student it is definitely one of the times when a preliminary sketchbook drawing will be of enormous help.

The first thing one notices is that masterpiece of universal design known as the Fibonacci sequence where the seeds spiral around the teasel head. This pattern needs to be quickly established but unlike, say, the pineapple where the sequence is clear, here only the area directly facing the artist – about one-third – is clearly discernible. The lightest golden-brown wash was applied to a relatively small egg shape, making sure the edges were washed out with no hard outlines. Then the diamond pattern was carefully worked, drawing with the brush to shade and give depth to each little section.

Next the bristles were painted, using a negative technique to leave some very golden on the lightest side but becoming darker away from the light. This ensured that the rounded appearance was upheld.

The ribbed stem is very prickly, with little spikes emerging from the top of the ridges along its length. Those at eye level appear as tiny triangles and only in silhouette show their vicious little points. For the artist this is always something to beware of. Take care not to paint something just because you know it is there – each prickle is equally sharp but you will not see them with equal clarity. The Poppy seed-heads made a nice contrast of texture and form for this composition and the lateral dissections show us what lies within, which creates added interest.

Watercolour, Kay Rees-Davies

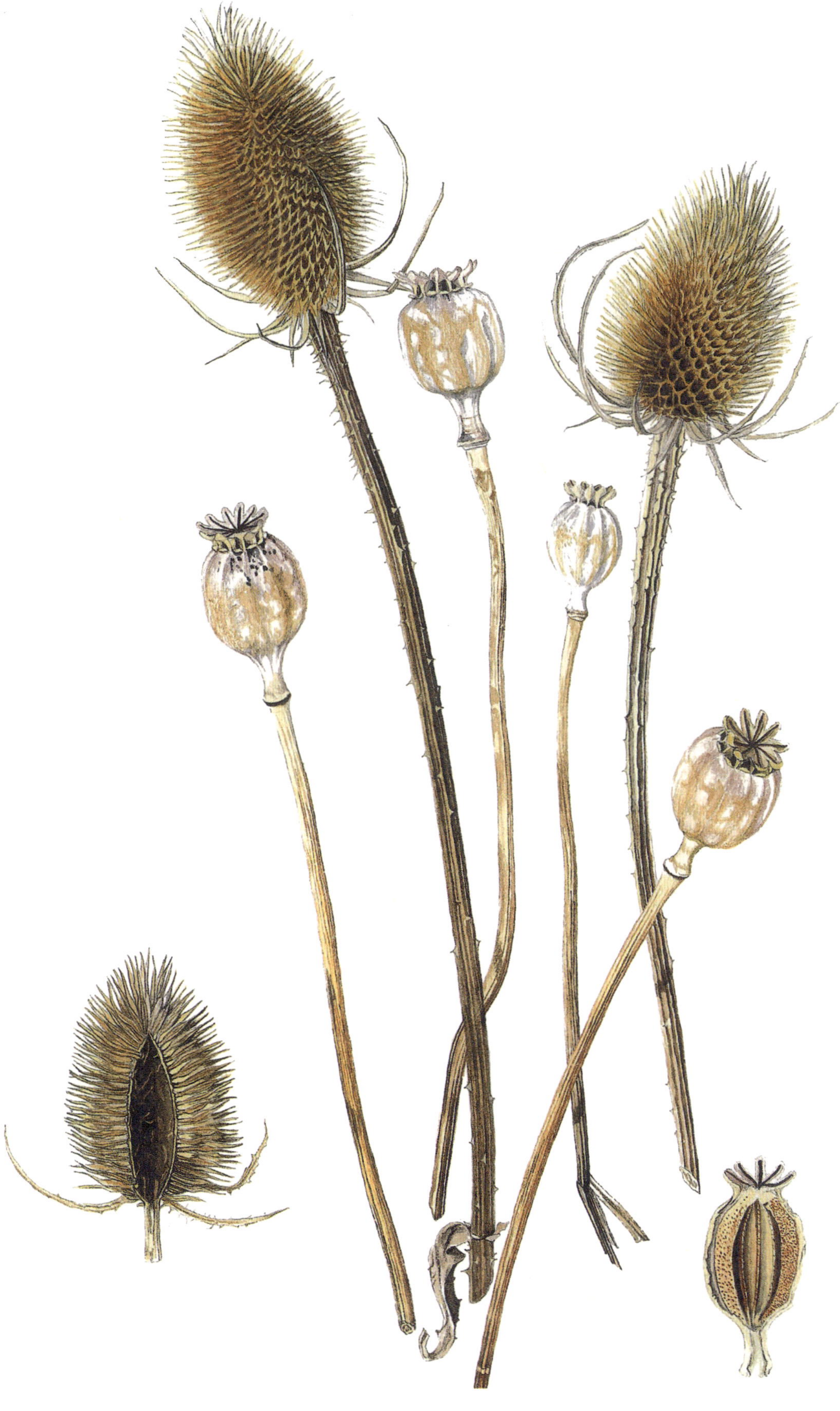

HEATH FAMILY *Ericaceae*

Rhododendron

Ericaceae

Rhododendron has formed for so long a conspicuous feature as an ornamental evergreen shrub in parks and private grounds, that we can quite look upon it, at least, as a naturalised tree.

The leaves, which are thick and glossy, grow spiral-wise or in whorls round the stems, and are oblong-lanceolate in form, with entire margins. The flowers appear early in May and June, and are in terminal groups; each has five petals or divisions, ending in a tube attached to the ovary, and twice as many stamens; the calyx is minute and five-toothed. Colour of flowers pink, purple, and red. EC

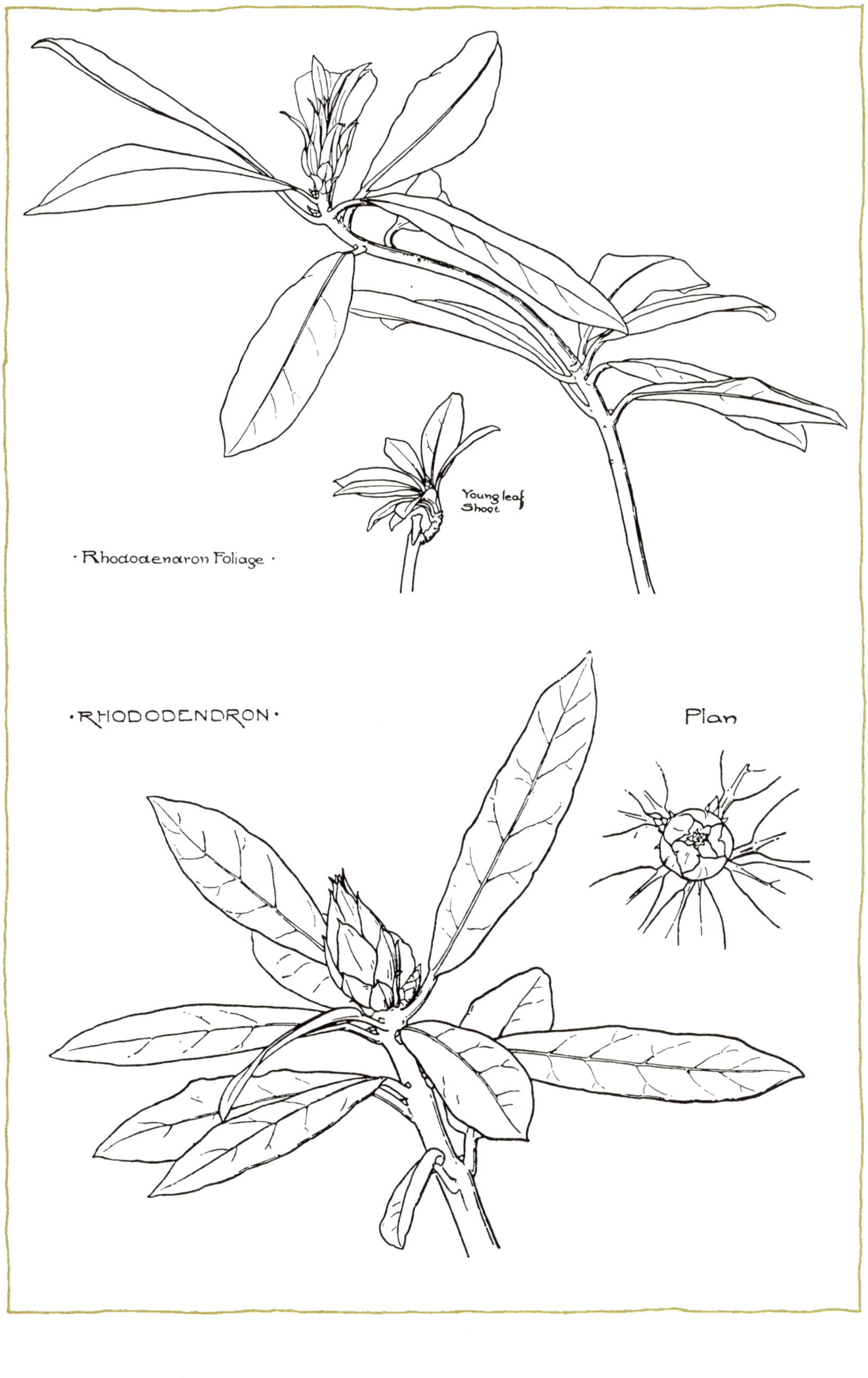
Young leaf Shoot
· Rhododendron Foliage ·
· RHODODENDRON ·
Plan

Rhododendron

Rhododendron 'Nobleanum Venustum'

The artist was lucky enough to be able to find this obliging specimen for her Diploma portfolio – obliging because it flowers at any time between November and March and sometimes manages a second flowering after frost. This painting shows the flower cluster as it emerges from the bud, when it is still a very rosy pink. Like many of its kind it will fade to pale pinkish white when the dark red blotches become more noticeable.

She made a few mistakes with this study but overall her style was still developing and this work shows a great deal of promise. The leaves, for example, look healthy and vigorous, thanks to the wet-on-wet washes where she left good highlights. Too often a student will play around with these and in trying to improve them end up overworking and spoiling what was already acceptable, even if not perfect. Knowing when to stop is important and, like so much else, becomes easier with practice.

The aritst showed a tendency to outline the petals instead of allowing lighter areas of colour to merge with the edges, particularly those on the left-hand side of the cluster which is in full light. Surprisingly she did this only on the petals, not on the leaves.

When deciding what to show for dissection, students should ensure that they are not repeating something which can clearly be seen in the main picture. Hence the leaf was unnecessary, and to be of value the flower section needed enlarging for the sake of clarity. Above all, each should have been numbered to match a key, which in this case should have been on the reverse.

By including this work I am emphasizing that we value the work of all our students, not just the lucky few with exceptional talent. Most of us, including the tutors, had to learn by our mistakes, and while it can be a hard process it is very worthwhile.

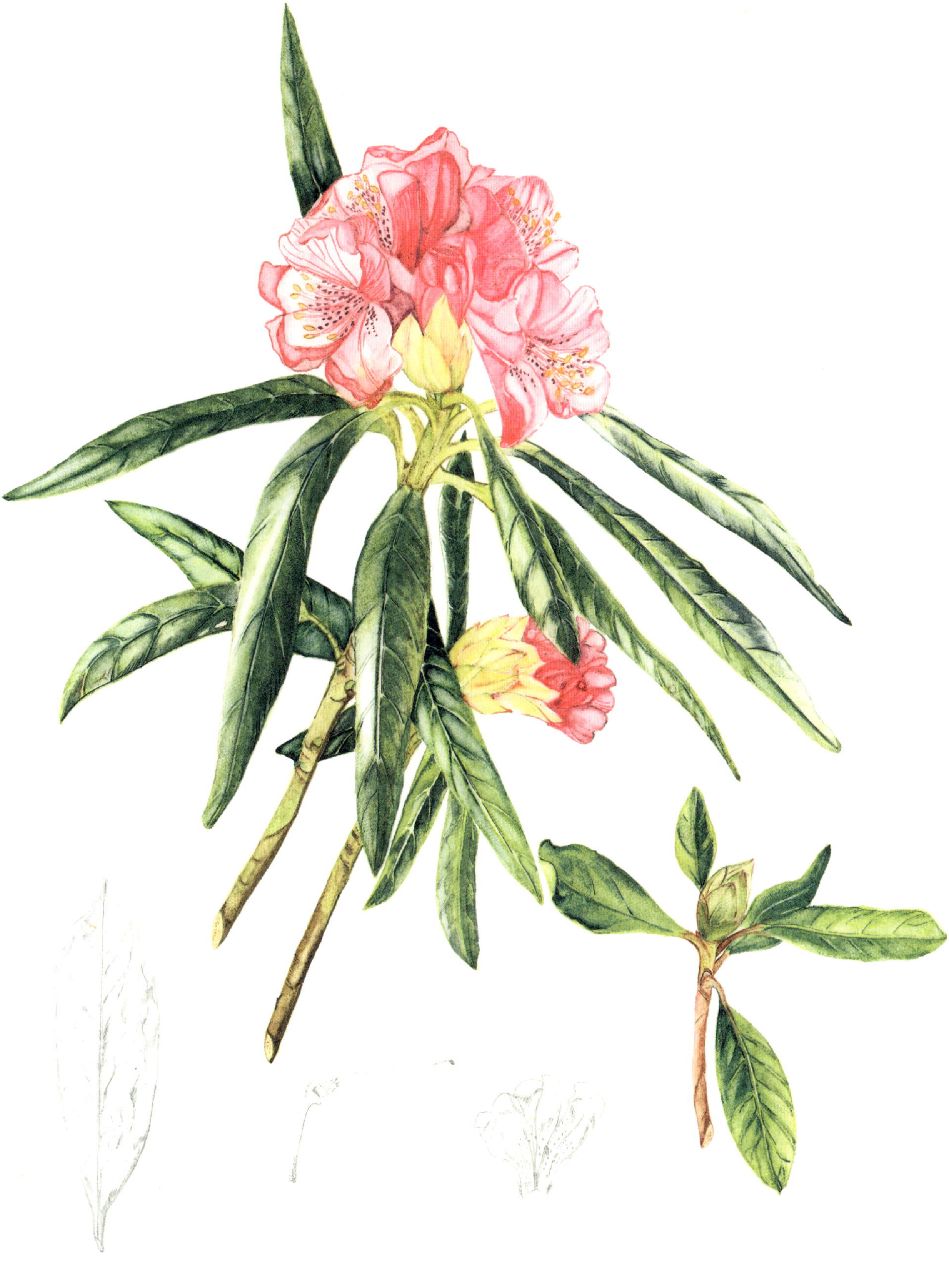

Rhododendron

Rhododendron 'Hoppy'

This very attractive member of the Yakushimanum hybrids has a compact habit and grows well in a large tub. The colour ranges from deep rosy purple as the buds open, through to the delicate lilac shade of the mature flowers, which gives continuing interest since the flowers do not all reach maturity at the same time.

I was working from a newly acquired plant in a very large pot which I was able to carry indoors during the day. Speed is quite important to me as I prefer to paint from life and never make drawings or colour notes in the more usual way. First I worked on the central flower-head, drawing the whole head, stem and leaves, but only painting the actual flowers. Once they were completed I moved on to the half-open flowers, again drawing the stem completely but only painting the blooms. Tucked slightly behind the main stem and with richer colouring, they gave depth to the painting. Working in this manner enabled me to add the shoot with new growth on the left-hand side, again tucking it in to create a middle perspective. The flowers had long fallen by the time the leaves and stems were completed.

It is some years since I painted this and I no longer remember the colours I used, except that a first wash of pale Naples Yellow gave the warm glow to the flower centres and the little bee blotches required the delicacy of Raw Sienna.

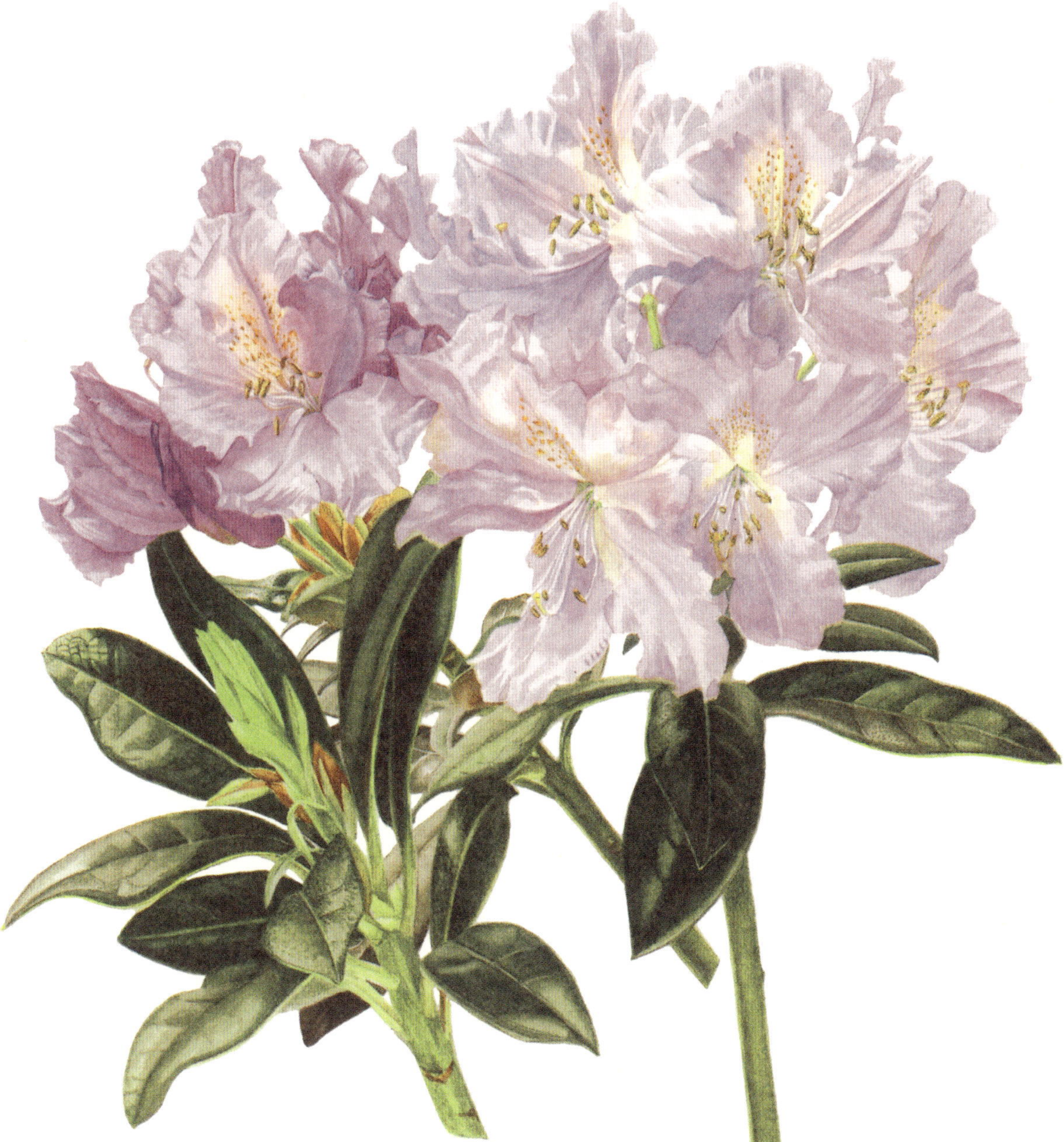

Watercolour, Margaret Stevens

PEA FAMILY *Fabaceae*

Sweet Pea

Lathyrus odoratus

Sweet Pea is one of the numerous cultivated varieties that adorn our gardens through the summer and autumn. It climbs by its tendrils to a height of seven or eight feet. The flower is of the papilionaceous order, having five petals, one, the standard, being very broad. Stamens ten, the style and stigmas single. The leaf-stalks are flattened or winged, terminating in a branched tendril, and bearing a broad oblong leaf consisting of two leaflets. The stipules are arrow-shaped. The peduncles or main flower-stems are six or eight inches in length, carrying several large flowers, the colours of which vary from white, through pinks, purples, and blues. The pod or seed-vessel varies from one to several inches long; the seeds are numerous and rather flattened. The Everlasting Pea (*L. latifolius*) is very similar in every respect, but the leaves are more lanceolate than oblong. EC

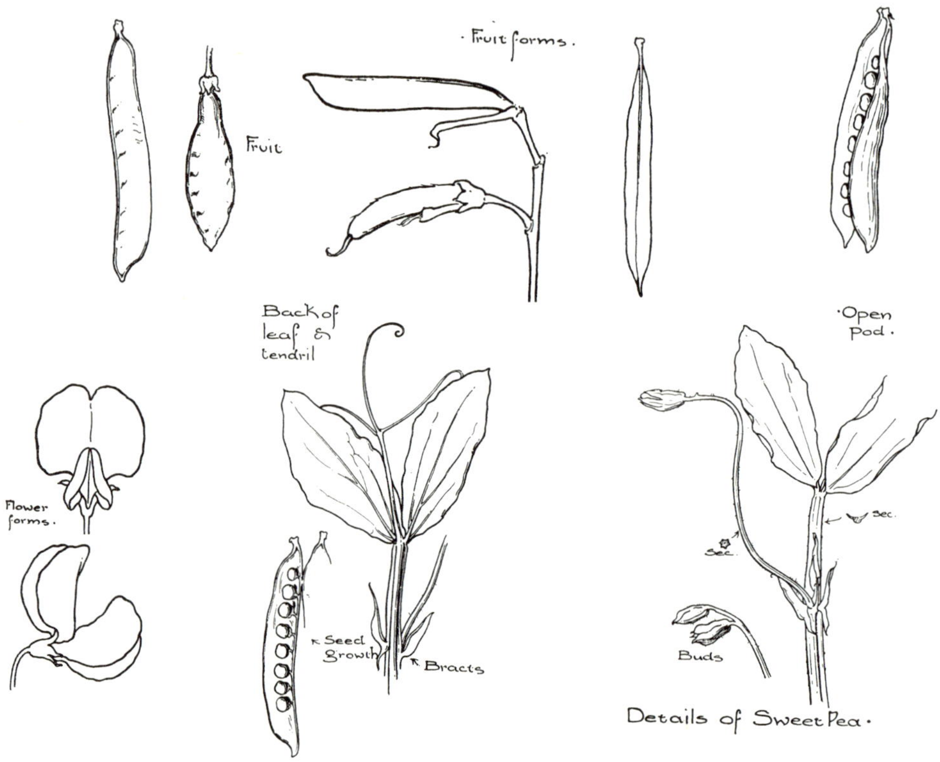

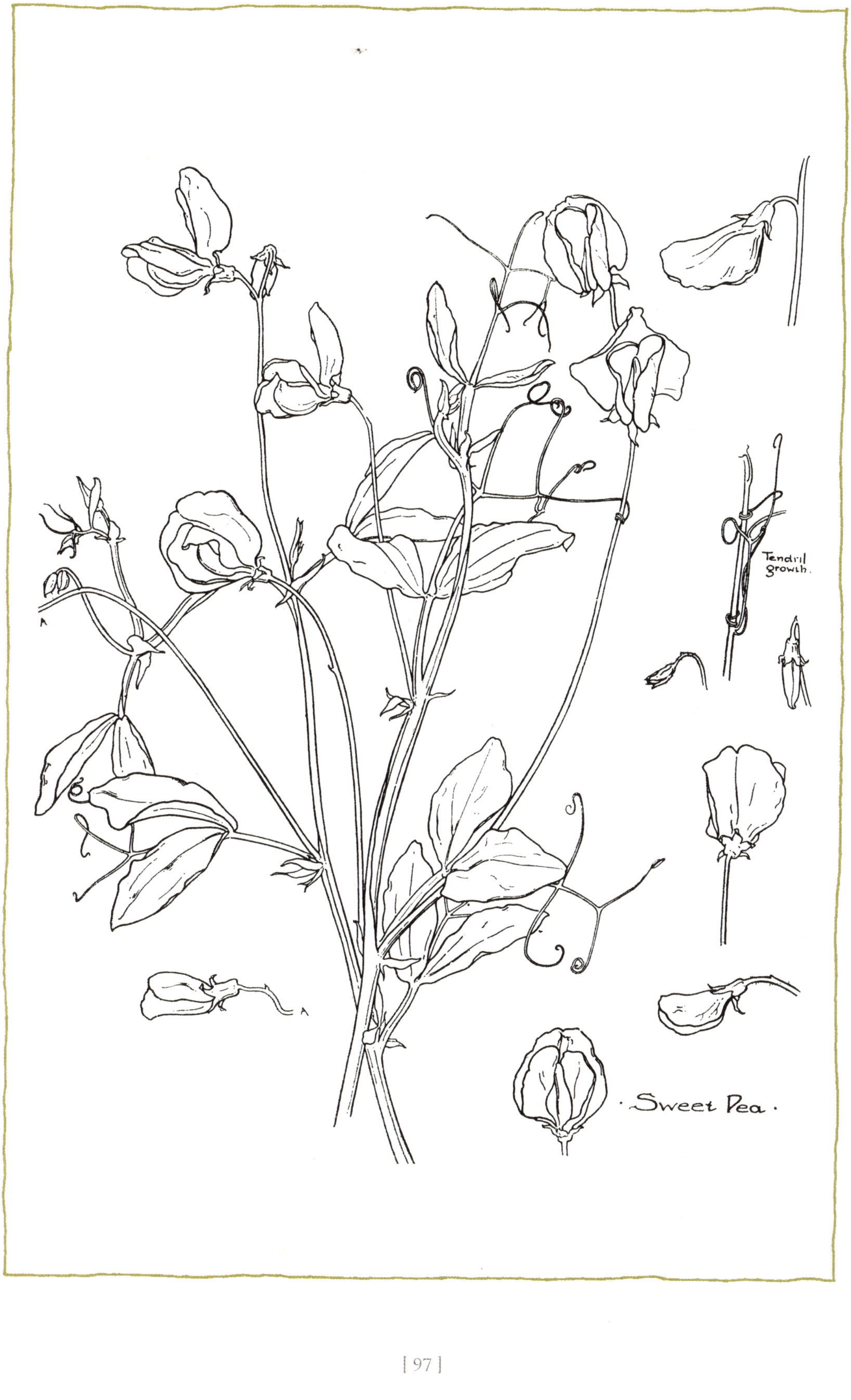

Tendril growth.
A
A
· Sweet Pea ·

Sweet Pea

Lathyrus odoratus 'Cupani'

Sweet Peas are such a familiar sight in Britain that many people assume they are a native plant. In fact they did not arrive on these shores until 1699, from Sicily – although that is not their true country of origin, which remains unknown. 'Cupani' is the original Sicilian Sweet Pea, small-flowered but prolific and with the most wonderful perfume which can be beaten by only a few of the modern large-flowered blooms. They are easy to grow from seed and they will be worth a corner in any artist's garden, where the flowers will chase over a twiggy support like a flock of tiny butterflies.

The standards are rich maroon and the wings have an iridescence where soft pink and blue merge. Here the artist used Schmincke Manganese Violet and Winsor & Newton Permanent Rose to capture this fleeting beauty. Note the carefully ribbed stem, particularly the attention paid to the cut ends. As always, a steady hand is needed to negotiate the spiralling tendrils and although they are fine and delicate these too have been shaded away from the light source. Tonal variation is important, no matter how tiny the detail.

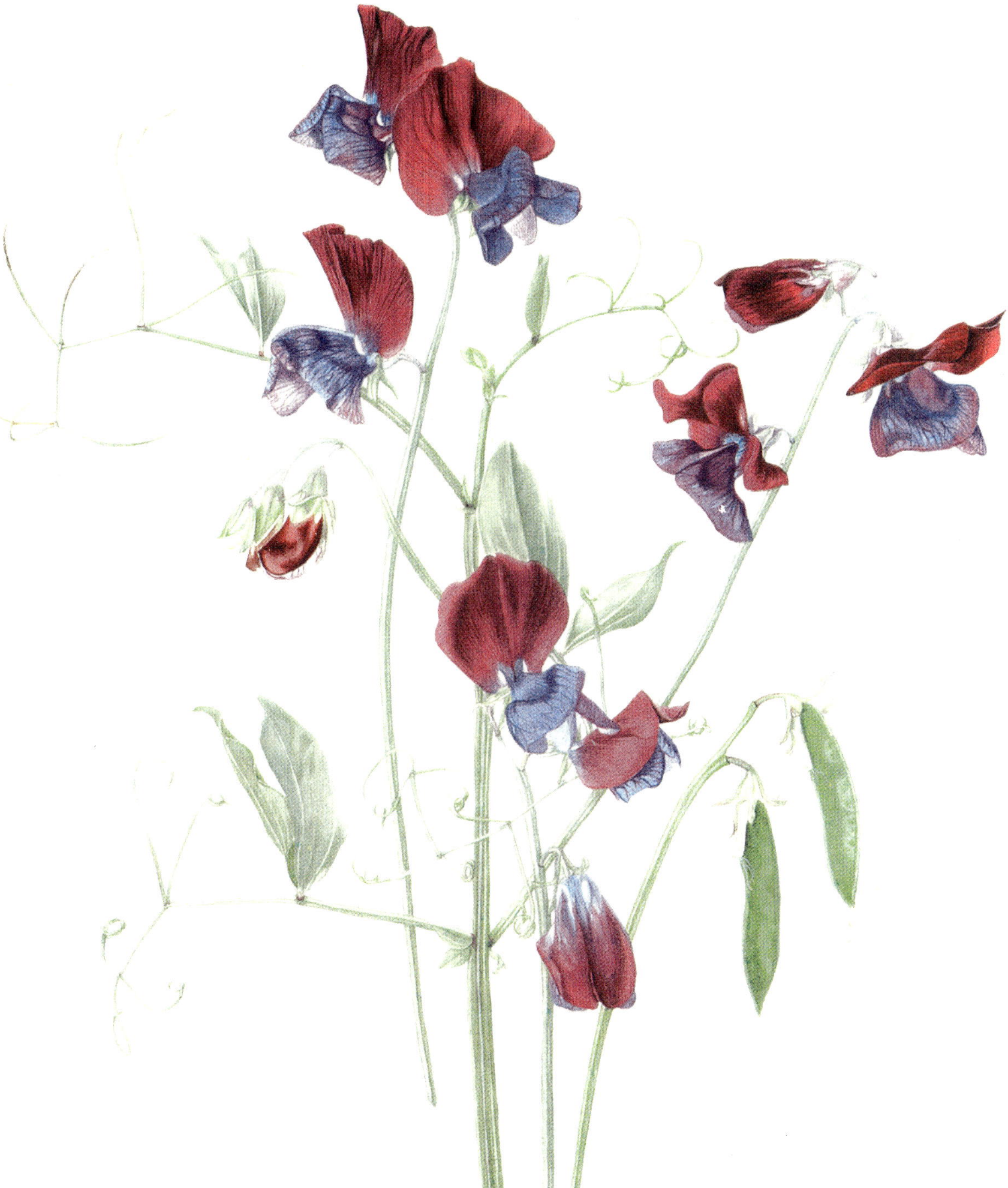

Watercolour, Kay Rees-Davies

Rattlebox

Sesbania punicea

This exotic member of the Pea family makes a striking contrast to the previous delicate *Lathyrus odoratus* 'Cupani'. It is native to South America and the artist grew it in her conservatory, where it begged to be captured on paper. Its arching foliage and racemes of vibrant flowers made composition relatively easy, as the wise artist will always go along with the growth habit of the plant. However, an easy composition does not always mean a straightforward drawing and much careful measuring was required in order to show the multipl e planes created by such a dense specimen.

This care followed through to the painting stage, when cooler, softer shades of green were used to denote the backward-facing leaflets, thus creating recession. The same attention to detail was equally important when painting the flowers, which are so tightly massed that it would be easy to end up with all-over spots of orange paint. The artist noted the way every flower has a variety of planes – reflex, convex and concave – each capturing the light differently. By varying the intensity of the pigment she was able to show this individuality, so that foreground flowers really stand out, while those to the back are allowed to retain some of their mystery.

The artist was helped in this by using transparent Winsor Orange, with Winsor & Newton Scarlet Lake, Transparent Yellow and Sepia. Had she been tempted to use opaque Cadmium Orange the effect would have been heavier and less airy. The seed-pods at the top right are well balanced by the lateral dissection shown below, where the seeds and flower parts add interest to this true botanical painting.

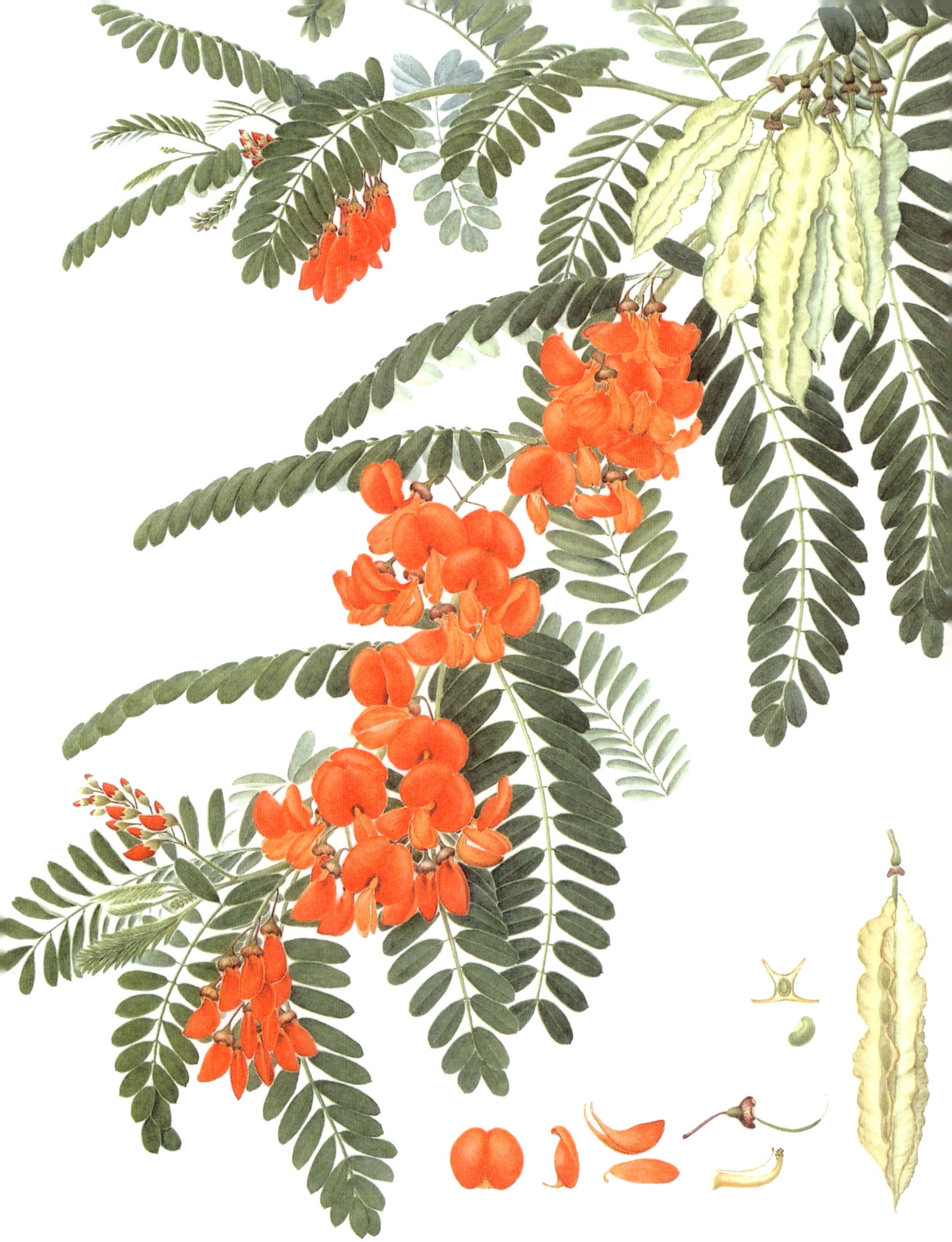

Watercolour, Yvonne Edwards

BEECH FAMILY *Fagaceae*

Oak

Quercus robur

Speaking of the oak is like speaking of one's oldest friends. Perhaps no school-boy remembers the time when he knew nothing of acorns and oak-apples. The English Oak is the longest-lived among the native trees of our islands. The leaves are short-stalked, sometimes sessile, and are obtusely lobed. The fruit, which is the well-known acorn, is carried in a shallow cup, consisting of a series of closely-knitted scales forming an involucre. They grow sometimes in clusters, sometimes in spikes. The tree flowers in the spring, when the leaves are growing. There are many varieties, and the leaves vary considerably. EC

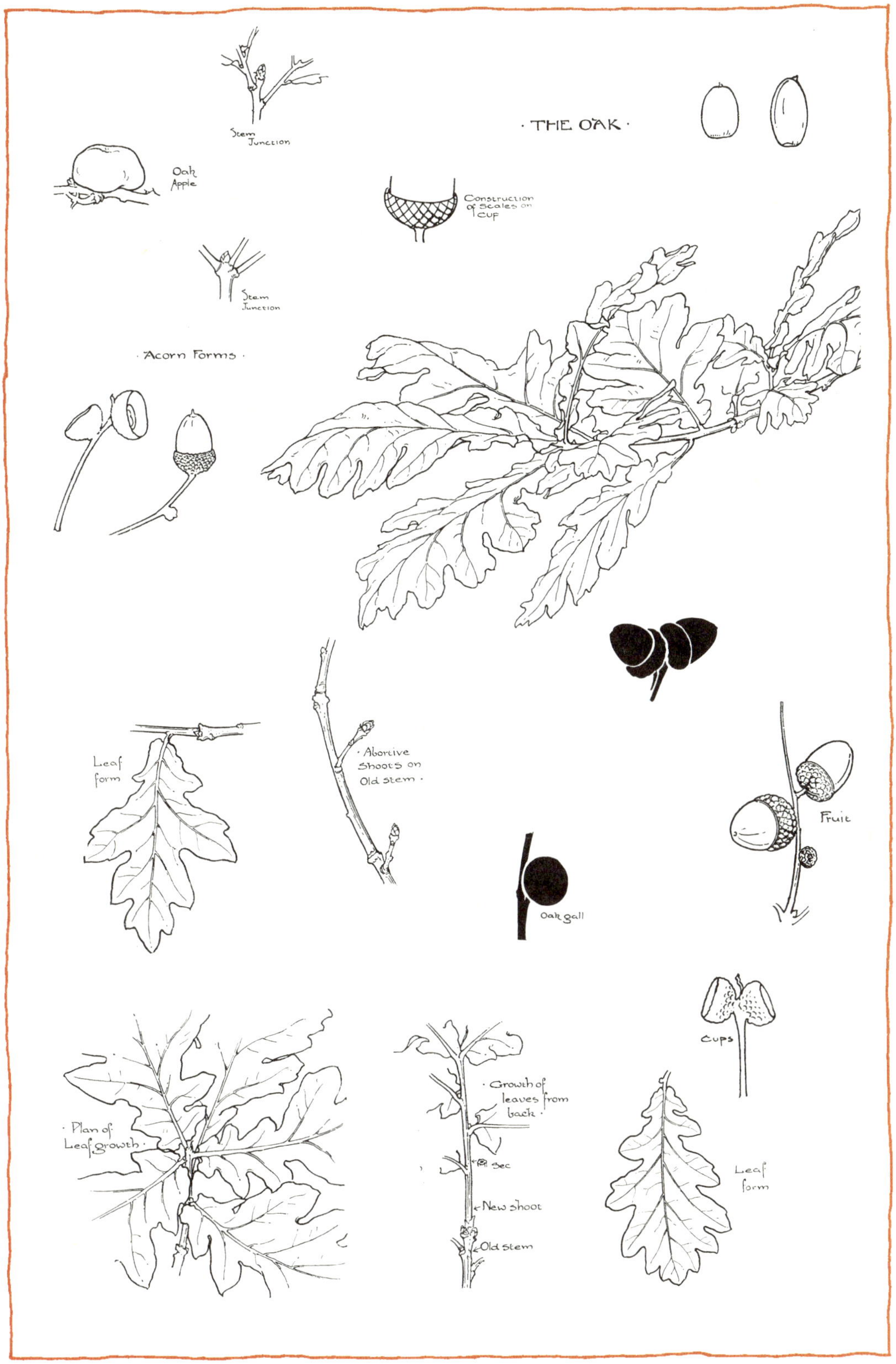
· THE OAK ·
Stem Junction
Oak Apple
Construction of Scales on Cup
Stem Junction
· Acorn Forms ·
Leaf form
· Abortive Shoots on Old stem ·
Fruit
Oak gall
Cups
· Plan of Leaf growth ·
· Growth of leaves from back ·
Sec
New shoot
Old stem
Leaf form

Oak

Quercus robur

This illustration shows a complete year in the life of an English oak, from the pale green leaves and lime-green flowers of spring through fruitful maturity to the rich brown of late autumn, when acorns fall from their cups.

Once again the artist used graphite to lighten the composition and it provides diagonal symmetry to the layout. With the addition of the bare twig, empty cup and foliage with just a hint of colour wash, it also suggests the barren winter months. A lot of thought goes into an illustration of this kind where a seemingly casual arrangement conceals a level of deeper meaning.

This artist always does a preliminary drawing of a leaf in order to plot the position of the veins before starting on the main picture. She then uses a wash of the lightest green to match the vein and midrib colour. When this is dry she paints in towards the veins and, using them as a map, works carefully on each section of the leaf, painting toward the midrib and following the direction of growth. This method helps to make sense of what can otherwise seem complicated and daunting. Done properly, it will ensure that perspective and form are accurately portrayed and that a full tonal range will be shown.

Watercolour and graphite, Vickie Marsh

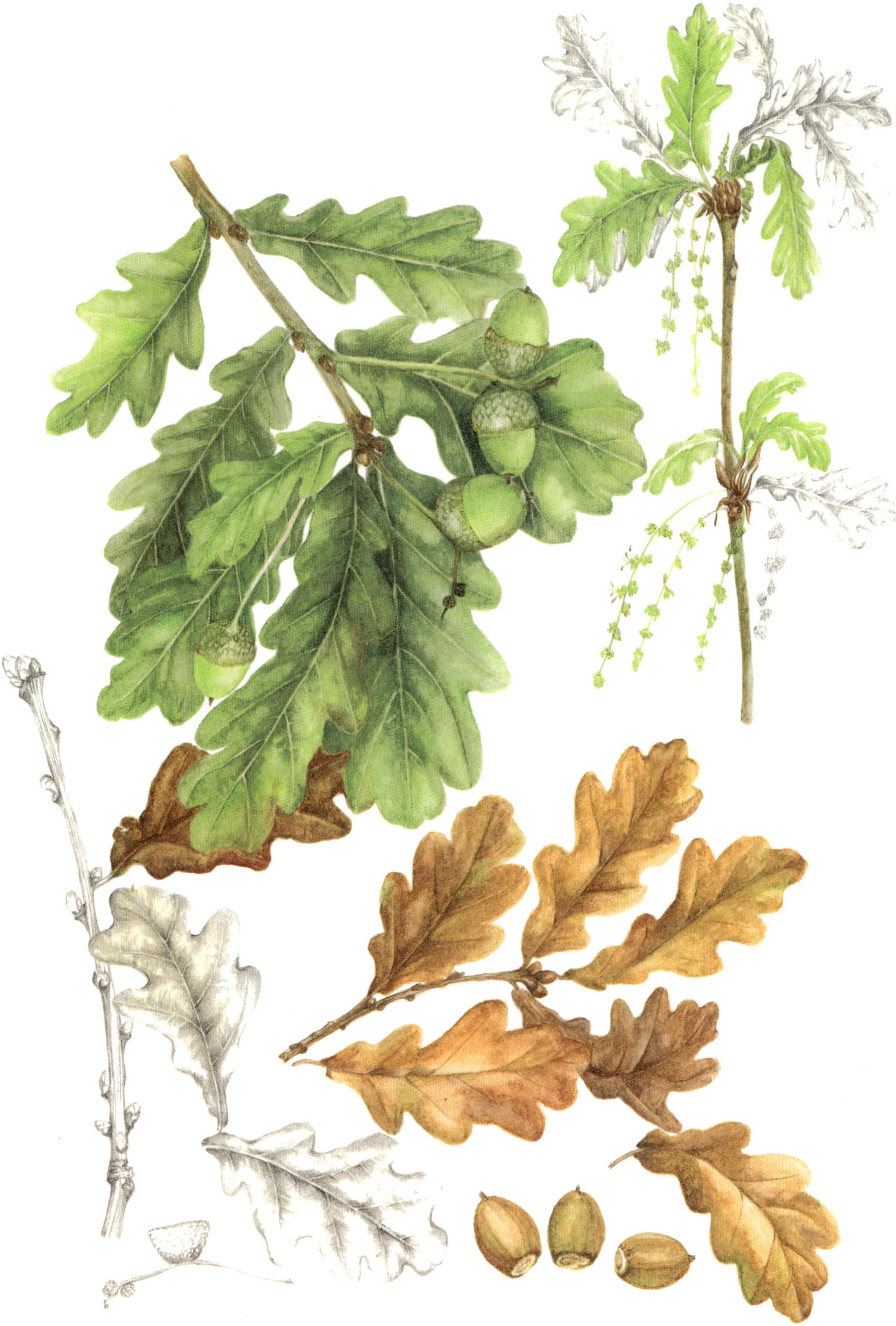

GERANIUM FAMILY *Geraniaceae*

Meadow Cranesbill

Geranium pratense

Where it is found the Meadow Cranesbill is a striking feature, with its large bluish-purple flowers and reddish-purple veins, its erect branching growth, and large dull-green leaves. It is mostly to be seen in low-lying land and moist pastures, very often enriching with its purple blooms the long mowing grass, and growing from one to three feet high. It bears five petals distinctly marked by purple veining, a calyx of five sepals slightly hairy, ten stamens, five long and five short, the ovary is five lobed, terminating in a long beak with five stigmas. The flowers grow in pairs, each with a separate stalk or pedicel. The lower leaves are large and palmate, having five or seven separate segments coarsely serrated and of a rather dark green, the radical leaves are borne on long stalks. At the junction of the flower-stalks are thin pointed bracts, sometimes resembling small leaves, while at the leaf-stalk junctions stipules of a fibrous nature are found. The inflorescence is known botanically as a loose panicle. The root-stock is thick and woody, covered with the thin brown stipules of the older leaves. The stems are much forked towards the top, and are somewhat swollen at the nodes or joints.

The leaves in the autumn take on the most brilliant colours, varying from a yellow to a deep scarlet. The flowers are to be found from May to September, and measure about an inch to an inch and a half across. EC

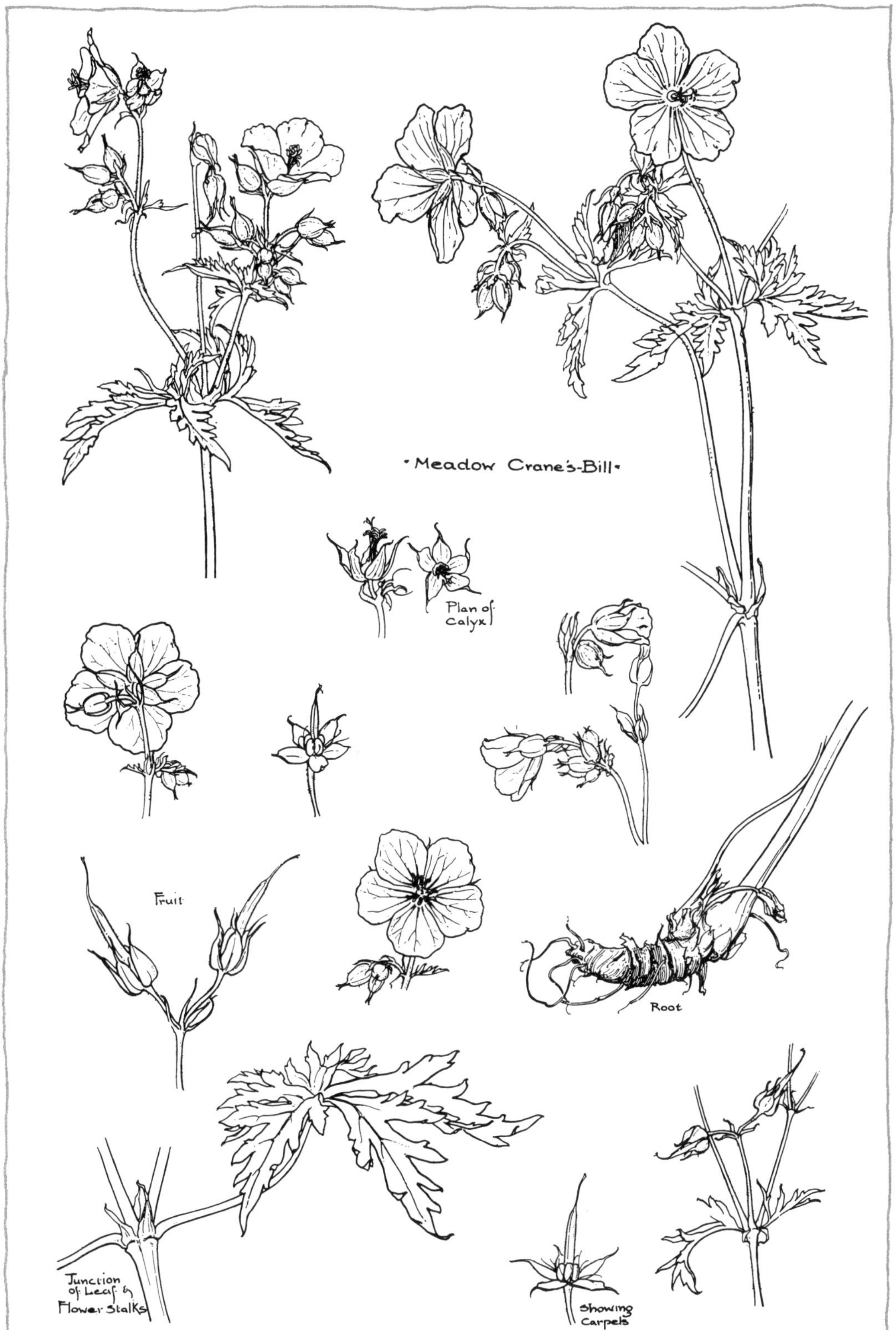
• Meadow Crane's-Bill •
Plan of Calyx
Fruit
Root
Junction of Leaf & Flower Stalks
Showing Carpels

Hedgerow Cranesbill

Geranium pyrenaicum

This is an excellent sketchbook page which records in detail a Hedgerow Cranesbill, one of the plants the artist chose for her Field Study assignment. The pencil drawing is crisp and clear, with some excellent shading. The texture of the root has been enhanced by a pale wash of colour and her colour notes show that she used Winsor & Newton Quinacridone Magenta with Winsor Violet, and Winsor Red with Winsor Violet for the flowers, which she doubled in size. The dead growth on the root was painted with a mix of Indigo, Winsor Yellow and Winsor Red, while the sepals required Winsor Lemon with Cobalt Blue.

The artist's note that the plant has an angular growth habit and 'popping' seed-heads is enhanced by her calligraphy, indicating that she does not look on keeping a sketchbook record as a chore but rather as a diarist might want her written word to record time, place and atmosphere for posterity. In fact the artist filled two such books throughout the course and I suspect this will become the habit of a lifetime – a wonderful legacy for her family.

Sketchbook page, Sandie Hawkins

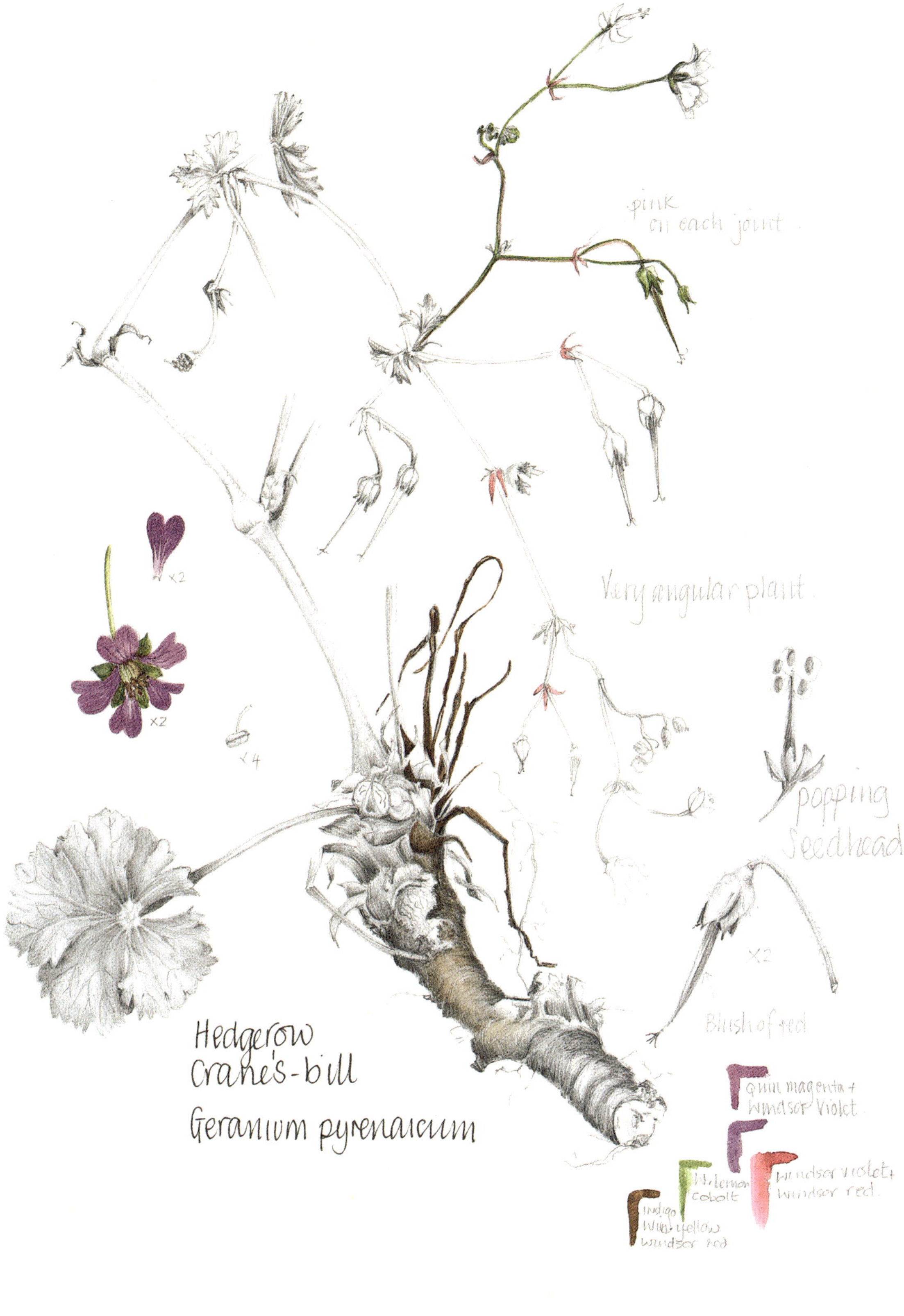
pink on each joint.
Very angular plant.
x2
x2
x4
popping Seedhead
x2
Blush of red
Hedgerow Crane's-bill
Geranium pyrenaicum
Quin magenta + Windsor Violet.
Windsor violet + Windsor red.
W. lemon cobolt
indigo
Win. yellow
Windsor red

HORSE CHESTNUT FAMILY

Hippocastanaceae

Horse Chestnut

Aesculus hippocastanum

What was said of the oak might as fitly be said of the Horse-chestnut. It is not a native of the British Isles, but has been long-enough introduced (1629) to become quite naturalized. It bears a beautiful cluster of flowers, varying from white to pink, in the form of a panicle or thyrsus. The leaves are palmate, consisting of five or seven leaflets, and grow in opposite pairs. The young leaf buds (illustrated on page 111) and fruit form extremely decorative forms, as does the flower (see page 112). EC

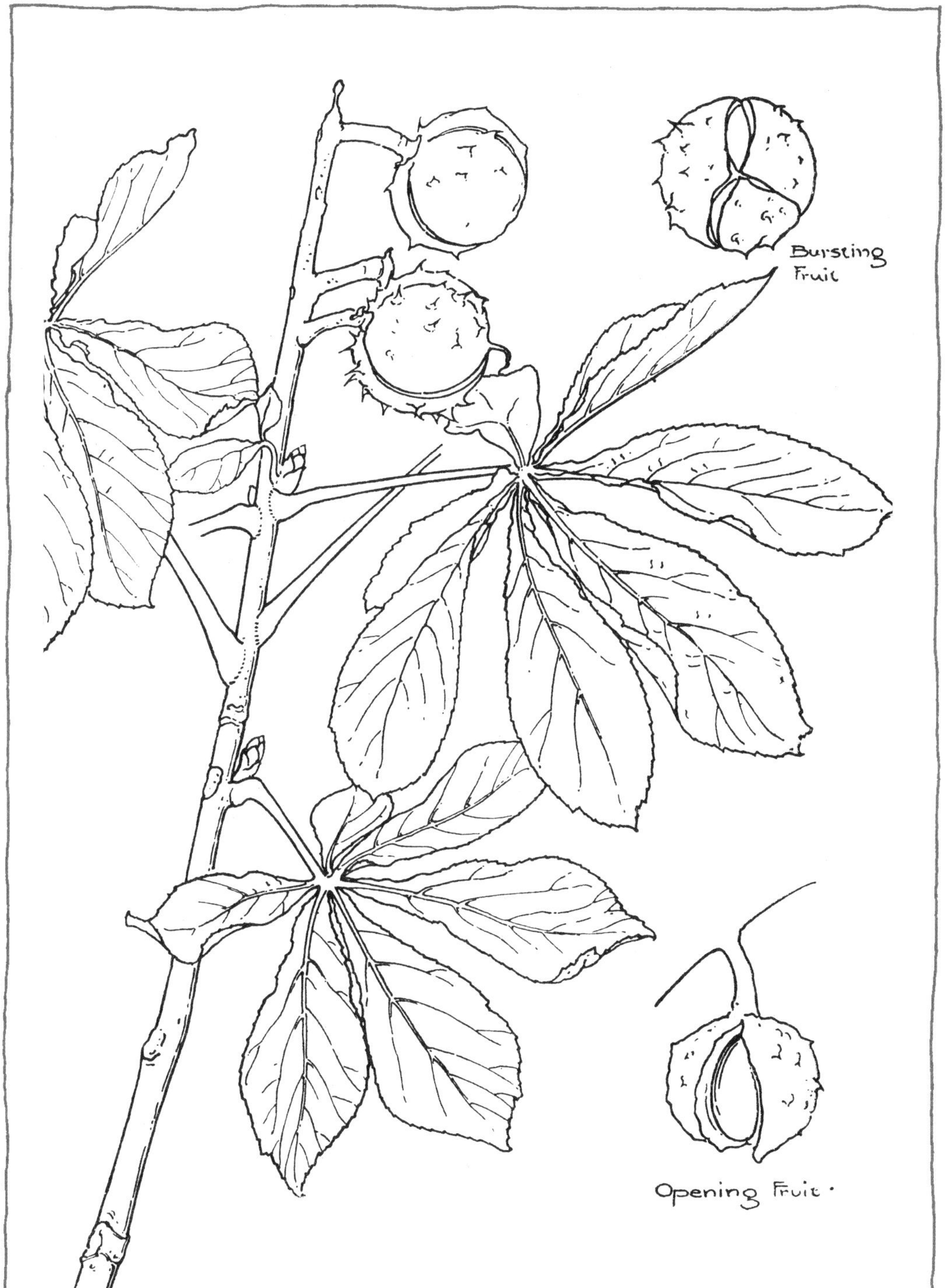
Bursting Fruit
Opening Fruit ·
· HORSE CHESTNUT ·

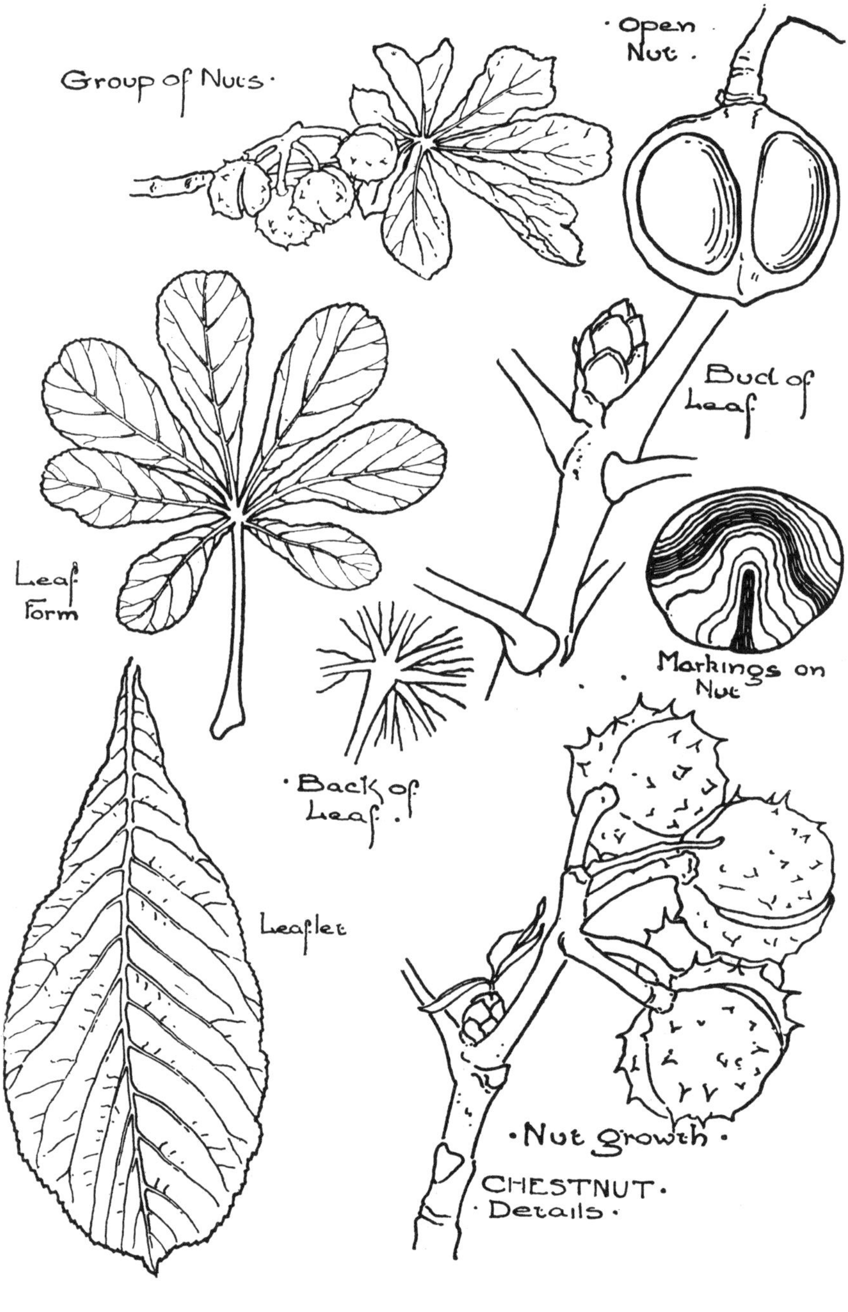
Group of Nuts
Open Nut
Bud of Leaf
Leaf Form
Markings on Nut
Back of Leaf
Leaflet
Nut growth
CHESTNUT
Details

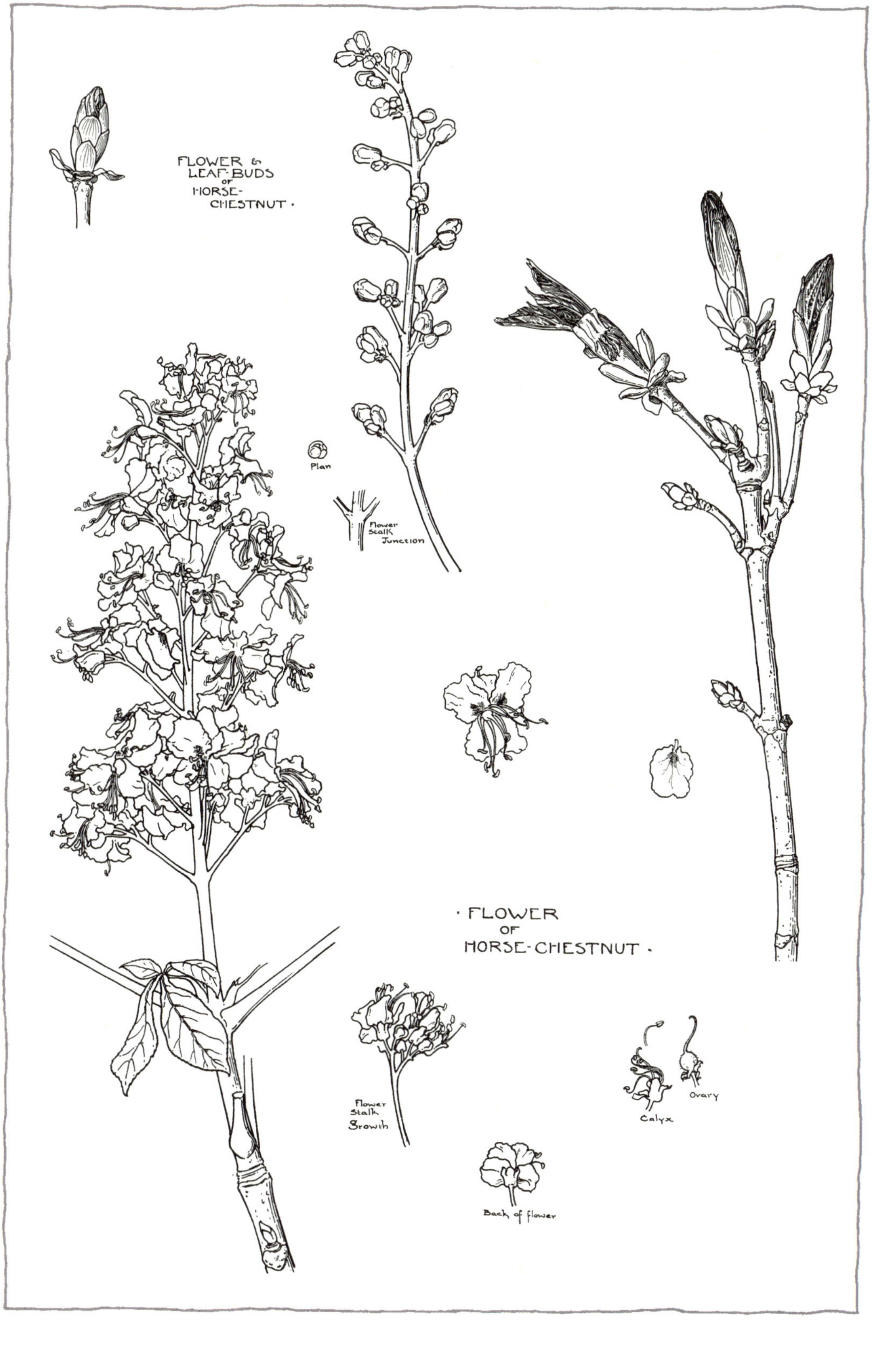
FLOWER & LEAF-BUDS OF HORSE-CHESTNUT.
Plan
Flower Stalk Junction
· FLOWER OF HORSE-CHESTNUT ·
Flower Stalk Growth
Calyx
Ovary
Back of flower

Horse Chestnut

Aesculus hippocastanum

The artist's colour blending and attention to detail in depicting the venation of the large leaf is unsurpassed in this painting. She has controlled the washes well, taking her time to build up layer upon layer of colour and leaving these washes to dry completely before using the brush to draw in the side veins. Only then could she add the finishing touches of colour such as the green, painting it up to the veins and using a clean damp brush to blend and soften the outer edge. With such large subjects it is best to work on one section at a time.

The green leaves and conkers in their husks had to be drawn in first in order to show the large leaf positioned well behind them. You cannot depend on nature to put things in the right place for composition purposes, and it is sometimes necessary to tweak a leaf or stem to achieve this, or perhaps to show a feature to its best advantage.

Removing an unwanted leaf or bud is also permissible, though if possible you should show where you have made the cut so that the observer knows that something grew in that position.

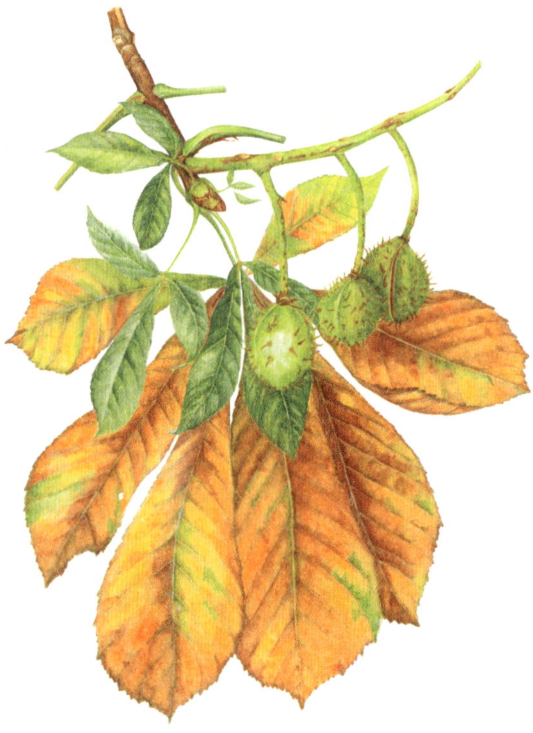

Watercolour, Vickie Marsh

Horse Chestnut Conkers

Aesculus hippocastanum

This simple study of conkers teaches us two things: first, that clean lines and an uncluttered triangular space on the right-hand side makes a very appealing composition. Note the way in which the twisted end of the twig on the left gives depth to the arrangement without the use of shadows, which would have turned this into a still-life painting rather than a botanical study.

Secondly, the artist used, in this case, a limited palette of Burnt Sienna, Permanent Rose, Cobalt Blue and Winsor Yellow, which unifies the whole and makes it hold together by harmonizing the colour. Burnt Sienna with Permanent Rose gave her the vibrant colour of the conkers, with Cobalt Blue added in the darker areas. The inside of the husks and the twig were shaded with a mix of varying proportions of Burnt Sienna and Cobalt Blue, while the outside of the husks required a mix of Winsor Yellow and Cobalt Blue. The artist has achieved some lovely textures both on the prickly husks and the glossy conkers by carefully blending the highlights and then painting in the delicate grain on the shells.

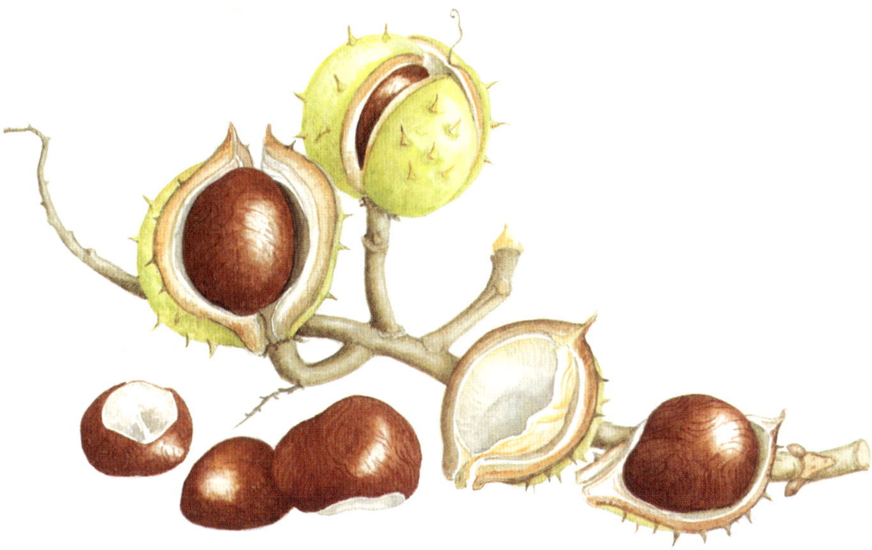

Watercolour, Jenny Jowett

IRIS FAMILY *Iridaceae*

Crocus

Crocus vernus

An early-flowering spring plant, bearing flowers of purple, yellow, and white. When the Crocuses begin to push up their heads through the earth in spite of biting east winds, we begin to realize that 'Springe ys i-comen in'. Its root is a bulb with a scaly covering and white rootlets. The leaves are narrow, linear and radical, dark green in colour, enclosed at the base by fibrous sheaths, they grow nearly as high as the flower and are angular in section. The flower, which in the example figured was purple, has nearly six equal petals or sepals, ending in a very long tube the same colour as the perianth, and which does duty as a flower-stalk, reaching to the root. The stamens are three, and the pistil has three stigmas, which are wedge-shaped and notched. Both stamens and stigmas are a deep bright yellow. EC

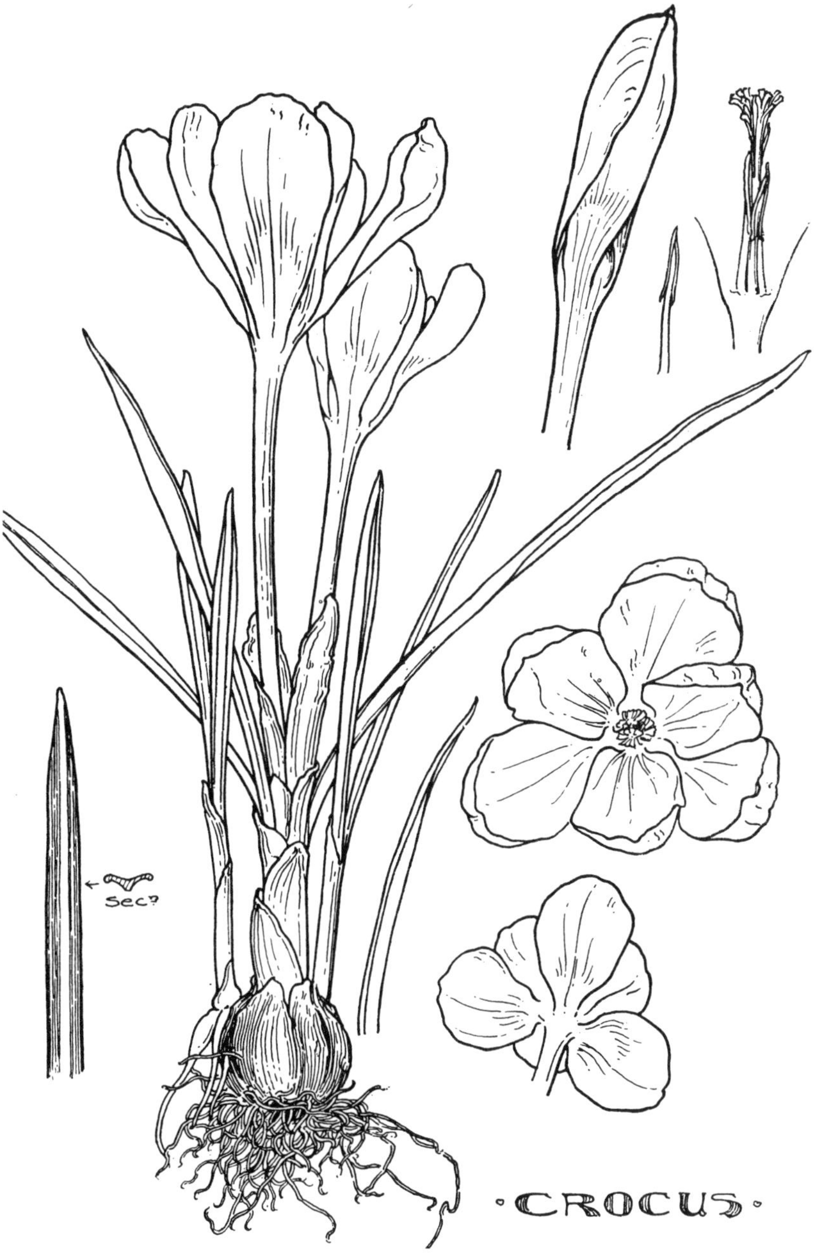
Sec?
·CROCUS·

Purple Crocus

Crocus vernus var. unknown

The artist has shown this large-flowered variety of crocus in every stage of growth from bud to open flower. It was important to capture the shine on the petals, which not only gives shape to the curved cups but helps to emphasize the depth of colour. This is one of those occasions when it is important not to paint all over the palest first wash but to allow the darker shades to suffuse the light areas, gently blending the colour to create the silky texture which is such a feature of these flowers.

Note how the colour warms as the flower matures, and what is just a rosy hint as they open gradually takes over from the blue shade of purple. Growing the bulbs in a pot so that they can be put outdoors in the cold at night helps the flowers to last longer. Painting in a chilly room is also a good idea!

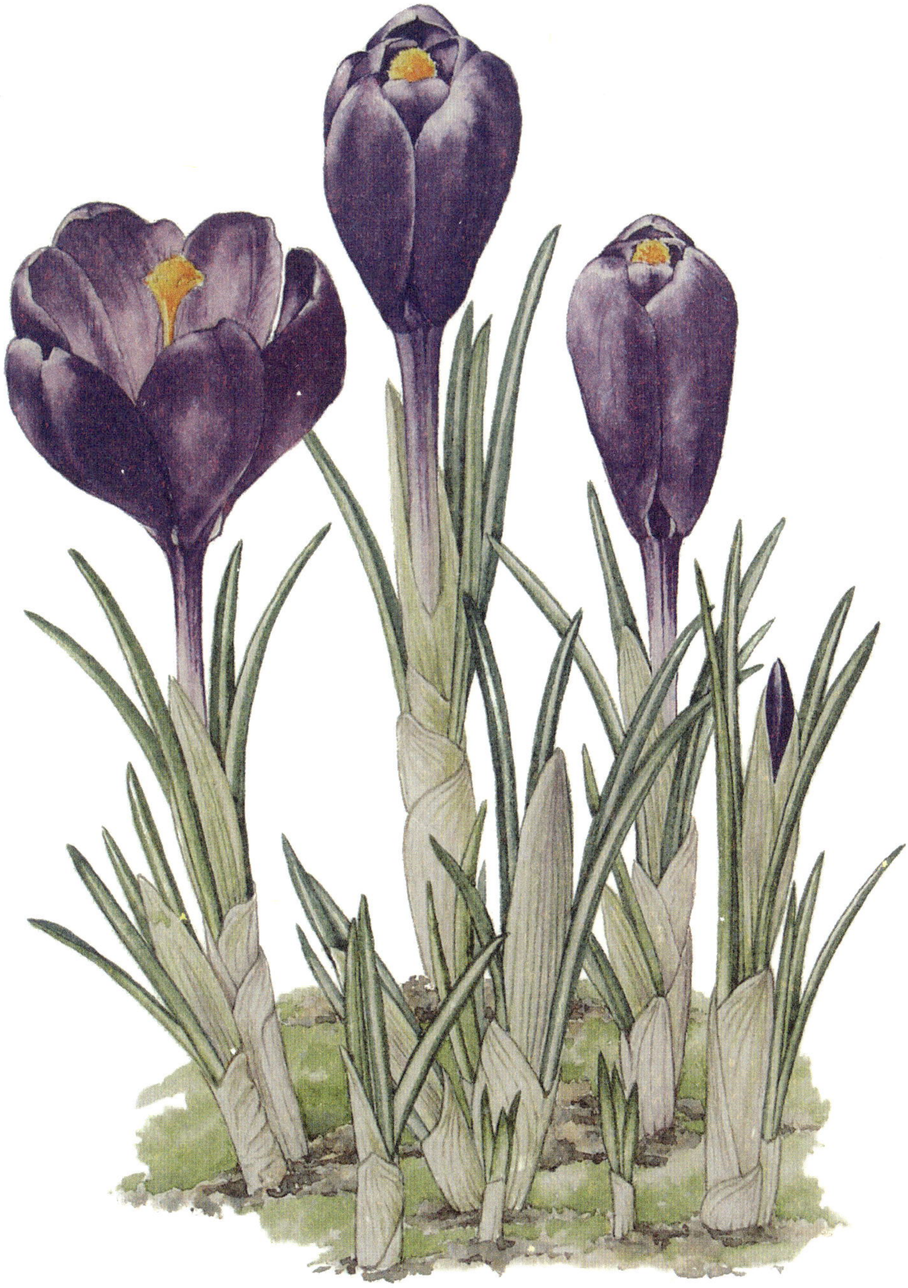

Watercolour, Reinhild Raistrick

Dutch Iris

Iris x *hollandica*

Dutch Iris are among the easiest of the early summer bulbs to grow, as well as one of the least expensive. Planted in tubs, they reappear year after year and once the untidy foliage has died back, shallow-rooted summer bedding will provide ongoing colour. They are also excellent flowers for the house, particularly when cut in the bud, and by the same token they are good for the artist, allowing reasonable time for painting as their heraldic shapes unfurl. Included here are 'Bronze Beauty', 'Golden Emperor' and 'Silvery Beauty'.

Composition using stiff, upright flowers is often tricky and this particular painting languished for four years as I tried to find a way to soften it. The torrential rains of 2012 were not good for the flowers but resulted in masses of grassy foliage quite early on, so I took a handful up to my workroom and settled on one elegant strand to provide a much-needed curve that would hold the whole thing together.

There were so many lovely shapes that I was tempted to add more, but part of the challenge with this kind of painting is knowing when to stop.

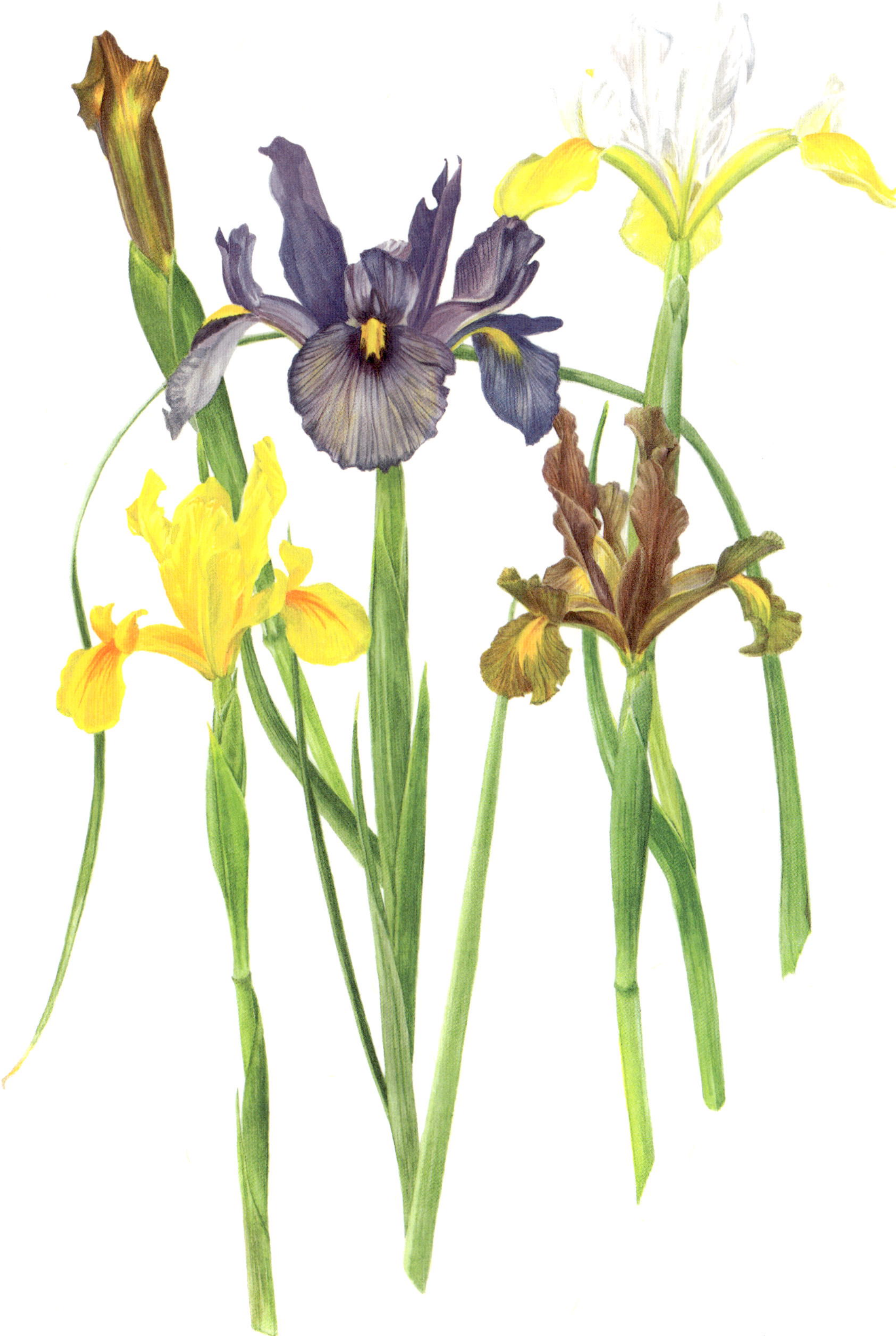

Gladiolus

Gladiolus ramosus

This plant is usually seen in its cultivated state in our gardens, where it forms a conspicuous feature, assumes a greater variety of colours, and grows to a greater height than it does in its wild state, when it is known as *Gladiolus communis*. The root-stock is bulbous, the leaves are those known as linear-lanceolate, and are shorter than the flower-stem. The flower is a perianth, and grows in a one-sided spike; it has six petals or segments which are oblong, three stamens, style three-lobed, larger than the stamens. The flowers are all turned to one side and sessile between two bracts. A spike usually consists of from four to eight blossoms.

EC

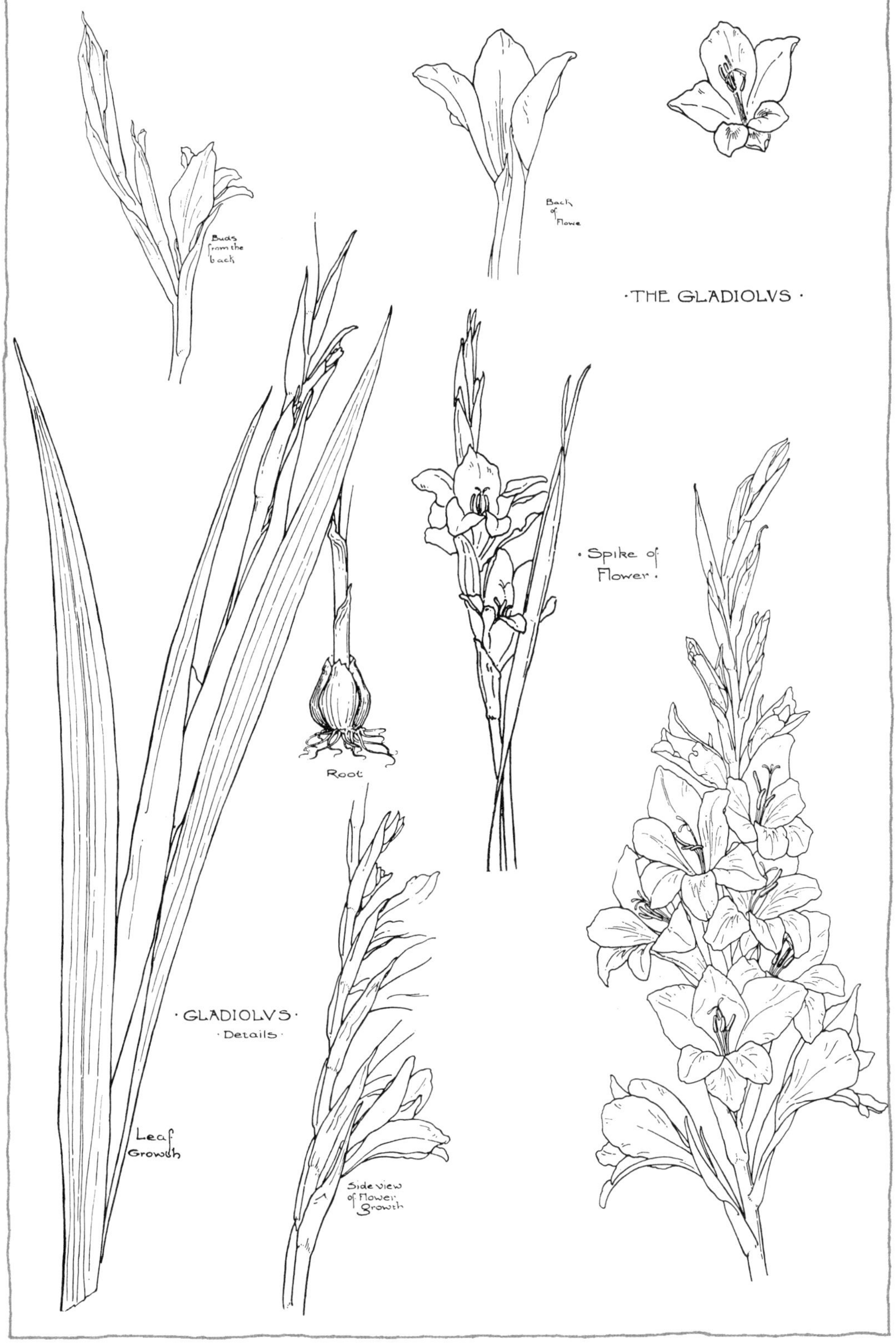
Buds from the back
Back of Flowe
·THE GLADIOLVS·
·Spike of Flower·
Root
·GLADIOLVS·
·Details·
Leaf Growth
Side view of Flower Growth

Gladiolus

Gladiolus 'Georgette', Grandiflora group

The sketchbook of this artist is a thing of beauty, with all her working drawings, colour notes and trial paintings stuck in either individually or in transparent polythene pockets. From them I was able to work out exactly how she arrived at this very attractive painting of an often overlooked flower.

I could see that originally she planned three stems of flowers, no doubt thinking that the odd number would work best in her composition. She went on to reach the sensible conclusion that this would result in an overcrowded painting on the A3-size paper demanded for the assignment, a constraint that is imposed purely for the convenience of posting, often from one side of the world to the other – distance learning means exactly that.

The artist overcame this by placing one of the long, sword-like leaves on the inner side of the page, thus adding weight and balance to the composition and enabling the eye to read successfully from left to right. You could say that the short leaf provides the full stop. Flowers with this erect growth habit are ideal for cutting off straight at the bottom and the picture could be mounted with or without visible bleed – the area between the mount and subject matter.

The artist wisely photographed her flowers for future reference as they would open out and change quicker than she could paint them. Providing she worked out her colour chart she was had what she needed to make her painting, and I could see from the chart that she used Cadmium Yellow Pale as the underlying shade, with Permanent Rose and sometimes a little Alizarin Crimson touched with French Ultramarine where the darkest note was needed.

The foliage was painted using a mix of Winsor & Newton's Cadmium Yellow Pale and French Ultramarine, sometimes adding Winsor Blue (Green Shade). For the dark reddish-green leaf edges she mixed Alizarin Crimson with French Ultramarine. As a final touch, she washed Cadmium Yellow Pale in the centre of the flower petals to add a fresh, vibrant glow. The end result is a delightful painting which helped the artist gain her Distinction.

Watercolour, Minna Keeler

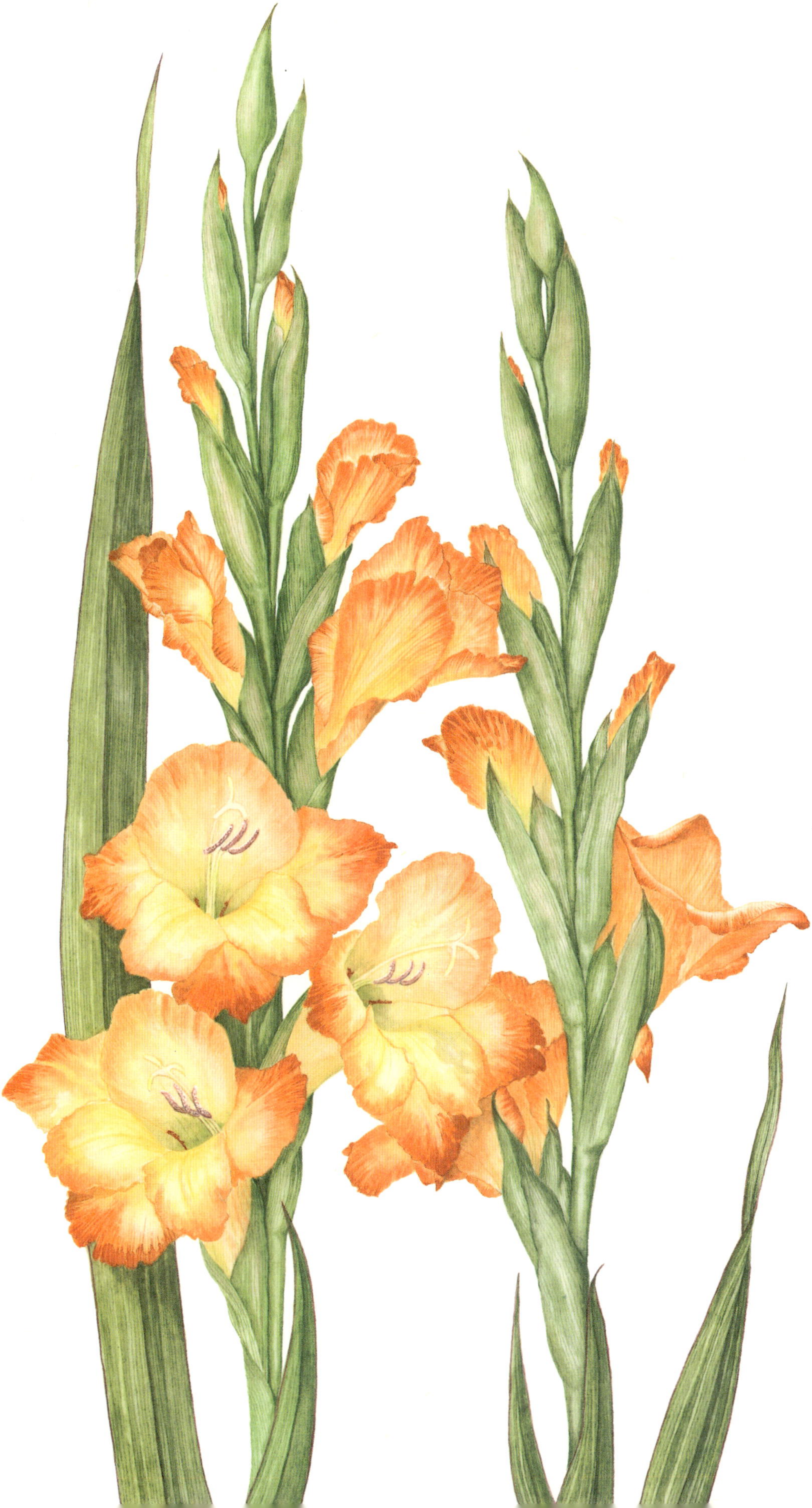

LAUREL FAMILY *Lauraceae*

Laurel

Prunus laurocerasus

'Daphne' is the name by which this shrub was known among the ancient Greeks; it was sacred to Apollo. The drawings illustrate the Common or Cherry Laurel, which, along with the Portugal Laurel, forms a conspicuous feature of most ornamental shrubberies and gardens throughout Britain.

It is an evergreen and has large ovate-lanceolate, smooth and sometimes remotely serrated leaves growing alternately up the stem. The flowers appear in the spring in long racemes, succeeded by small fruit of a nauseous taste.

The Laurel of the Victor's Crown (*Laurus nobilis*), or Sweet Bay, is the true laurel, and is a native of Asia Minor, but now common in this country. It has rather large lanceolate, leathery leaves, and bears axillary clusters of yellowish white flowers. The point is oval, bluish black, and about half-an-inch long. EC

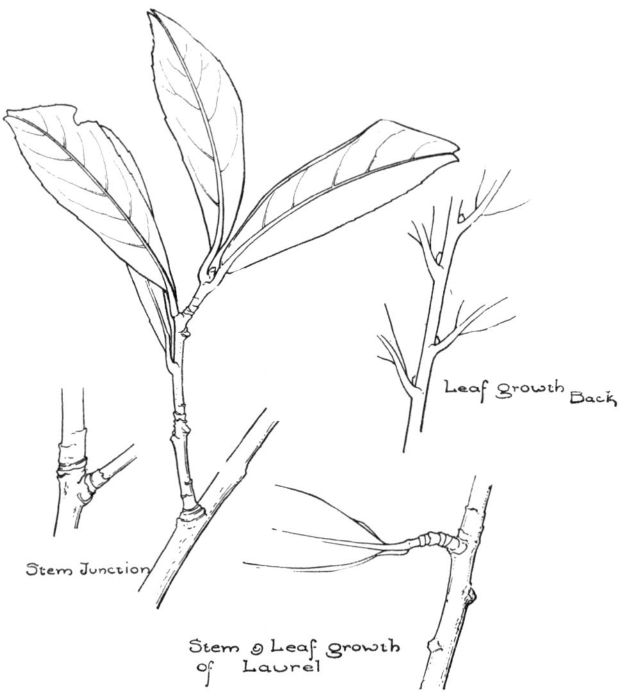

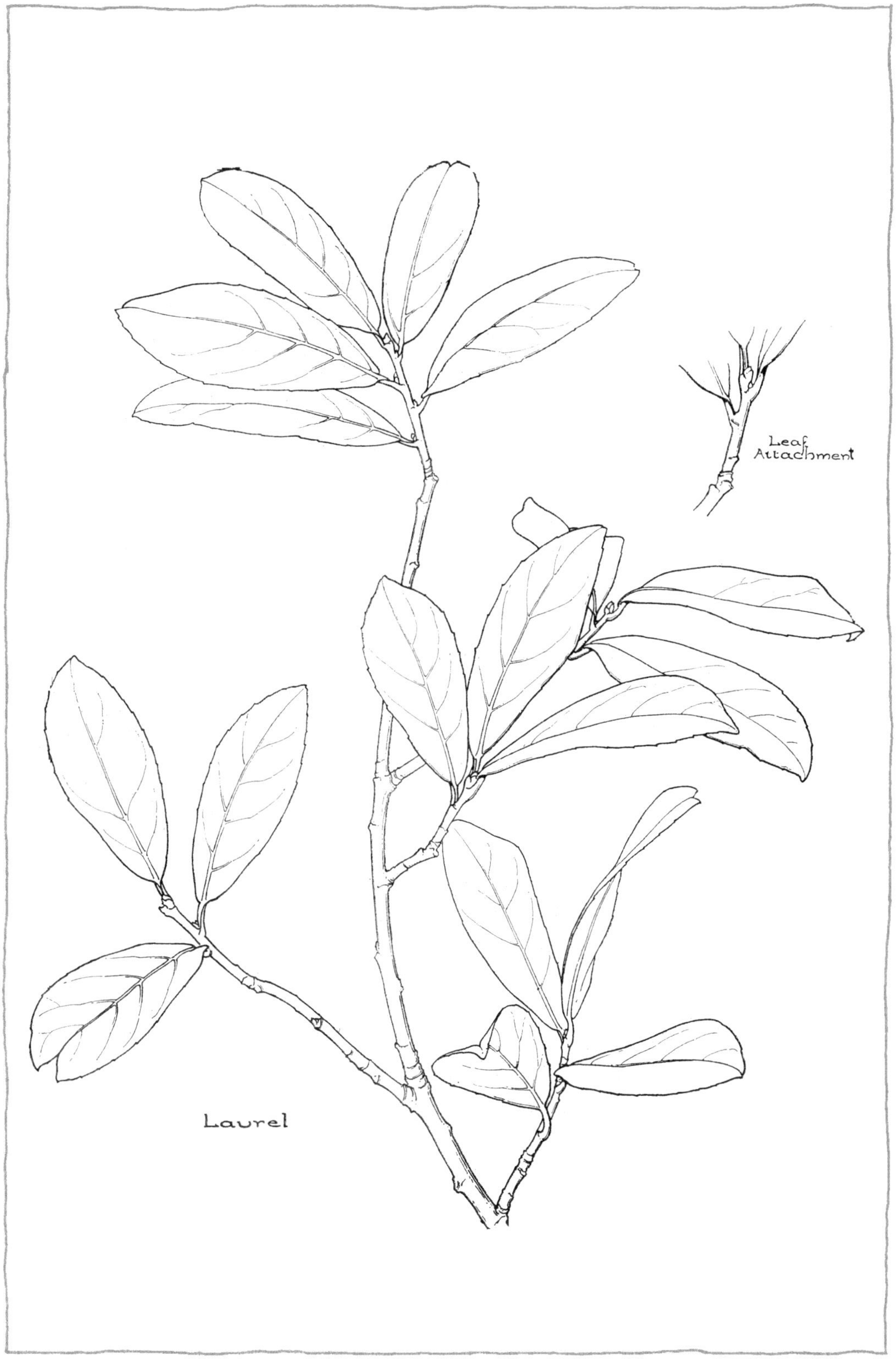
Leaf
Attachment
Laurel

Avocado

Persea americana

This is a fine study of avocados, executed in coloured pencil on Fabriano Classico 300gm paper. This surface works well with coloured pencil as there is just the right amount of tooth to hold the pigment, allowing multiple layers and blending to be successfully accomplished.

The growth habit of this plant is rather unusual; as the leaves mature some turn in such a fashion that the underside of the leaf is presented. This can clearly be seen here and the artist was right to show it as it is an important distinguishing feature of her specimen. Her clearly wrought venation, particularly on the underside where the midrib stands proud, is beautifully done and she has captured the avocado peel in a way which leaves the viewer in no doubt of its texture. There are beautifully soft highlights on both fruits, although they could have been improved by a softer outline on the side away from the light source where there is a disappearing edge of reflected light.

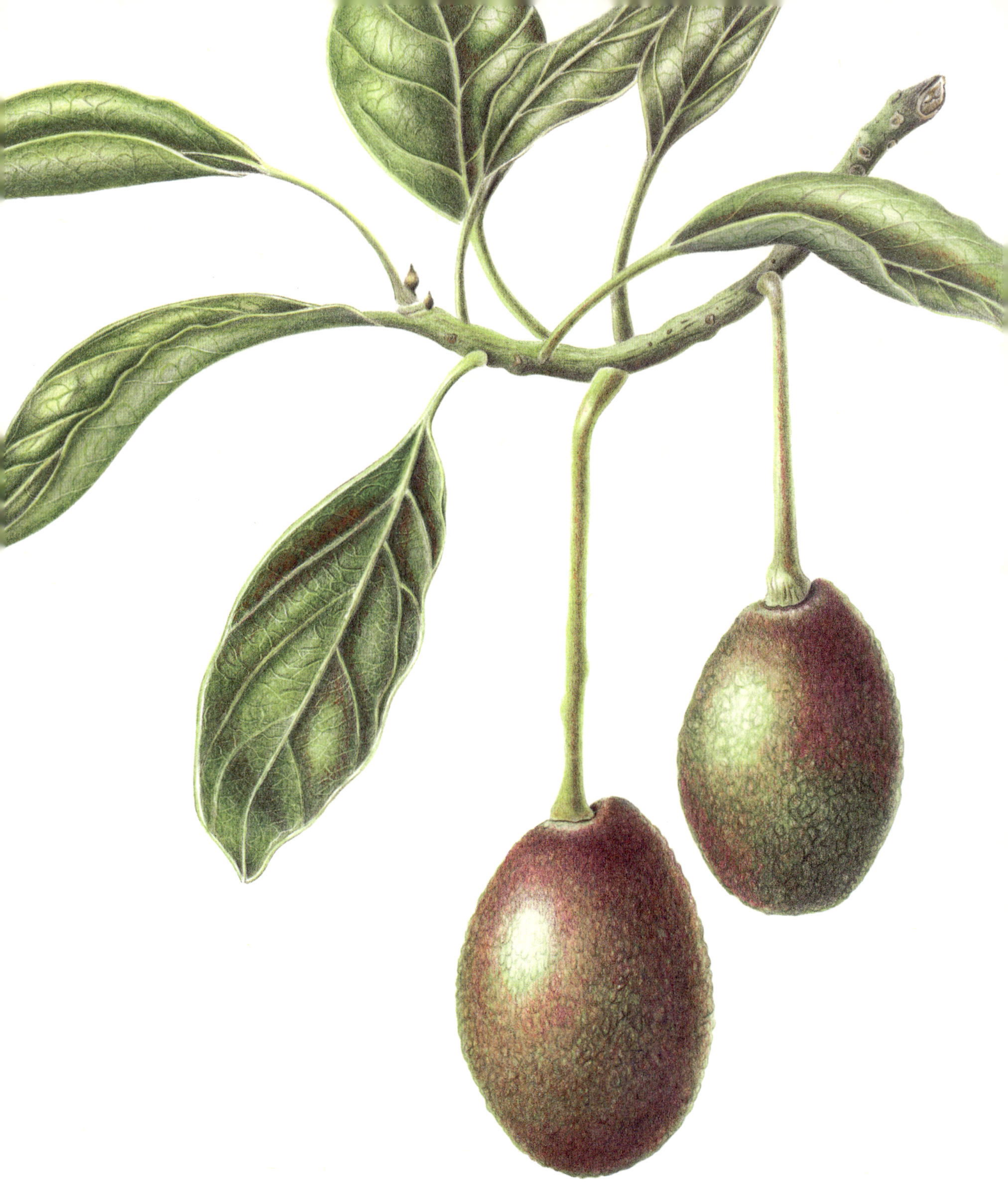

Coloured pencil, Jacqueline Pemberton

LILY FAMILY *Liliaceae*

Bluebell or Wild Hyacinth

Scilla nutans

This must not be confounded with the Scottish Bluebell, which is the same as the English Harebell. In the early spring the leaves of the Hyacinth begin to break through the earth, and are soon followed by the pale buds of the flower. Its root is a small bulb. The leaves are linear and slightly grooved, growing straight from the bulb and attaining in cases to fully a foot in height, but they do not reach the height of the flower-stalk. The growth of the flowers is a terminal, one-sided raceme of drooping flowers. The flower itself is a perianth, and is a long bell-shape, divided into six segments, reflexed at their extremities. There are six anthers attached to the inside of the flower, a style, and stigma. The bracts grow in pairs at the base of the flower-stalks. The fruit is a capsule containing black shiny seeds. This flower is to be found in plenty in woods and copses during May and June, giving a rich depth of colour to the undergrowth, and furnishing, one may imagine, a practical illustration to the fairy tale that the 'sky has fallen'. EC

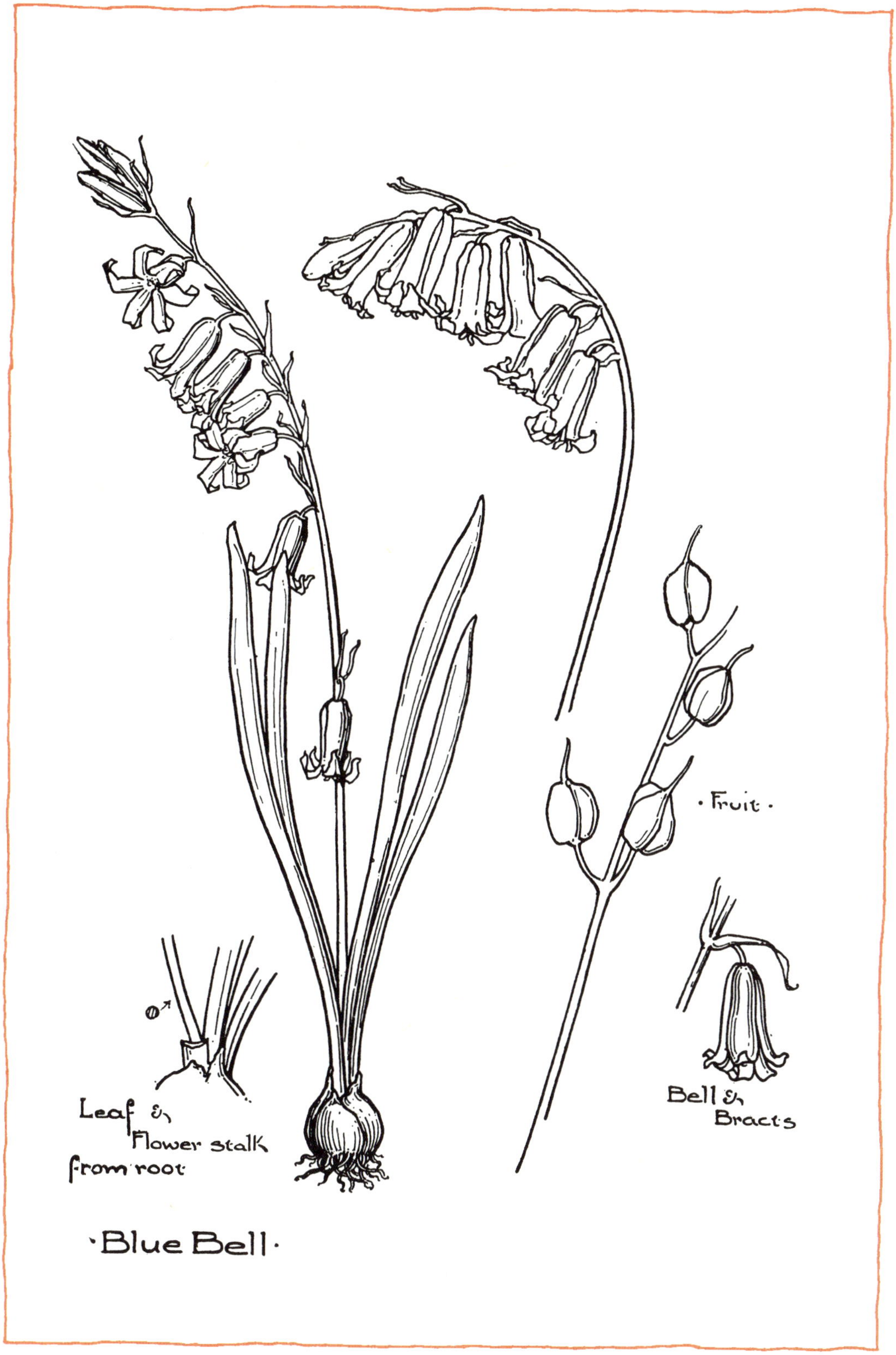

·Blue Bell·

Snake's Head Fritilleries

Fritillaria meleagris

The artist chose this beautiful specimen of the Snake's Head Fritillary for part of her Diploma portfolio and not surprisingly it contributed to her Distinction. The sensuous nature of the plant helps to create a lively composition, full of movement to enchant the eye. Using graphite for some leaves prevents a 'sameness' of greens and gives depth where one might blur the furthest elements in a less formal composition. She has observed the flowers well and not fallen into the trap of making the reptilian pattern too regimental. Painting the forward-facing tepals with the greatest detail then fading or shading to left and right has made the flowers three-dimensional and bell-like. The top flower gives an enticing glimpse of the soft patterning inside the tepals and the lime-yellow stamens immediately catch the eye, the brightest note in the entire painting.

The delicate markings of the immature buds are reflected in the graphite dissection and the whole thing is rounded off by the very attractive bulb with its emerging shoot. Again the artist has captured the texture of this bulb and given as much care and attention to it as to the flowers.

It is worth mentioning something here that may seem obvious but is often overlooked when a flower is shown in half section. Because the flower has six tepals and six stamens the artist has been careful to show three stamens, not two or four, which sometimes happens in the hands of the inexperienced. Botanical illustration is all about producing work that is capable of identifying the plant, so that even a seemingly trivial discrepancy could lead to a wrong conclusion. When caught up in the enjoyment of creating a beautiful image this aspect of the work can sometimes be forgotten.

Students can learn a lot from this piece, which leans heavily in the direction of the classical botanical illustrators without any modern gimmicks of composition. Such work will, like its predecessors from Georg Dionysius Ehret (1708–70) or Ferdinand Bauer (1760–1826), be admired for centuries to come.

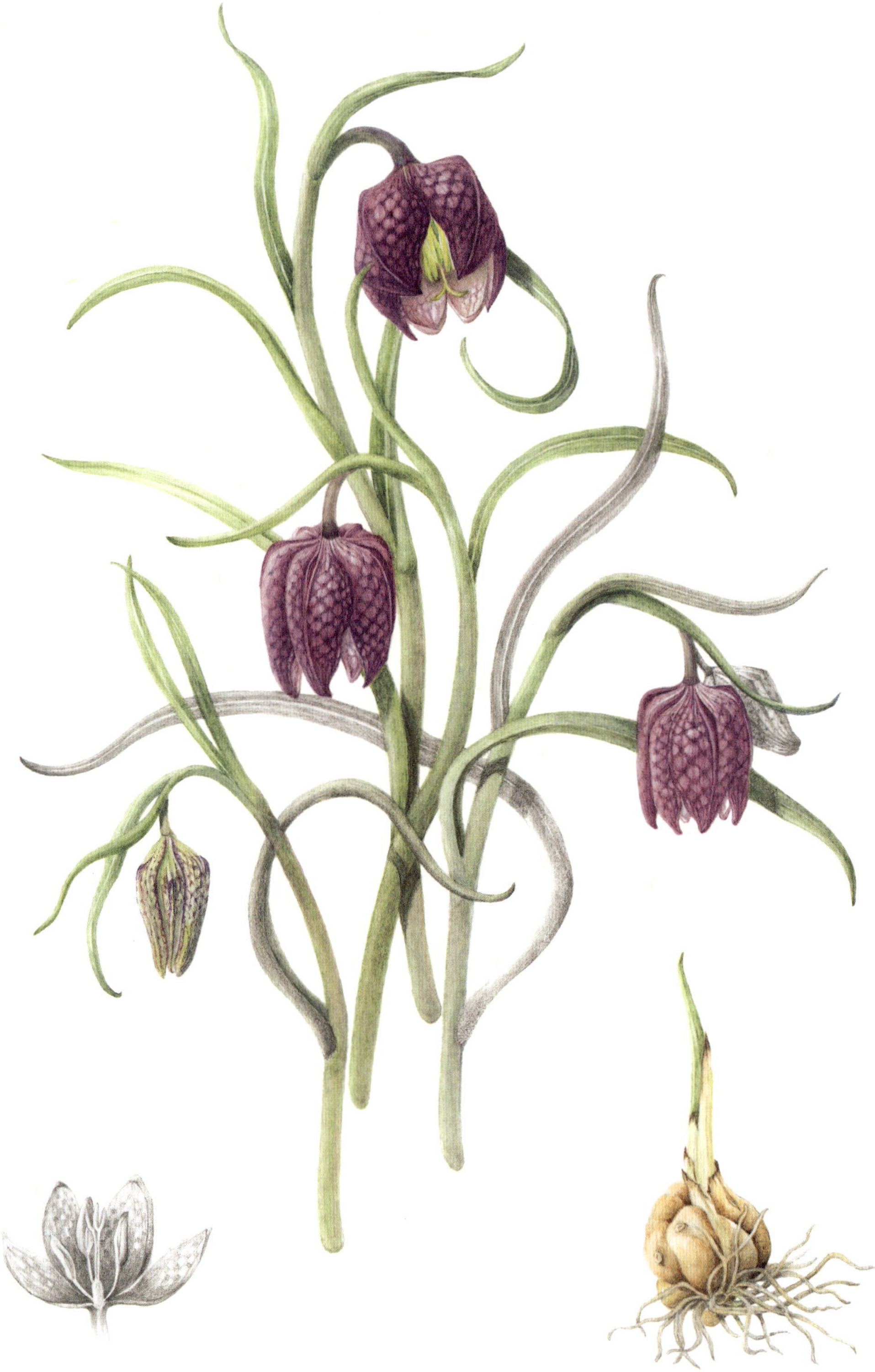

Easter or Bermuda lily

Lilium longiflorum harris

This beautiful lily is so well known to artists that a description seems superfluous; but as this might also be said or many other flowers figuring here it is not a sufficient excuse for omitting it. The flower is a perianth, and is terminal. It has six oblong and pointed segments, creamy-white with distinct parallel markings, terminating in a tube. The stamens are six in number, the anthers of which are a deep yellow, the pistil is long and has a three-lobed stigma. The leaves are lanceolate and sessile, with parallel veining, and grow spirally round the stem. The main stem is branched and round in section. Flowers in spring and summer.

EC

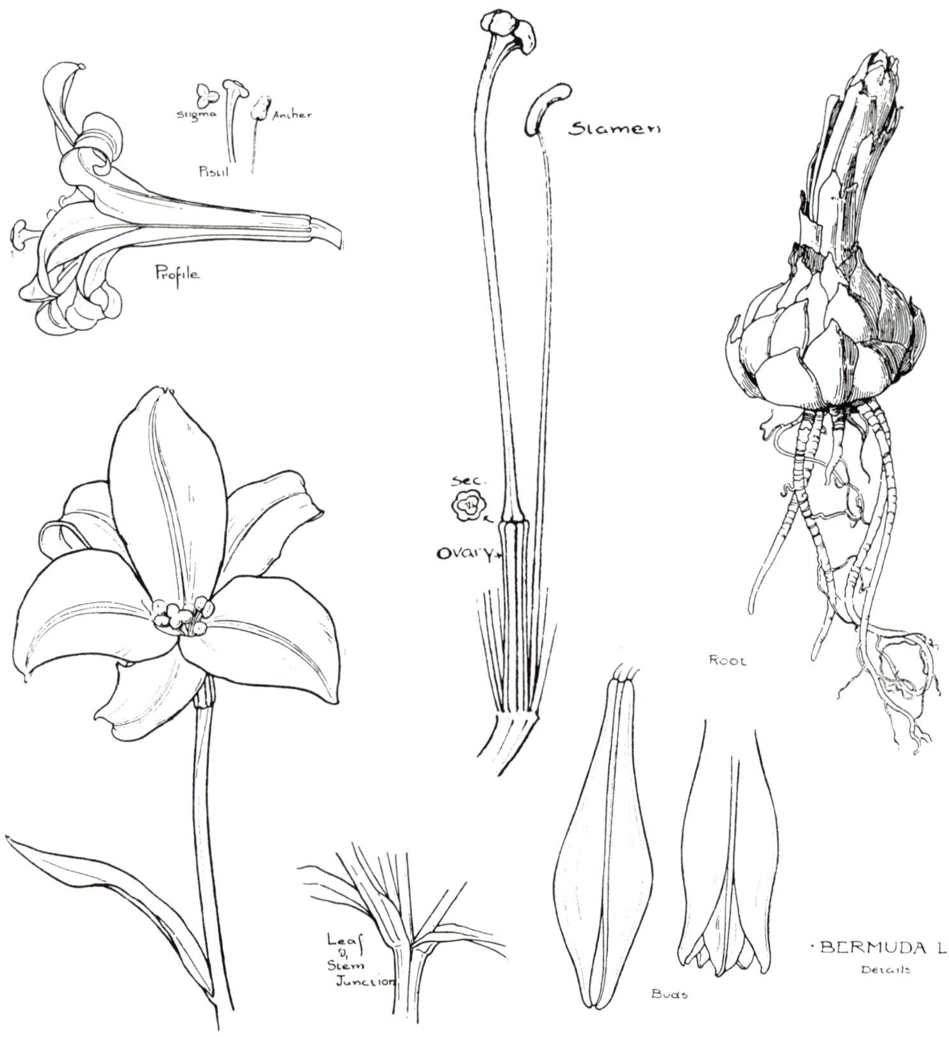

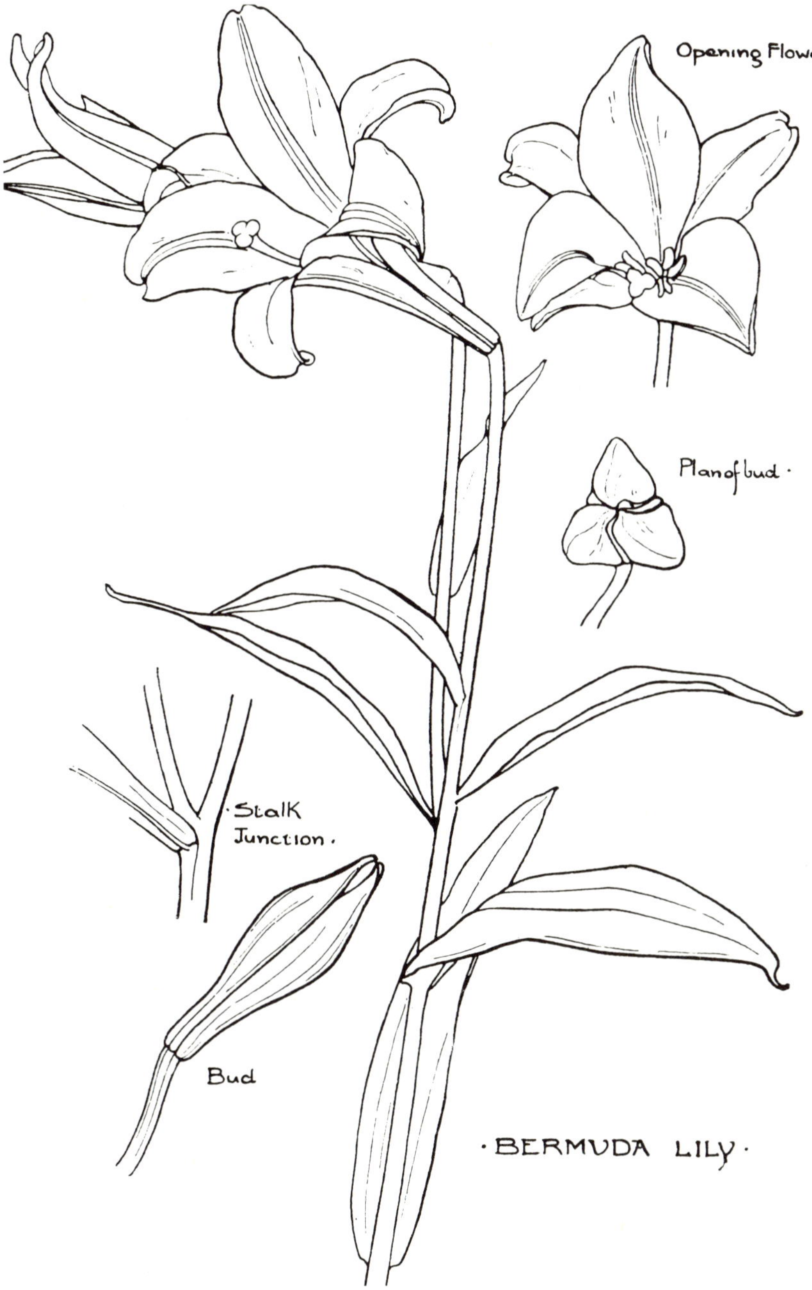
Opening Flower
Plan of bud ·
· Stalk
Junction ·
Bud
· BERMUDA LILY ·

Asiatic Lily

Lilium 'Matrix'

In an earlier assignment this artist had been criticized for painting red flowers in a way which made them flat and dull, so she was determined to do better with *L.* 'Matrix', a member of the Asiatic hybrid group of lilies. Here she has handled her washes beautifully on both the tepals and leaves by ensuring that sufficient white paper has been left untouched. This enables the stronger pigments to be gently blended in to create soft highlights and a silky sheen. Redouté had a masterly touch in this area, as you would expect, and any true botanical artist will aim to emulate his skill at creating the texture of silk, velvet or satin on the surface of a petal.

The artist is working close to perfection here. She chooses not to mix pigments but to use many layers of thin glazes of transparent or semi-transparent pigments. This gives her, in her own words, 'lots of thinking time and creates a lovely glow which I find hard to reproduce when mixing colours on the palette'.

There is some excellent blending of red pigment on the stems and the use of stippling to achieve this has again created texture which contrasts with the smooth tepals and foliage. The dissections are precise, with good brush drawing, and it is a very good example of a large flower-stem composed in a way which allows all its main features to be shown on a relatively small piece of paper.

The colours used (Winsor & Newton unless otherwise stated) were, for the flowers, Permanent Sap Green, Indian Yellow, Daler-Rowney Warm Orange, Quinacridone Red, Winsor Red and Permanent Rose; and for the leaves, Indanthrene Blue, Aureolin, Perylene Green, Perylene Violet and Daler-Rowney Terre Vert, which is less sticky than Winsor & Newton's Terre Vert and easier to work with.

Taken as a whole, this painting made a very satisfactory contribution to the artist's Distinction award. A very neat key on the reverse of the painting allows the parts to be identified.

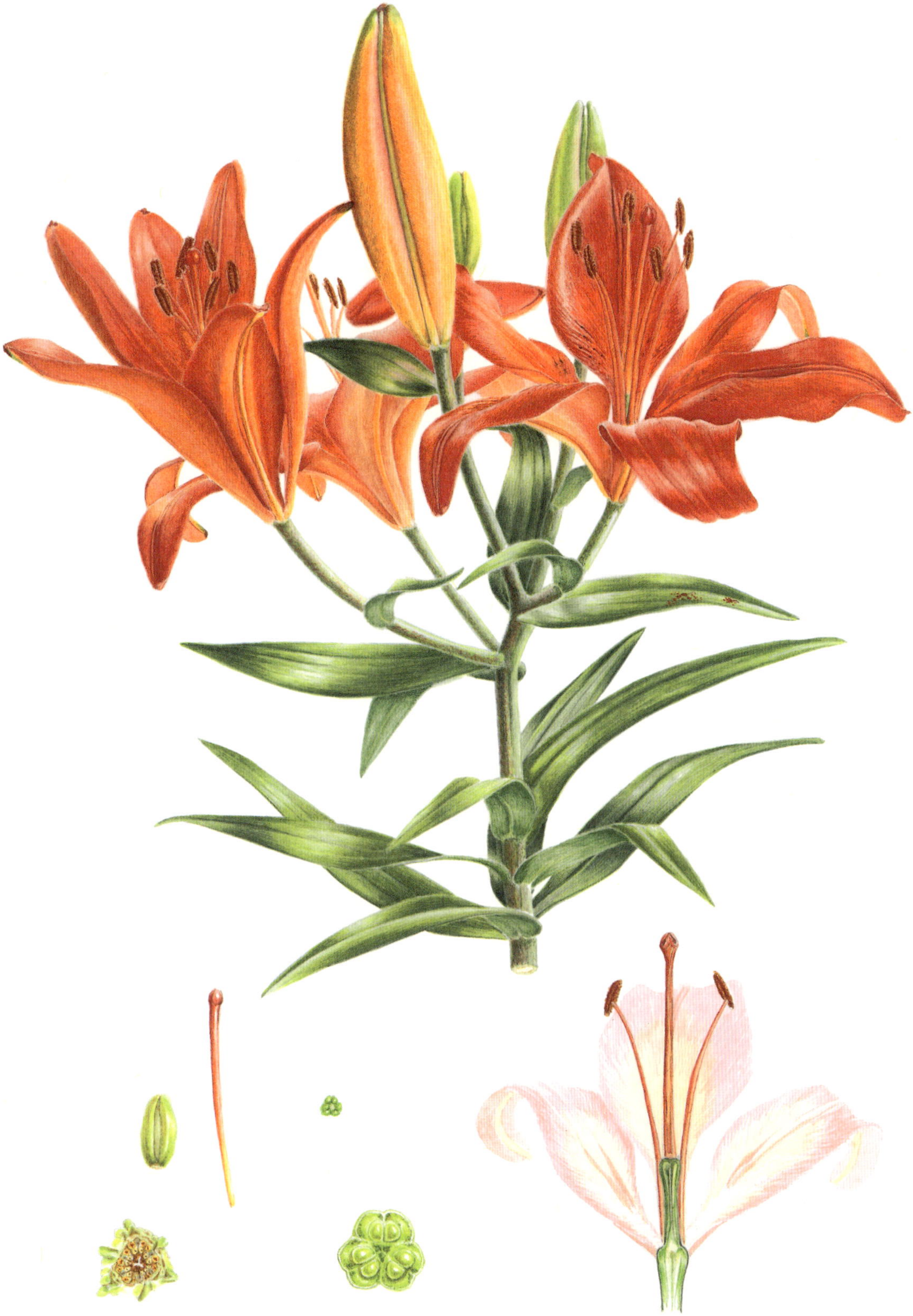

Tulip

Tulipa gesneriana

'The tulip', it has been said, 'is nature's mistake'; it is a mistake, then, from which artists may profit. The varieties are innumerable, the one figured here is one of the many garden varieties. It grows from one to two feet high, bearing a large bloom on a smooth erect stem. The flower is a perianth with six distinct segments, a three-lobed sessile stigma, six stamens with anthers erect attached by their bases. The leaves generally of a pale green, ovate-lanceolate and smooth, some are radical, and some grow from the flower-stem sheathlike. The bulb is fleshy and covered with a brown crisp skin. The Tulip is a native of the Levant; is largely cultivated in Holland, especially at Haarlem; it is prized for the size and colour of its flower. Our gardens and parks would lose some of their spring glory were it not for the Tulips. EC

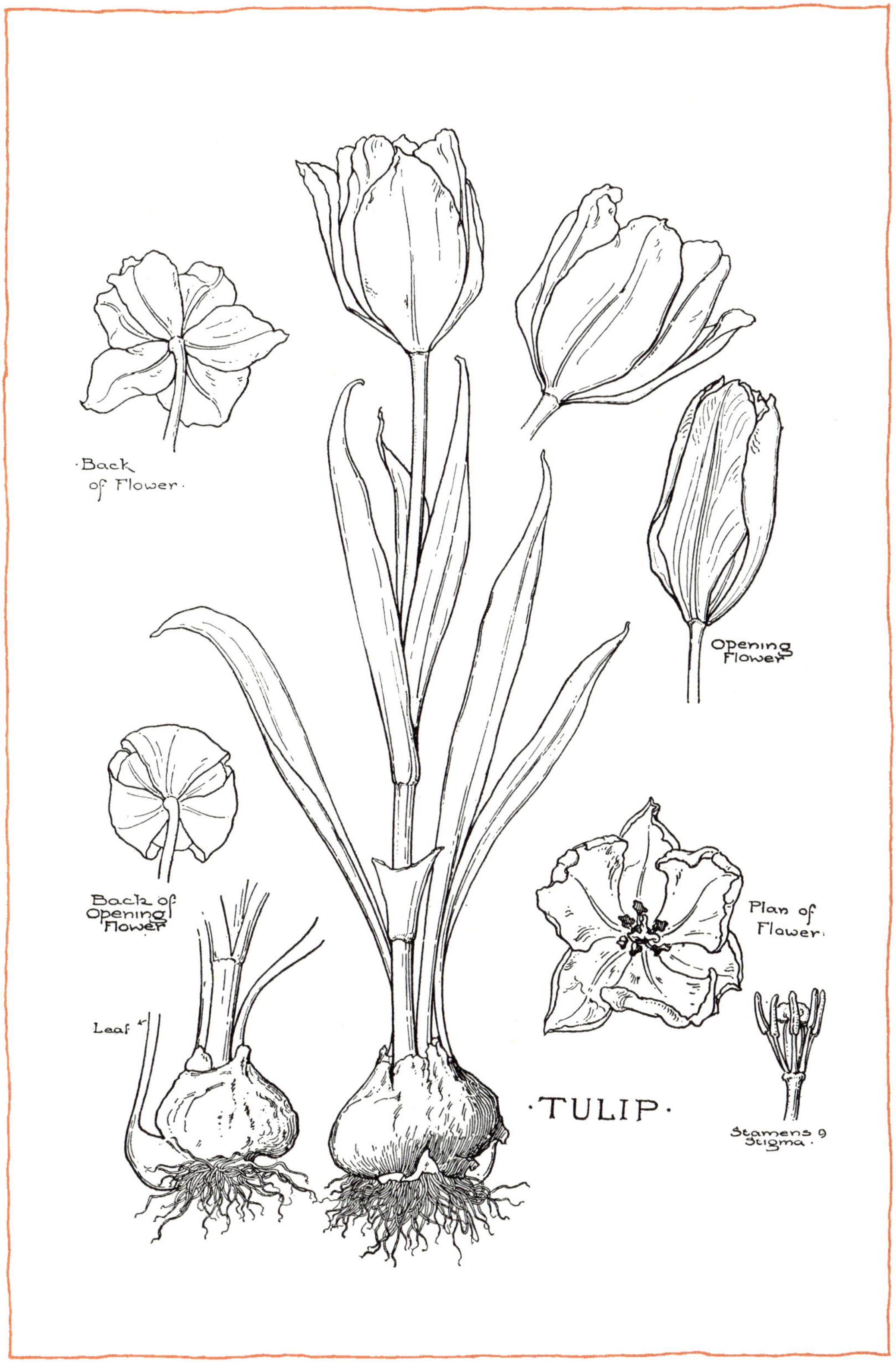
·Back of Flower·
Opening Flower
Back of Opening Flower
Plan of Flower·
Leaf
·TULIP·
Stamens & Stigma·

Parrot Tulip
Tulipa 'Rococo'

Like all Parrot Tulips, 'Rococo' is showy and it takes considerable skill to paint the detailed frills and fringes of the tepals,while making sure they are each given their separate identiy. Tonal variation is important with good reflective highlights on the left-hand side and the really dark tones of cast shadows helping to differentiate one tepal from the next. This same tonal variation also creates a dramatic study of the yellow-tinged bud in its cradle of leaves and with a hint of transferred red in the leaves and stem. Note the highlight on the beautifully painted bulb where the disappearing edge shows up the division on its surface. 'Rococo' was painted as a pair with 'Flaming Parrot' (right) and the artist made sure the composition of each mirrored the other, which is important if you hope to sell the work to one buyer who wants to hang the paintings together.

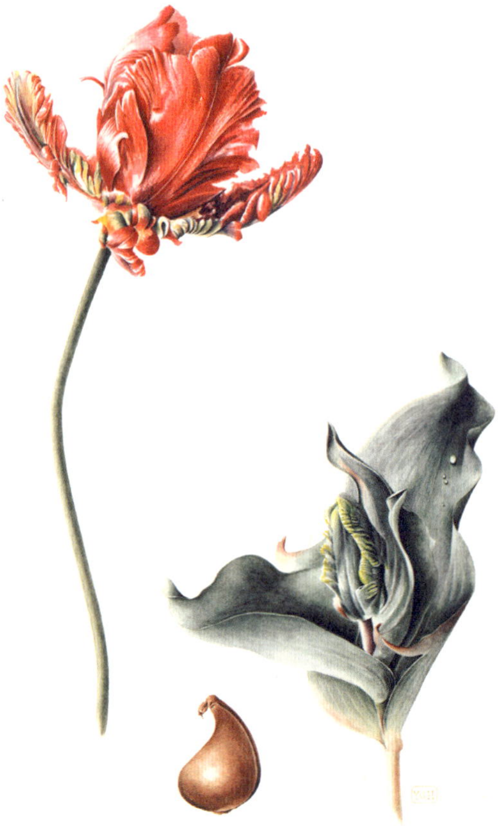

Watercolour, Yvonne Glenister Hammond

Parrot Tulip

Tulipa 'Flaming Parrot'

A full-faced study is never the easiest angle to choose, particularly when the flower is as fussy as a Parrot Tulip. The basic structure of three inner and three outer tepals has to be shown and the artist is helped by the flashes of crimson that follow the growth line of each tepal. These flashes show the furling and movement of each element, so the answer is to follow them and identify the curl inwards of the red feather-marking to the right of the tepal at 12 o'clock and the graceful flick over and outward movement of the feather at 4 o'clock. This alone separates these two tepals from the larger and bolder red markings on the two outer tepals at 2 o'clock and 6 o'clock.

A quick pencil sketch to establish these details would be a good way for a student to start on such a flower without feeling overwhelmed by its complexity. By taking note of individual details it is possible to tame the flower and control it rather than have it control you.

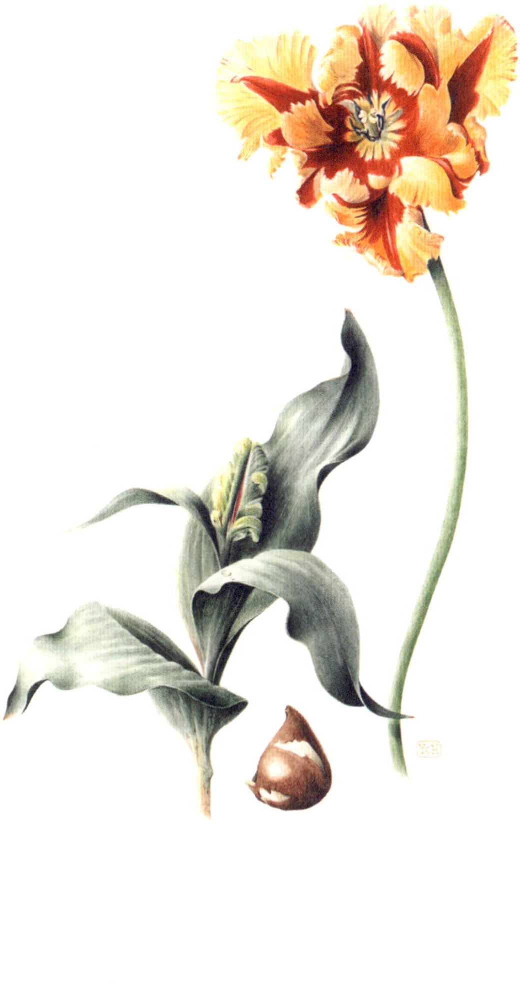

MISTLETOE FAMILY *Loranthaceae*

Common Mistletoe

Viscum album

The only British species of this order, and is to be found on a variety of trees, but particularly on the Apple, for which it seems to have a decided predilection, and rarely on the Oak. The stem is green and smooth, with bone-like joints. The leaves, which are thick and yellowish, grow in pairs opposite. It is most familiar to us in the winter, when bearing its whitish-green berries. The flowers appear in March and May, but are rather inconspicuous; they are nearly sessile in the forks of the branches, having four short, thick, triangular petals. The male flowers grow in groups of three and five, in a sort of cup-shaped bract. The female usually solitary, but sometimes two or three together. EC

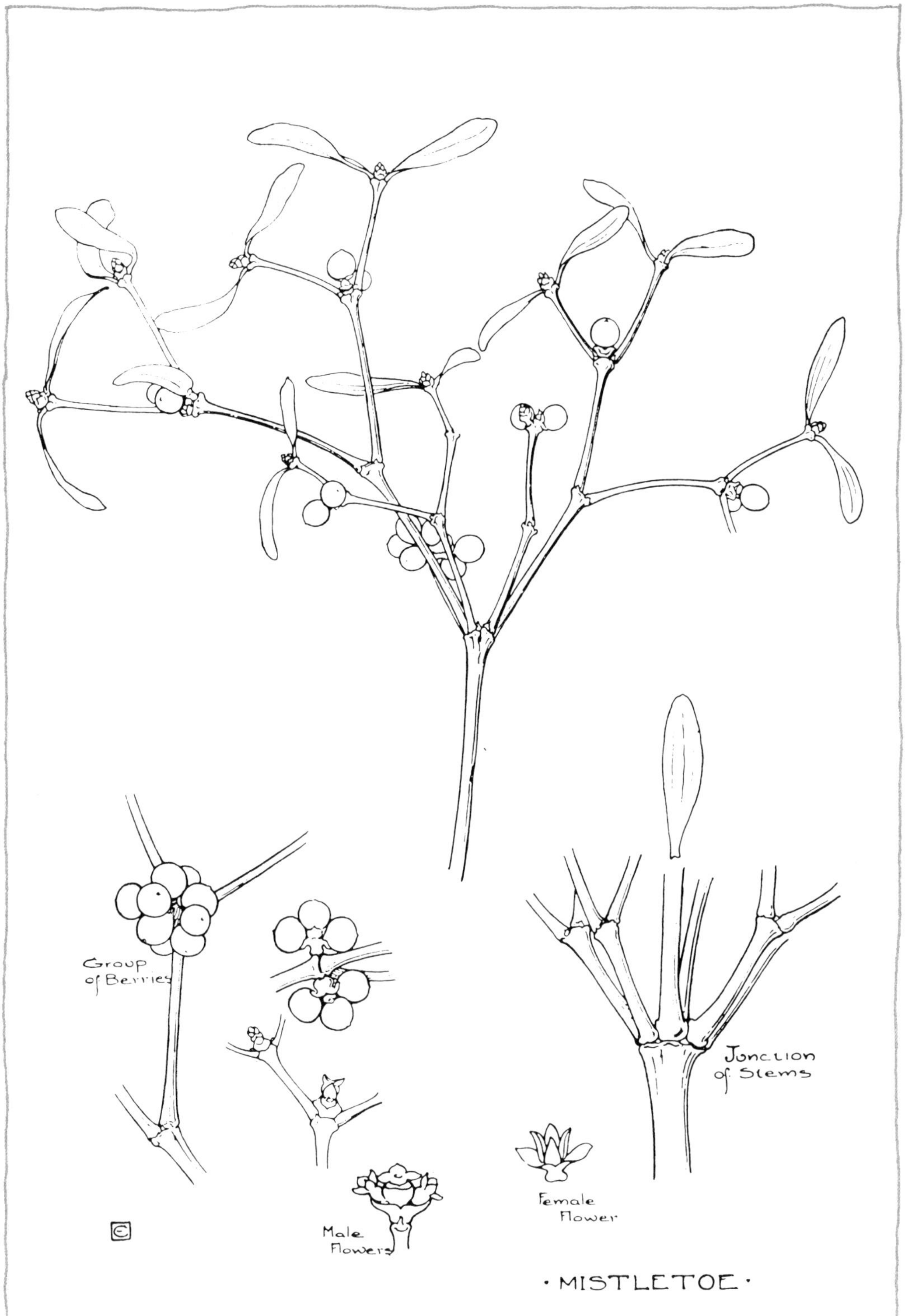
Group of Berries
Junction of Stems
Female Flower
Male Flowers
· MISTLETOE ·

Australian broad-leaved Mistletoe

Amyema miquelii

It is good to find a student who is happy to put time and devotion into a monochrome study of this complexity. Working with continuous tone, where the pencil is used to make repeated tiny elliptical movements that gradually build up darker areas of shading, is a slow process, but rewarding.

When the artist elected to work on this branch of Australian Broad-leaved Mistletoe she was already showing a natural bent for working in graphite. Most people want to excel in colour, but it is always good when the artist recognizes that their true calling lies with monochrome, and some of the most stunning work that is hung in our London exhibitions comes from such artists. Just as a black and white photograph often evokes a sense of mystery or a longing to know more, a botanical drawing stripped of the distraction of colour has the same effect.

One of around 35 varieties of this parasitic plant which is native to Australia, *Amyema miquelii* blends well with its host, the Eucalyptus. Red flowers are followed by sticky yellow seeds. These are, like our native species, enjoyed by birds and distributed in the same manner. There the similarity ends, although it is possible to imagine our familiar short leaves pulled and twisted into this more sinuous shape. The pale tones of the graphite suggest the grey-green shades of the Eucalyptus and by following the direction of growth the artist has depicted the form of the plant with clarity. It is important to maintain the direction of the grain even if this is more arduous when working on long slender leaves or petals.

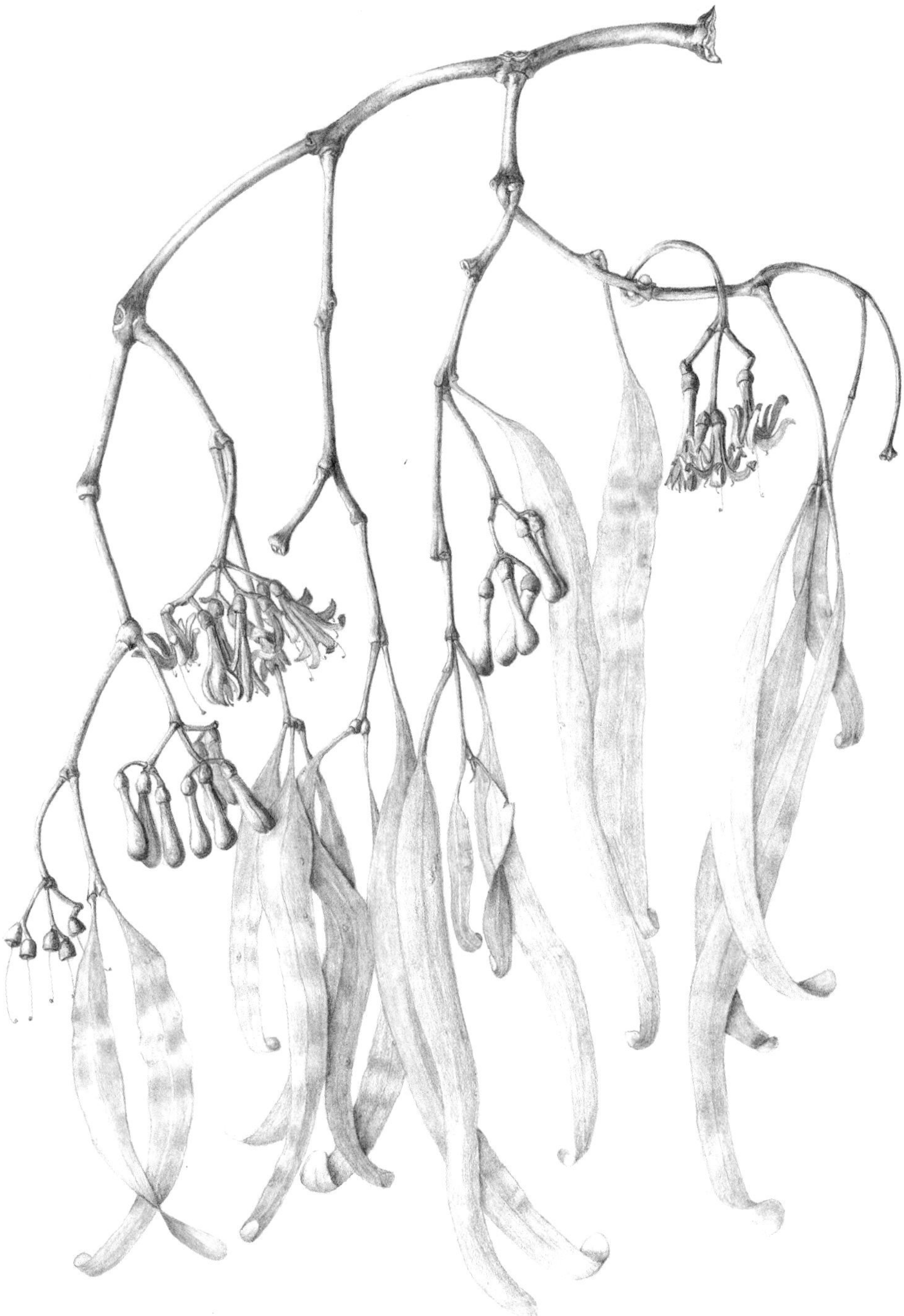

OLIVE FAMILY *Oleaceae*

Privet

Ligustrum vulgare

Privet is a hedge shrub, growing to six or eight feet in height, with long slender branches. Its beautiful groups of white flowers growing in compact panicles form a conspicuous feature in the hedges and thickets where it grows. In the autumn and winter bunches of dry purple succulent berries succeed the flowers. It is perhaps at this stage of greater use to the designer than when it is in flower. The leaves are lanceolate or oblong, nearly evergreen, growing on short stalks in opposite pairs (decussate), and are entire. Surface smooth and dark green in colour. The flower has four petals and a calyx of four small teeth, cup-shape. It has two stamens, a short thick style, and a two-lobed stigma. Petals terminate in a tube.

EC

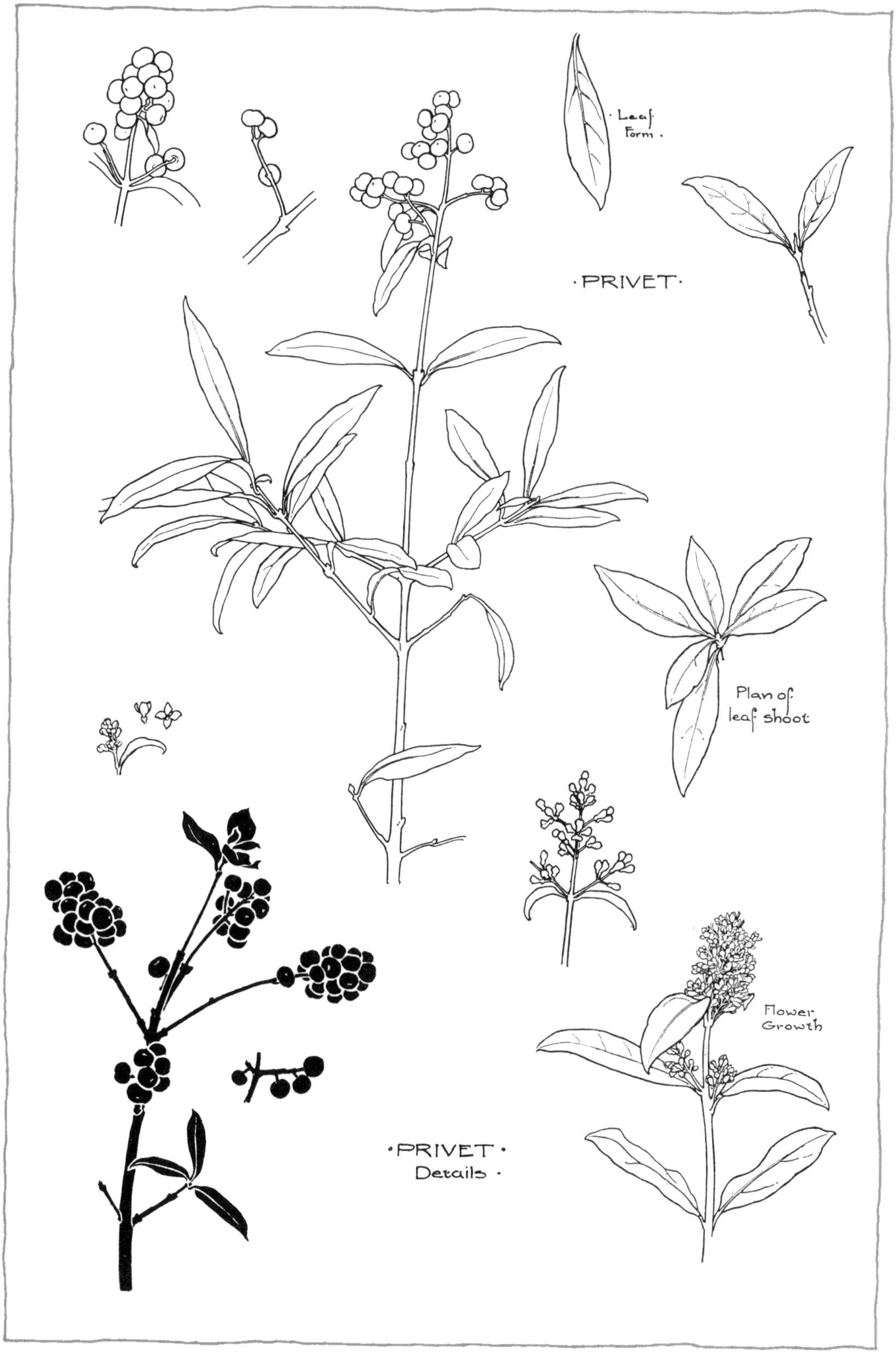

· Leaf Form ·
· PRIVET ·
Plan of leaf shoot
Flower Growth
· PRIVET ·
Details ·

Privet

Ligustrum delavayanum

This privet from north-west Yunnan in China forms a decorative shrub of some 2m (6 ¼ft) in height, with panicles of white flowers followed by clustered black berries. It caught the artist's eye because it was so different to the more familiar clipped privet hedge, which is usually grown from *Ligustrum ovalifolium* or *L. vulgare*. From the artist's point of view, the berries are more like miniature sloes as there are no bright highlights with which to denote form, just a tiny matt gleam to break the otherwise inky surface. Neither are there any conspicuous veins on the top or undersurface of the leaves and even the midribs are sunken. This again makes it a very tricky subject to paint and many would shy away from the challenge, because it is as if the markers on which we rely are no longer available.

The artist has never turned away from difficult subjects, often taking on those that most of us would have avoided at all costs. This made her stand out in those early days when she first studied botanical painting because it is a highly commendable attitude and ensures that such plants are recorded, not just the ones with obvious eye appeal.

Watercolour, Vickie Marsh

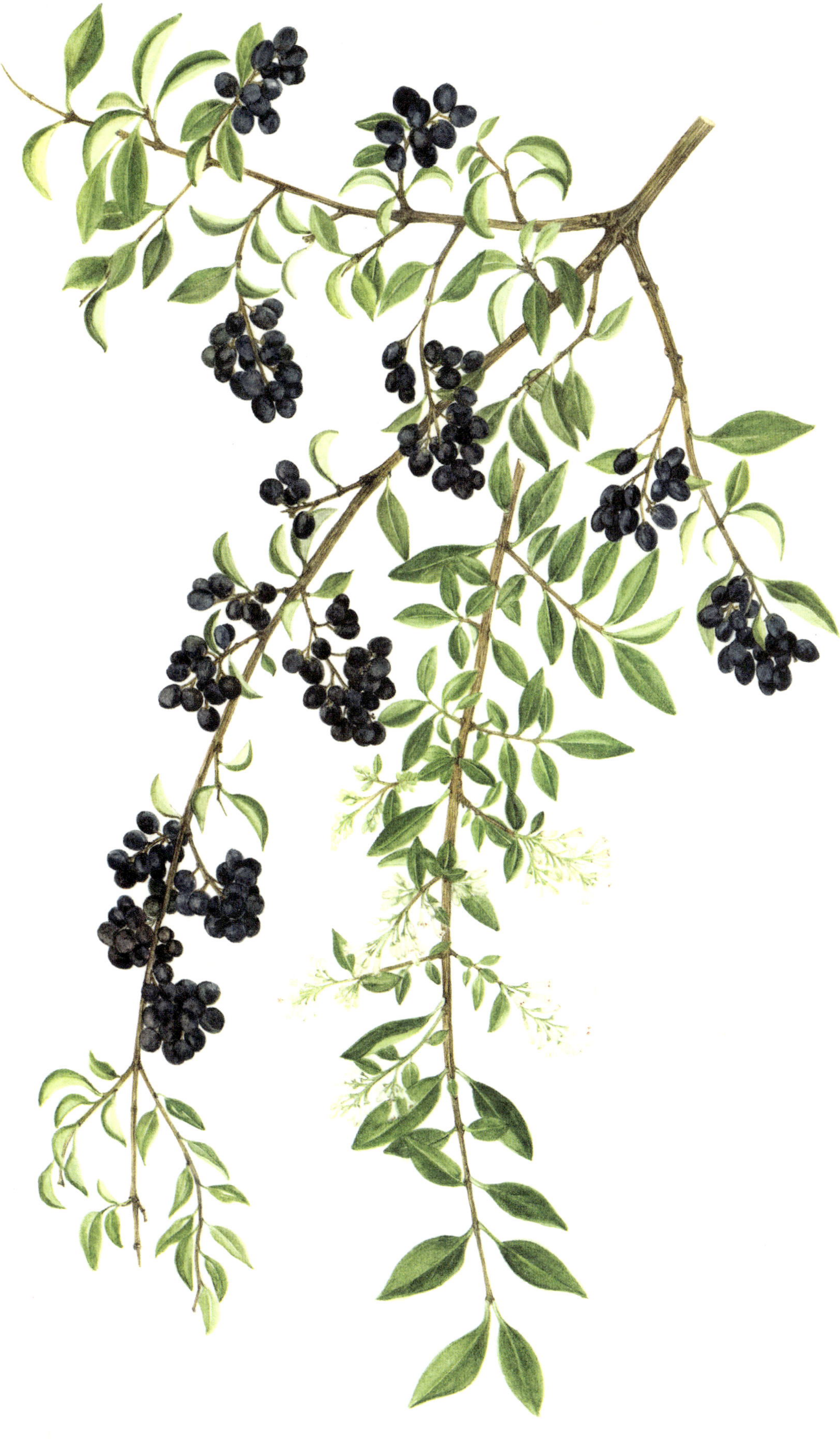

Ash

Fraxinus excelsior

Ash is a native of Britain. The Privet (*Ligustrum vulgare*) and this are the only native representatives of this order. The flowers appear in April and May, the leaves are very late in developing, and are amongst the first to fall in the autumn. The fruits, or 'keys' as they are sometimes called, each contain two seeds, and consist mainly of a membranous wing. The flowers have neither calyx nor corolla, but merely consist of the essential organs, a pistil and two stamens. The young leaf-buds are very beautiful. The leaf is an example of the pinnate form.

EC

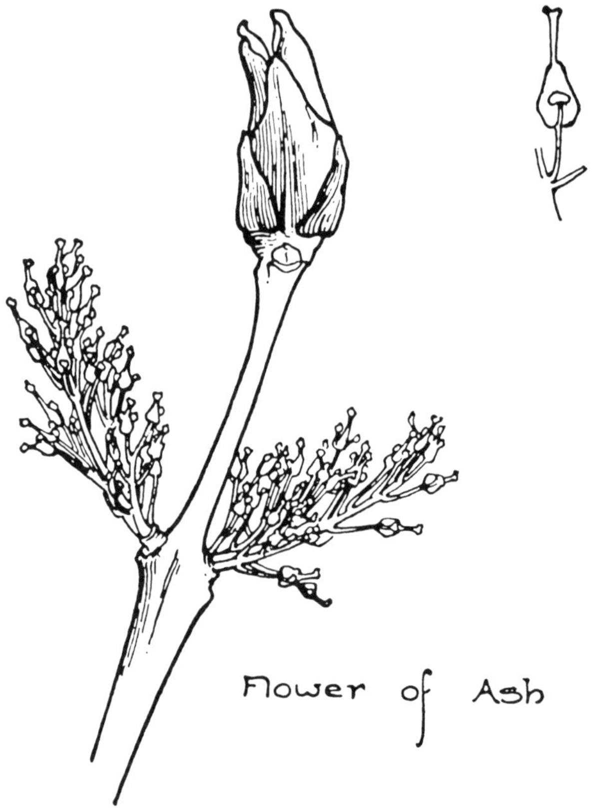

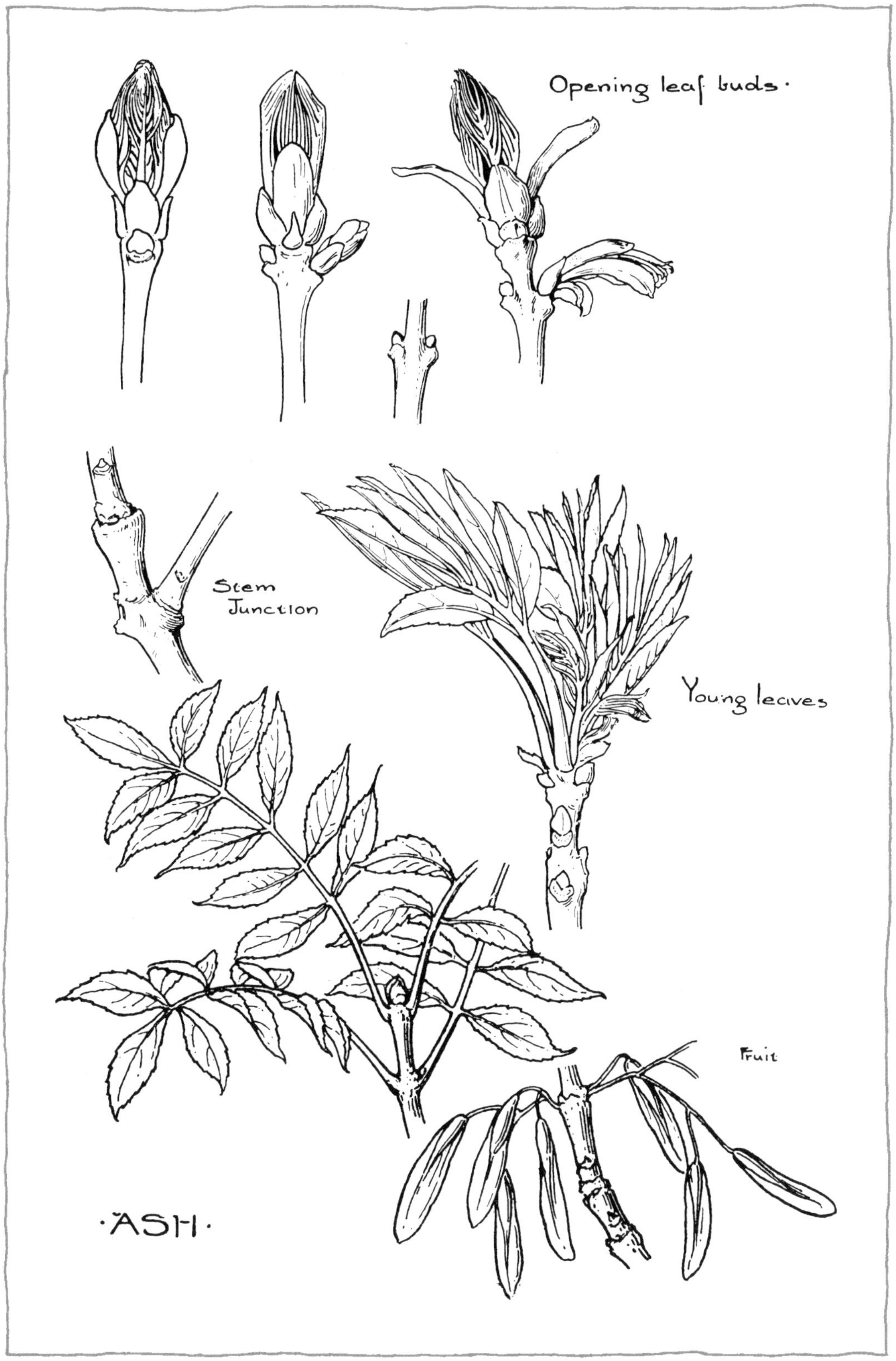
Opening leaf buds·
Stem Junction
Young leaves
Fruit
·ASH·

Olives

Olea europaea subsp. *europaea*

Repeatedly painting these olives in her sketchbook helped the artist come to grips with their varied colours, almost iridescent in places. Grapes and plums also lend themselves to similar practice studies but at that time olives were easily available to her at her home in Cairo. You can see how she recorded them, warts and all, and also the nuances of colour changes in the leaves from silver to burnished copper when at first glance they might all appear to be the same.

As the little strip on the left helps to indicate, 12 colour mixes went into the work on this page. From top to bottom, they are: Terre Vert with Indigo, Terre Vert with Cerulean Blue, Terre Vert with Lemon Yellow, Lemon, Raw Sienna, Raw Sienna and Winsor & Newton Thioindigo Violet (no longer available), Perylene Maroon, Caput Mortuum, Winsor & Newton Thioindigo, Indigo, Winsor & Newton Payne's Grey, and Winsor & Newton Natural Tint.

The artist's minute handwriting also records that she found the Neutral Tint too dull so she substituted a mix of Indigo and Caput Mortuum Violet. Around the dark olive at the bottom left she writes 'struggling to control these washes' and after using white paint to obscure a smudge, 'a bleed'. Trivial, you may think, but it shows a great attention to detail since she had no idea that anyone else would see this page.

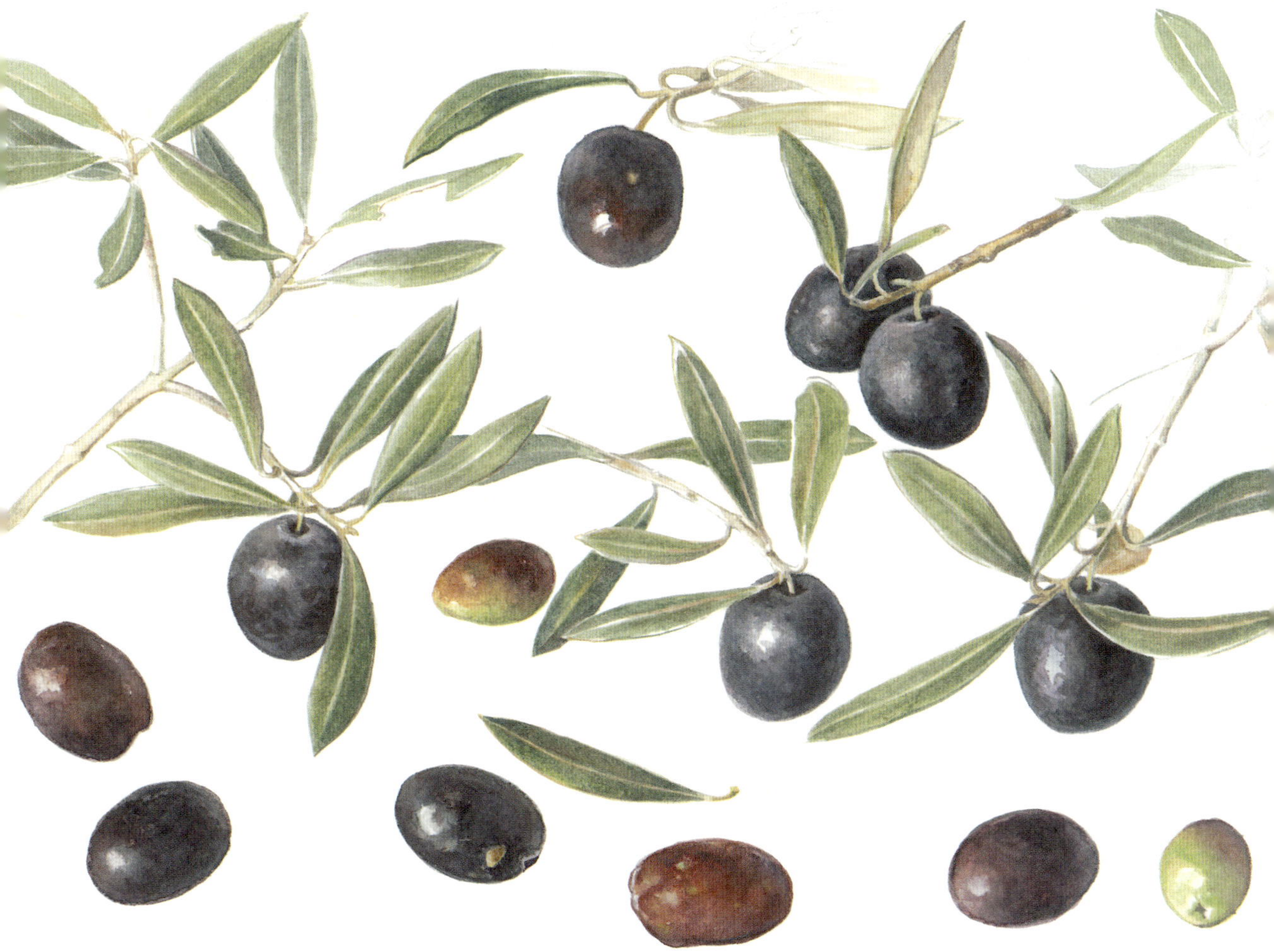

Sketchbook page, Shevaun Doherty

FUCHSIA FAMILY *Onagraceae*

Fuchsia

Fuchsia globosa

A plant or shrub of which there are many varieties, and the tendency of the gardeners is to keep on increasing them. This particular variety is one of the older ones, and its form is indicated by its species name, *globosa* – globe-flowered. It is a dwarf shrub from one to four feet in height.

The leaves are usually opposite, sometimes in threes, bright green, smooth, serrated, ovate in form, and pointed. The flowers are axillary and pendulous, the calyx is four-cleft and rich crimson, the petals are four, and purple, about half the length of the calyx. The fruit is a berry. Flowers in the late summer and autumn. EC

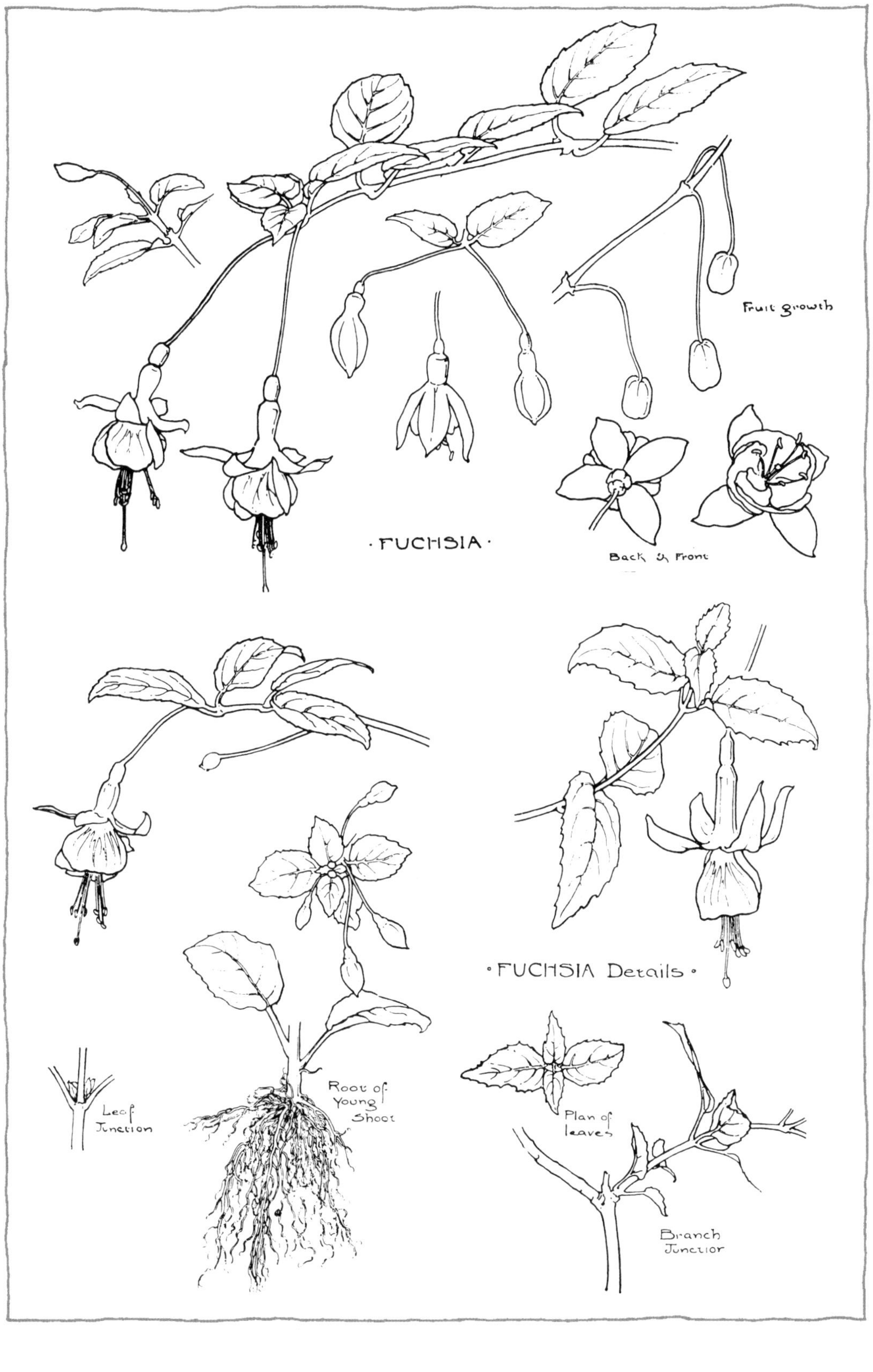
Fruit growth
·FUCHSIA·
Back & Front
·FUCHSIA Details·
Leaf Junction
Root of Young Shoot
Plan of leaves
Branch Junction

Fuchsia

Fuchsia 'Blacky', 'Dollar Prinzessin' *and* 'Beacon'

Over the years I have spent many happy hours capturing the beauty of these gorgeous flowers. There are so many to choose from and yet all offer something different, varying from the flamboyant showgirls, all flounced skirts and exuberance, to the singles with their simple lines suggesting the modesty of the Victorian governess.

Brightly coloured specimens such I have painted here give the artist a good opportunity to practise their glazing skills, laying one wash of colour on top of another so that the result is vibrant and glowing. I have used the same pigments for two of these flowers and I am still amazed at the difference in the end result, depending on the density of pigment to water and the order in which the glazes were applied.

Today we are spoilt for choice as it is so easy to obtain a huge range of paints from manufacturers worldwide and this was not the case even two decades ago. Over the years I have painted a lot of old roses, the majority of which are pink, white and crimson, often with only very subtle colour variations. Before the days of Quinacridone pigments, it was amazing what we could do with just Permanent Rose, Permanent Magenta and Crimson Lake, and I never failed to wonder at how the finished paintings varied using just those basic colours.

Much the same applied here. For 'Blacky' I used Schmincke Madder Lake Light and Winsor & Newton Crimson Lake, Quinacridone Magenta and Purple Madder; both 'Dollar Prinzessin' and 'Beacon' were painted with Winsor Red, Crimson Lake, Permanent Rose, Schmincke Magenta and Schmincke Purple Magenta. The leaves were painted in my usual haphazard fashion by mixing greens from whatever blue and yellow was left over on my palette, added to Daler-Rowney Sap Green. Winsor & Newton Light Red was useful for stems and midribs. For once I can answer the question which is so often asked: 'How long did it take?' The answer is approximately 11 hours.

Watercolour, Margaret Stevens

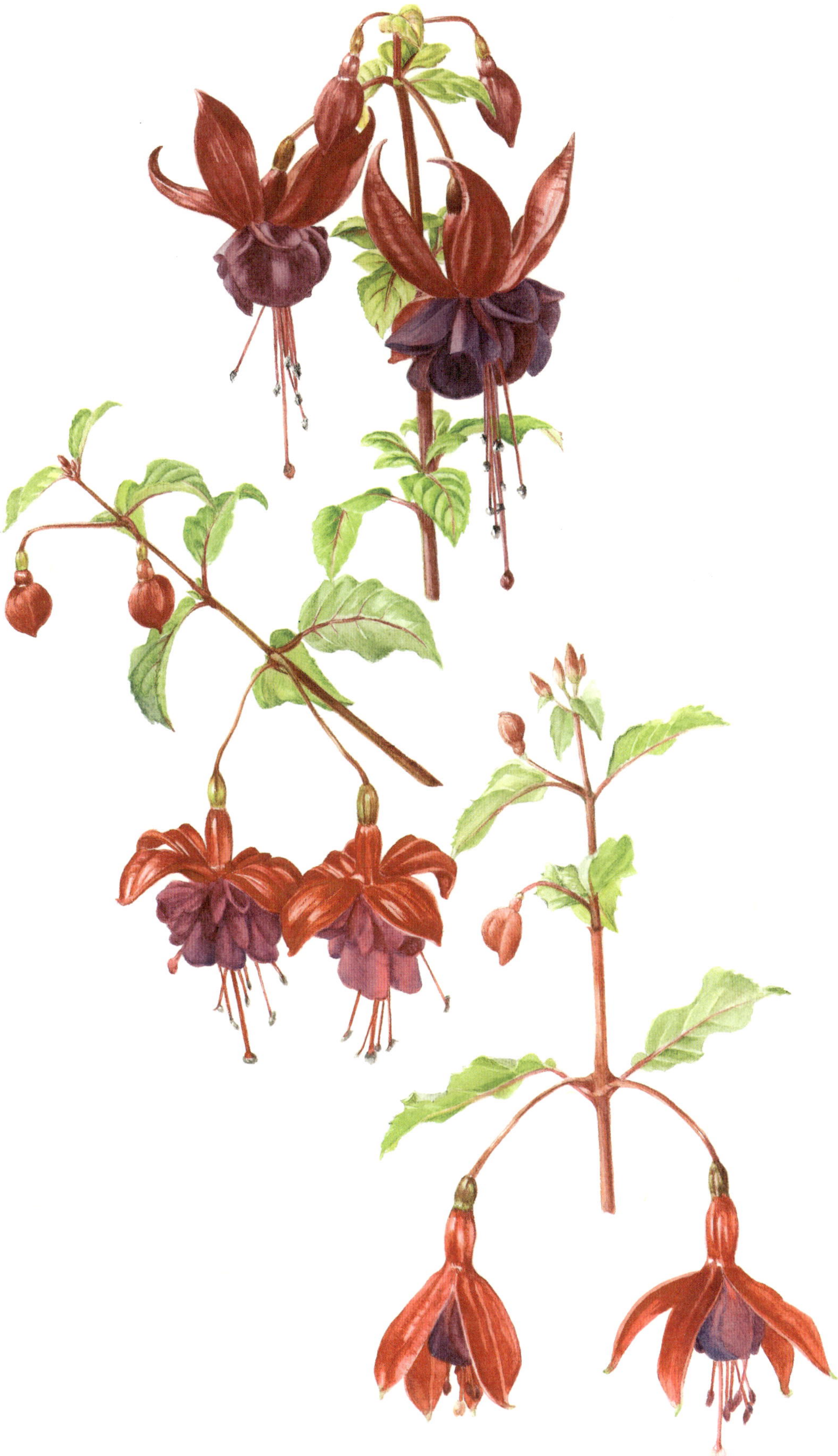

POPPY FAMILY *Papaveraceae*

Common Poppy

Papaver rhoeas

The cornfield would lose some of its beauty, and the railway embankment would become somewhat more monotonous, were it not for the abundance of the scarlet Poppy.

It has a calyx of two sepals, which fall at the opening of the bud, giving the flower the appearance of a perianth. The petals are four, and usually of a bright scarlet; the two outer ones are the larger; the buds hang gracefully down the stem covered with short hairs, as are the stems. The stamens are very numerous, and the stigma is sessile and rayed. The fruit is a capsule, nearly globular, opening by valves. The leaves vary in size and form; the lower ones are large and stalked, the upper ones stalkless or sessile; they are very much divided or pinnatifid and serrated. The plant is erect and branched, carrying its blossoms on long stalks.

Its flowers may be found the greater part of the summer, but mostly in July. The Shirley Poppy is a hybrid, having the same characteristics as the red common Poppy, but a greater variety of colours.

EC

Opium Poppy

Papaver somniferum

This is usually an occupant of the garden; occasionally one is found growing in a wild state, but this is mainly due to accident. The foliage is very beautiful; it is of a glaucous green, and the leaves clasp the stem by their base; they are slightly lobed, and are irregularly toothed. The flowers are usually bluish-white, with a purple splash at the base of the petal, but the colour varies a deal. The capsule is large and globular. Flowers July and August. Sepals two and petals four.

EC

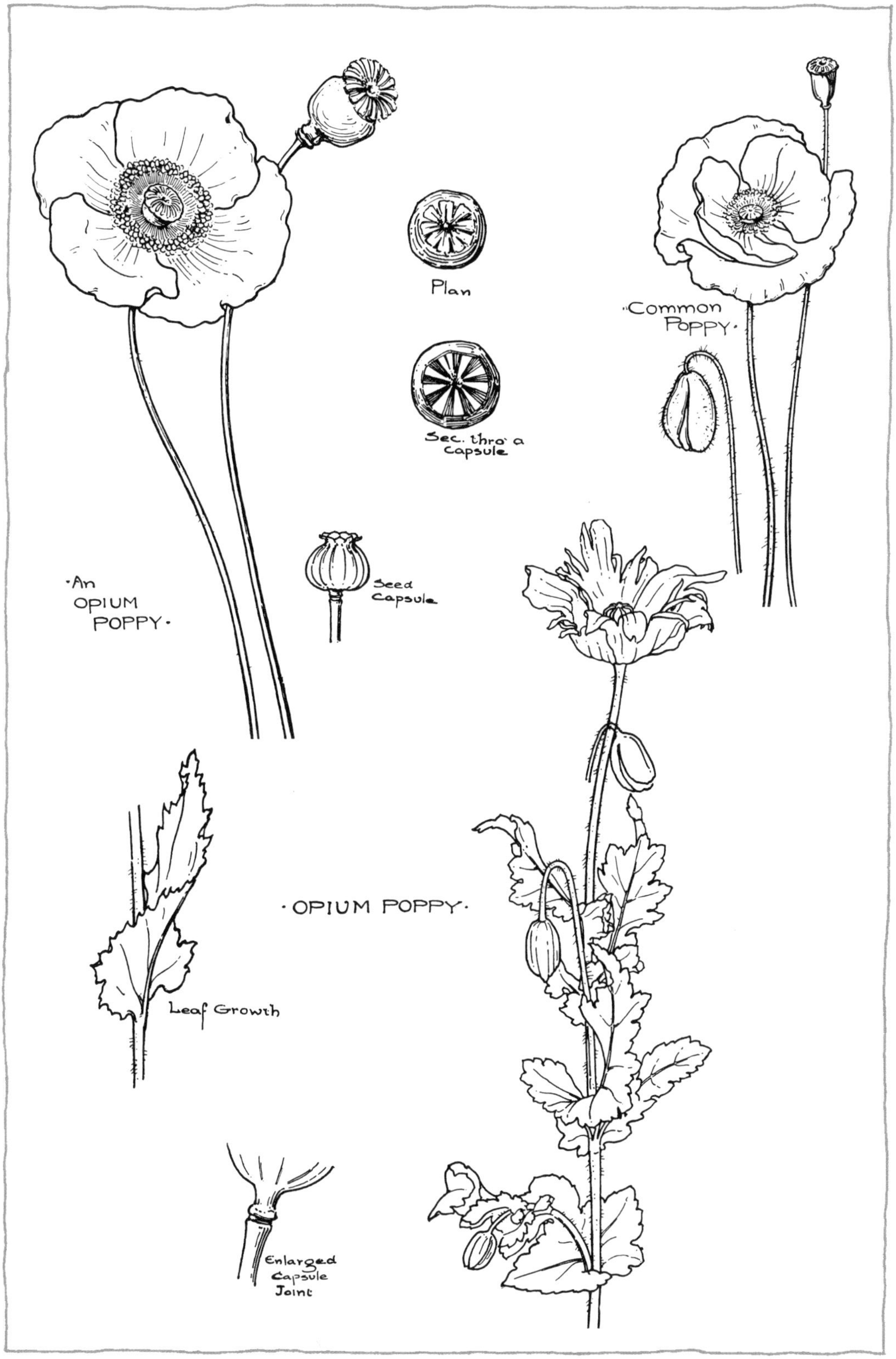

Plan
Sec. thro' a capsule
·Common Poppy·
·An OPIUM POPPY·
Seed Capsule
·OPIUM POPPY·
Leaf Growth
Enlarged Capsule Joint

Field poppies

Papaver rhoeas

The artist chose her specimen poppies from those growing traditionally in wheat fields, rather than along the roadside where new sowing has resulted in a variation in both colour and markings. The true Field Poppies have straight stems since they grow in competition with the grain as they reach towards the light, and the flowers are a more orange red. They are a difficult subject for any artist because of their fragility, and typically these started to droop and fade as soon as they were picked.

The artist worked quickly to establish the main features and aspects of the plants, sketching and photographing them *in situ*. She then drew them on tracing paper which she cut out and arranged in a pleasing composition for transferring onto Fabriano Classico 5 300gsm (140lb) Hot Pressed paper.

Painting the flowers first, she used as much live material as possible, which ensured their true colour. The lightest petal areas were first washed with Winsor & Newton Transparent Yellow, which made the subsequent use of red less staining so that it could be lifted out later if necessary. Shadow areas were washed lightly with Winsor Violet. A mix of Cadmium Red Deep and Transparent Yellow was then used on the lighter petal areas, with Alizarin Crimson and Transparent Yellow towards the centres and away from the light source. The fine lines on the backs of the petals were painted with Schmincke Brilliant Pink while a mix of Winsor & Newton Perylene Green and Permanent Magenta gave a purplish-black for the stamens, the sessile stigmas on the surface of the capsule and dark markings at the base of the backs of petals.

For the leaves, the artist used a mix of Permanent Sap Green and French Ultramarine with a touch of Alizarin Crimson, carefully avoiding the midribs. Later these would be softened with a light wash of Schmincke Cadmium Yellow Lemon. The same green mix, somewhat diluted, was used for the stems. The hairs were painted with this mix with a little Raw Umber added, using a very fine brush. The white spots on the buds were achieved by using a scraperboard tool, after making sure the paint was completely dry. The unripe seed capsule required the same green mix with additional French Ultramarine. As there were no ripe capsules available the artist tried to hasten the ripening process under the grill – which didn't work – as well as leaving them in the sun for a few days. The latter resulted in a 'ready to burst' capsule painted with Raw Umber touched with Burnt Umber; the open pores were added with a mix of Perylene Green and Perylene Maroon. As always she checked the edges for sharpness, deepened shadows and added some secondary veins before she considered the work complete. She used Winsor & Newton paint throughout unless otherwise stated.

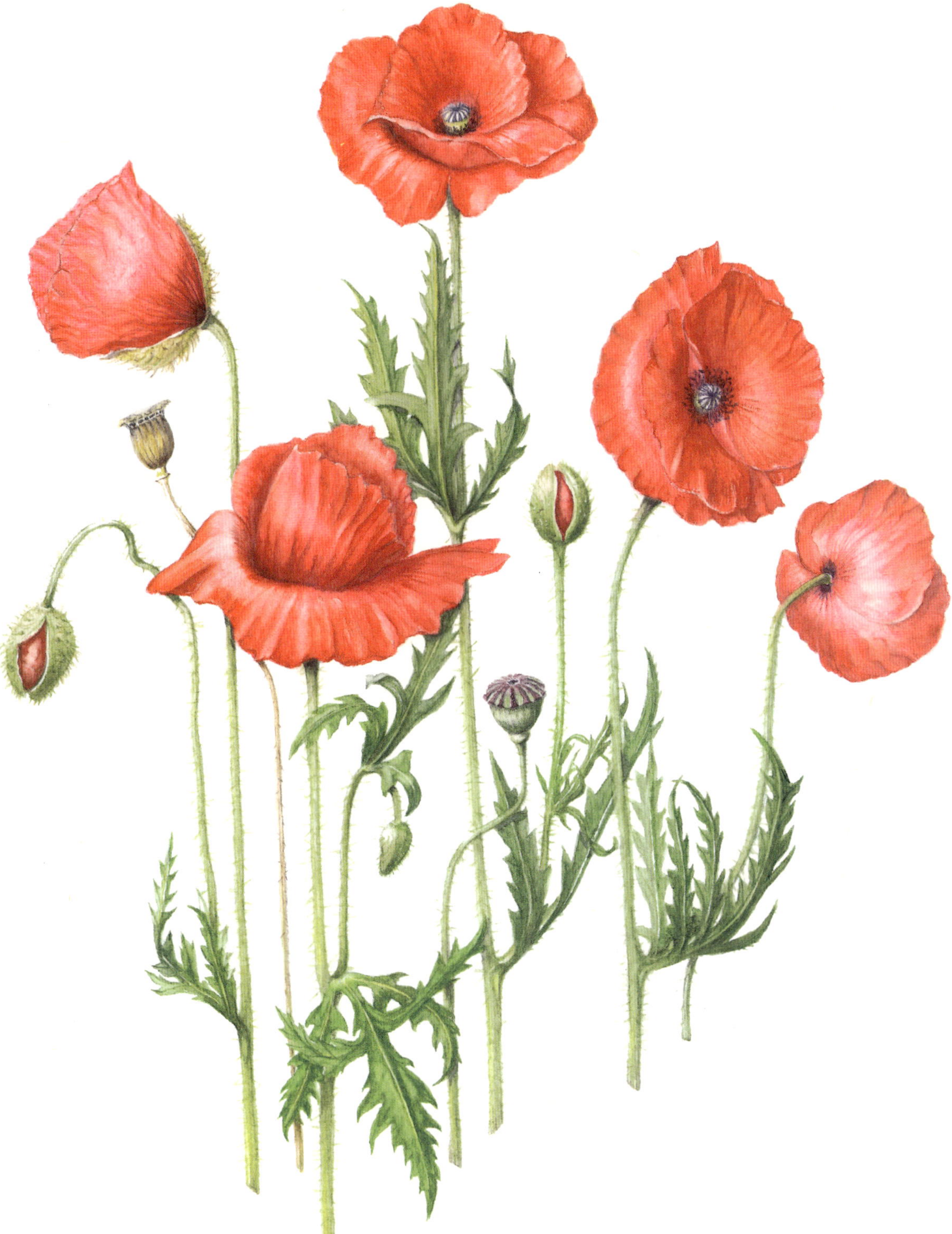

Opium Poppy

Papaver somniferum

Arthur Harry Church, a botanist at Oxford and a contemporary of Ernest E. Clark, was an exceptional botanical illustrator. He produced hundreds of paintings similar to the lateral dissection of an Opium Poppy shown here which were of enormous benefit to his students. His speciality was the construction and arrangement of flower parts and working in pencil, using Chinese White as body colour, he built up watercolour to produce vibrant and very fine images.

If Church was painting today, he would probably use gouache, but his method was familiar to me many years ago; I was born in the year of his death and in my teens painted chiefly in that fashion. The late Sally Keir was also using Chinese White as body colour to create her stunning images as recently as the early 1990s. Today we are spoilt for choice where artists' materials are concerned, but nothing can substitute for gaining mastery over a medium, even if this is difficult to achieve.

Note the way in which the petals have been halved, not just randomly removed, thereby showing that the whole flower has four petals. The seed capsule has been opened to show both interior and exterior surfaces and this lateral section therefore gives a very fine description of the subject within one image.

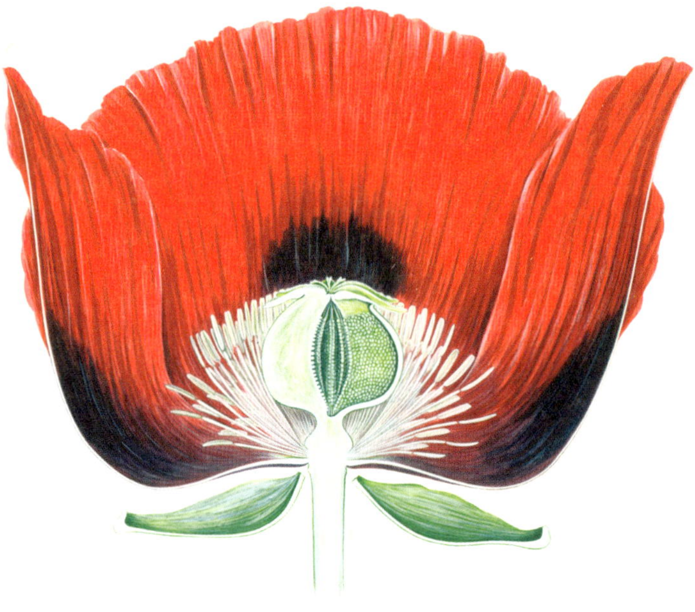

Watercolour, Arthur Harry Church (1865–1937) © Bridgeman Art Library

Oriental Poppy

Papaver orientalis

This study of an Oriental oppy flower is a charming piece of work in which the artist has captured the fragility and tissue-paper quality of each petal. Such small drawings are of great value as they enable the artist to spend time focusing on an individual flower and, when working in black and white, to concentrate on tone without the distraction of colour. The delicate nuances of shades in each petal will have taken a lot of controlled movement and each square centimetre shows this – try looking at it through a magnifying lens to fully appreciate the detail. Each dark blotch alone holds about five different tones and the flower centre has been drawn with exquisite accuracy. Every artist works with the pencils with which they feel most at home, but regardless of brand and grade, a cardinal rule is to keep a good point. A very fine emery paper or sharp penknife will help with this, so that you do not waste your pencils by constant sharpening of the wood, which is often the case with electric sharpeners.

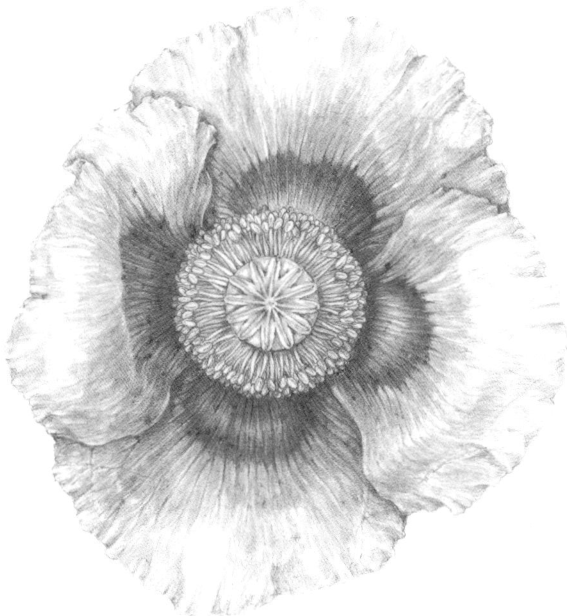

PRIMROSE FAMILY *Primulaceae*

Primrose

Primula vulgaris

Primrose is a general favourite among lovers of wild flowers, partly due to its early appearance in the spring. In April and May it can be found in profusion along the hedgebanks, in copses and pastures. Its pale yellow blossoms, measuring about an inch in diameter, grow singly on long radical, leafless stalks. The calyx is slightly inflated, and has five angular divisions of a pale milky green. The petals are five in number, each one being notched or cleft on the margin. There are five stamens enclosed within the tube of the corolla, a style and stigma. The leaves are about as long as the flower-stalks, and of a pale green, obovate in form, with a wrinkled surface, crenate along the margin and radical. The root-stock is thick and fleshy.

There are several native varieties of this plant, such as the Oxlip, the Bird's-eye Primrose, and the Scottish Primrose. It grows to a height of three to six inches. EC

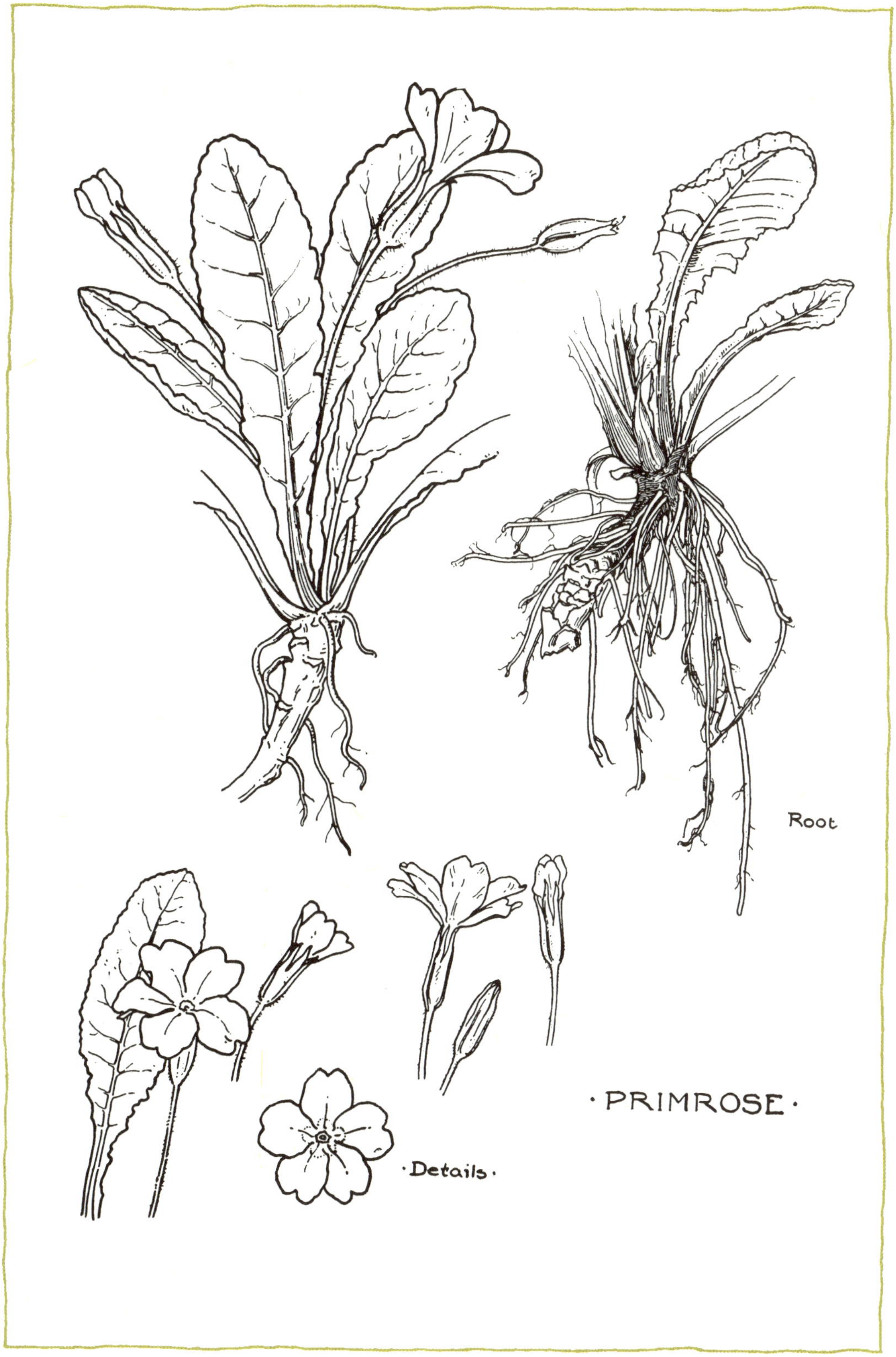
Root
Details
· PRIMROSE ·

Auricula

Primula auricula x *berninae* 'Windrush'

This delightfully fresh study of a Primula is a good example of what can be achieved using a limited palette, in this case with just four main colours. Painting on Fabriano Artistico 300gsm (140lb) Hot Pressed paper, the artist used Winsor & Newton Cobalt Blue in both flowers and leaves, adding Permanent Rose for the flowers and Lemon Yellow for the leaves. A touch of Yellow Ochre was mixed with the Lemon Yellow and Cobalt for the flower centres.

The artist has shown the fleshy texture of the leaves by carefully brush-drawing the edges, thereby showing their thickness. Like many auriculas the dusty farina is very much a feature and she used body colour to scatter this on the leaves and one flower. (Personally I favour Chinese White for this, sometimes with a little Naples Yellow, which will really make it sing out, particularly on a crimson auricula where there may be a dusting of golden pollen.) By holding the brush at right angles to the paper one can achieve really fine grains without any little 'tails'. The same technique works for hairs, such as those on a poppy stem, where you want them to be crisp and not bent at the tip.

Now that macro photography is within the reach of anyone with a reasonably priced camera it beholds the artist to be ever more precise in their brushwork. Set the camera on macro and go in close to the poppy stem or thorny rose, then see the detail enlarged on your computer monitor. We are all aware now of the help that 'modern' inventions such as the *camera obscura* or *camera lucida* gave to the revered artists of the past, so I think you can be assured that Canaletto (1697–1768), Vermeer (1632–75) and others would have been overjoyed if they had access to today's technology.

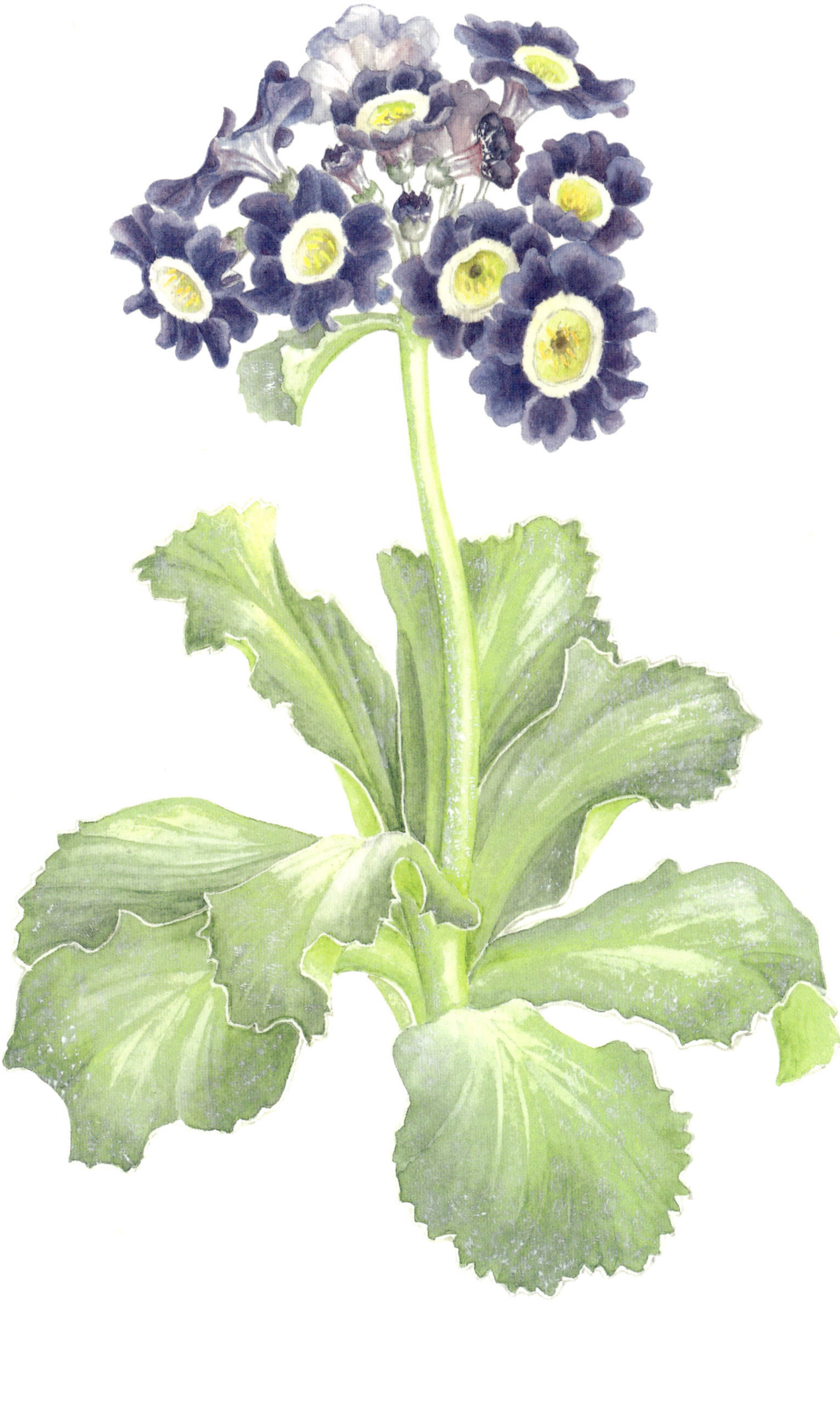

Cowslip

Primula veris

Cowslip, or Paigle, is another great favourite wild flower, and bears a close relationship to the Primrose. Although the inflorescence is in both cases an umbel, the arrangement of the blooms in the Cowslip is so distinctive as to make it appear a widely different plant. They grow on short stalks from the same point at the extremity of the long radical flower-stalk; from this point also two small bracts grow.

There are five small petals joining together to form a tube, which is mainly hidden by the calyx. The colour of the blooms is from a pale to a deep yellow, with sometimes a bright orange spot at the base of the petals. There are five stamens, and a pistil within the tube. The calyx is five pointed, resembling that of the primrose.

The leaves are radical, wrinkled and crenate along the margin, and pale green. It grows from three to six inches high in fields and pastures and hedgebanks. Its time of flowering is early spring. Very characteristic is the way in which the blossoms of the Cowslip hang their heads – 'cowslips wan that hang the pensive head'. EC

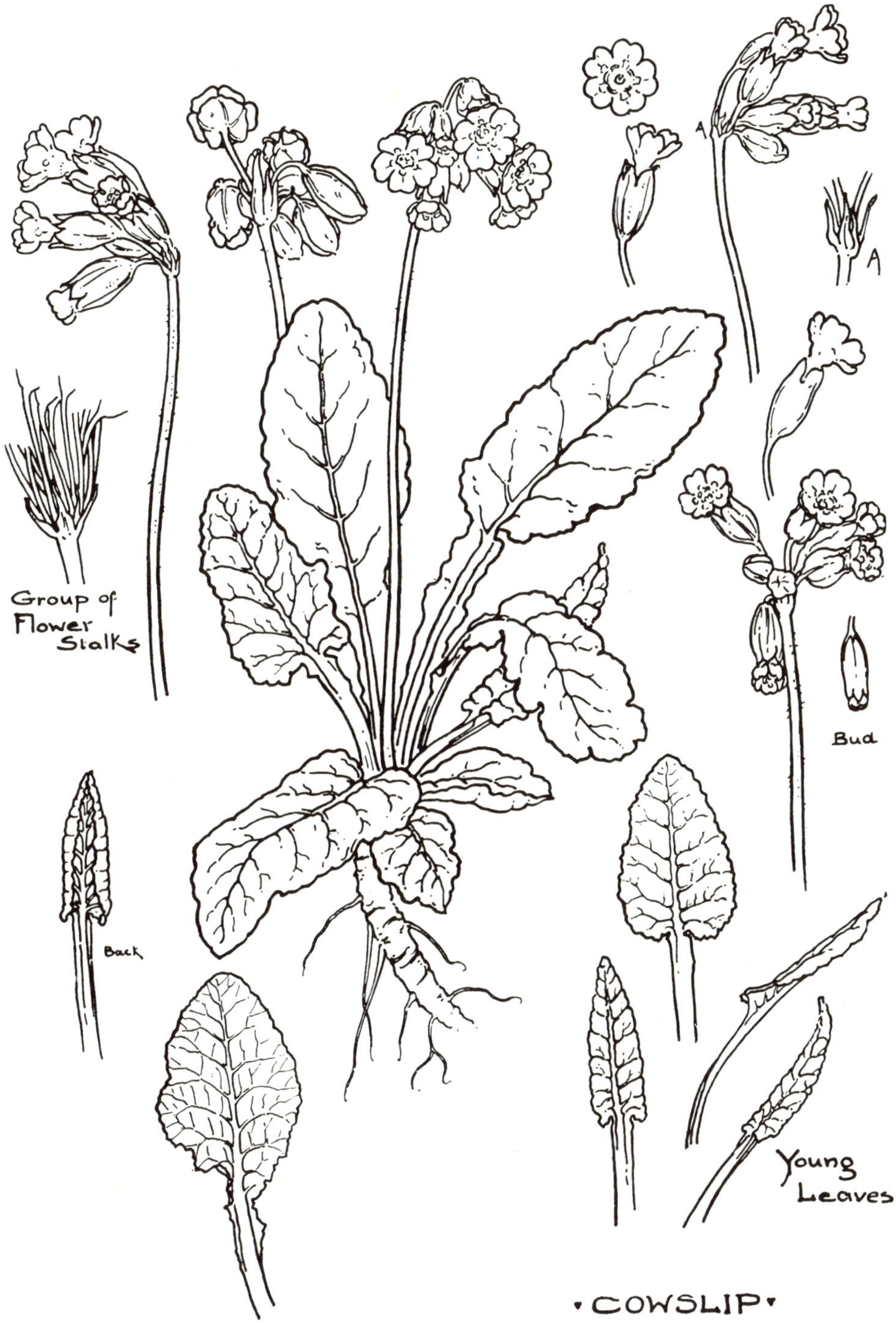

• COWSLIP •

Cowslip

Primula veris

I wonder if any reproduction could do justice to the quality of this painting of a Primrose. It combines two elements which are among the most challenging for the botanical painter, namely pale yellow flowers, with their attendant shading difficulties, and the almost reptilian venation of the primula leaves. Yet I doubt if there is an art class held in Britain during the spring where someone does not turn up carrying a primrose in a pot. They are so tempting after the dark days of winter, but students often rue the day when they struggle to make sense of such intricate patterns on the leaves.

The most common mistake is to draw in every vein regardless of whether or not they can be clearly seen. Notice here the way the artist has varied her initial green washes to create areas of leaf surface which catch the light, for example on the leaf at 9 o'clock. She has built up the veins, drawing with the brush but making sure that she does not lose the light sheen beneath. At the opposite side of the tonal scale, tiny veins are only hinted at in darker areas of cast shadow or hidden from direct light, as can be seen on the leaves at 4 and 12 o'clock.

The artist says she was surprised by the different shades of green she needed for the leaves and gives her mixes as follows. For the palest she mixed Daler-Rowney Sap Green with Schmincke Jaune Yellow (first wash), and Daniel Smith Deep Sap Green; Schmincke Green Earth mixed with Winsor & Newton Indanthrene Blue and Olive Green with Midnight Green and Schmincke Sap Green gave her the darker shades as required. The flowers were painted with Aureolin Modern and Vanadium Yellow, both by Schmincke. Winsor & Newton Transparent Yellow and Green Gold were used for shading.

Note how shading and varying tones show how the veins are indented on the upper surfaces of the leaves but stand proud on the reverse side, particularly the bold midribs with their strongly cast shadows.

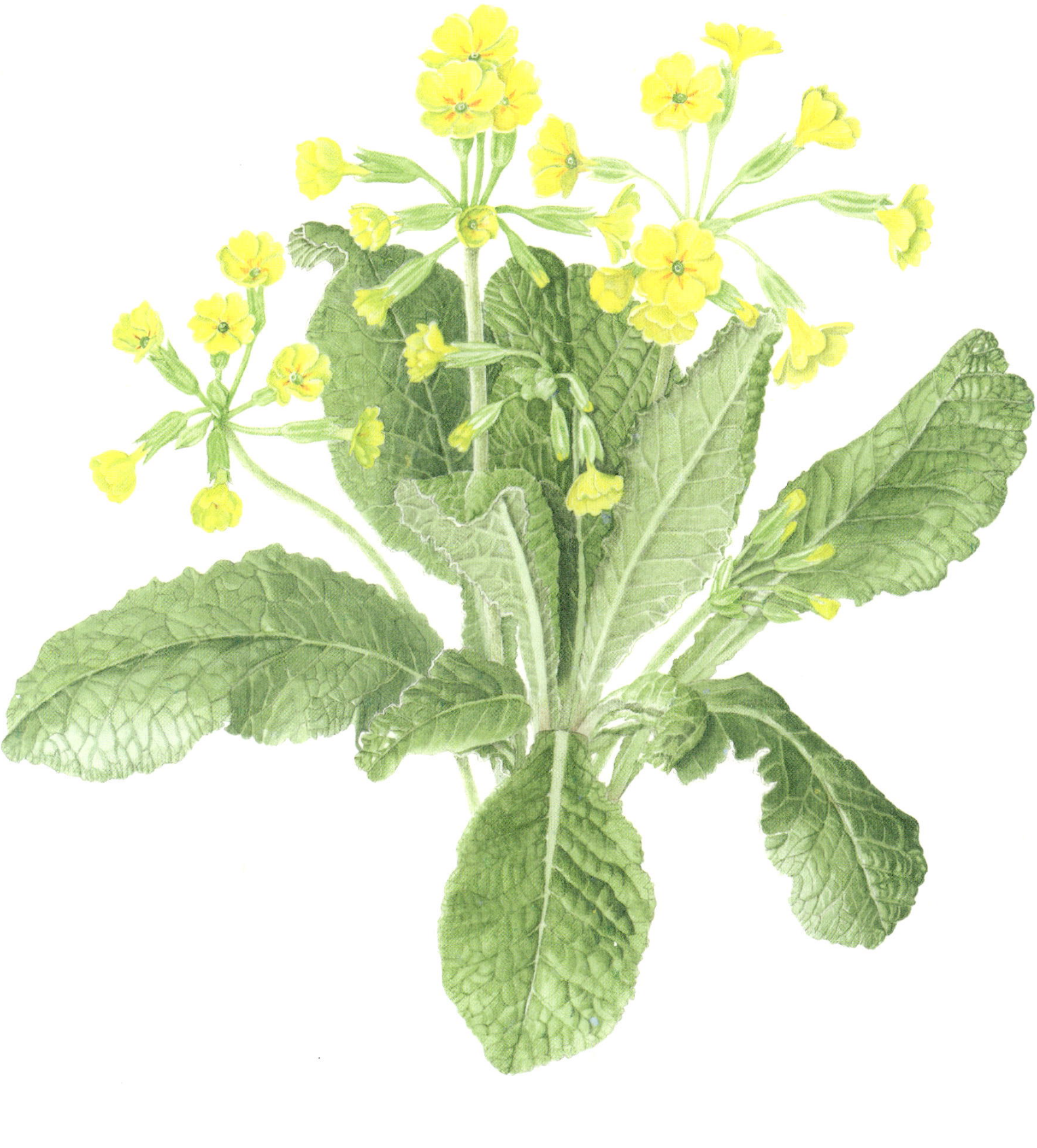

Watercolour, Kay Rees-Davies

BUTTERCUP FAMILY *Ranunculaceae*

Autumn Anemone

Anemone hupehensis var. *japonica*

Autumn or Japanese Anemone is in nearly all respects, except that of size, like the little Wood Anemone (*Anemone nemorosa*).

It grows from one to two feet high in rather a loosely branching manner. When in blossom its graceful growth and white, as in this case, or pinkish blooms, and its dull green vigorous-looking leaves, offer beautiful material to the student of plant form. The flower itself is a perianth somewhat irregular in form, consisting of six or more petals or sepals, delicately tinged with purple on the outside. The anthers are numerous and bright yellow, forming a ring of gold round the green globular stigma. The leaves are radical, excepting three involucral leaves placed on the stem at the junction of the flower-stalks, which are from six to eight inches in length. This whorl of leaves or bracts is one of the characteristics of the whole genus.

The radical leaves are large and three-lobed, rather sharply serrated, and with pronounced veining. The buds are roundish and vigorous-looking, enclosed by the three outer sepals. Flowers in the autumn. EC

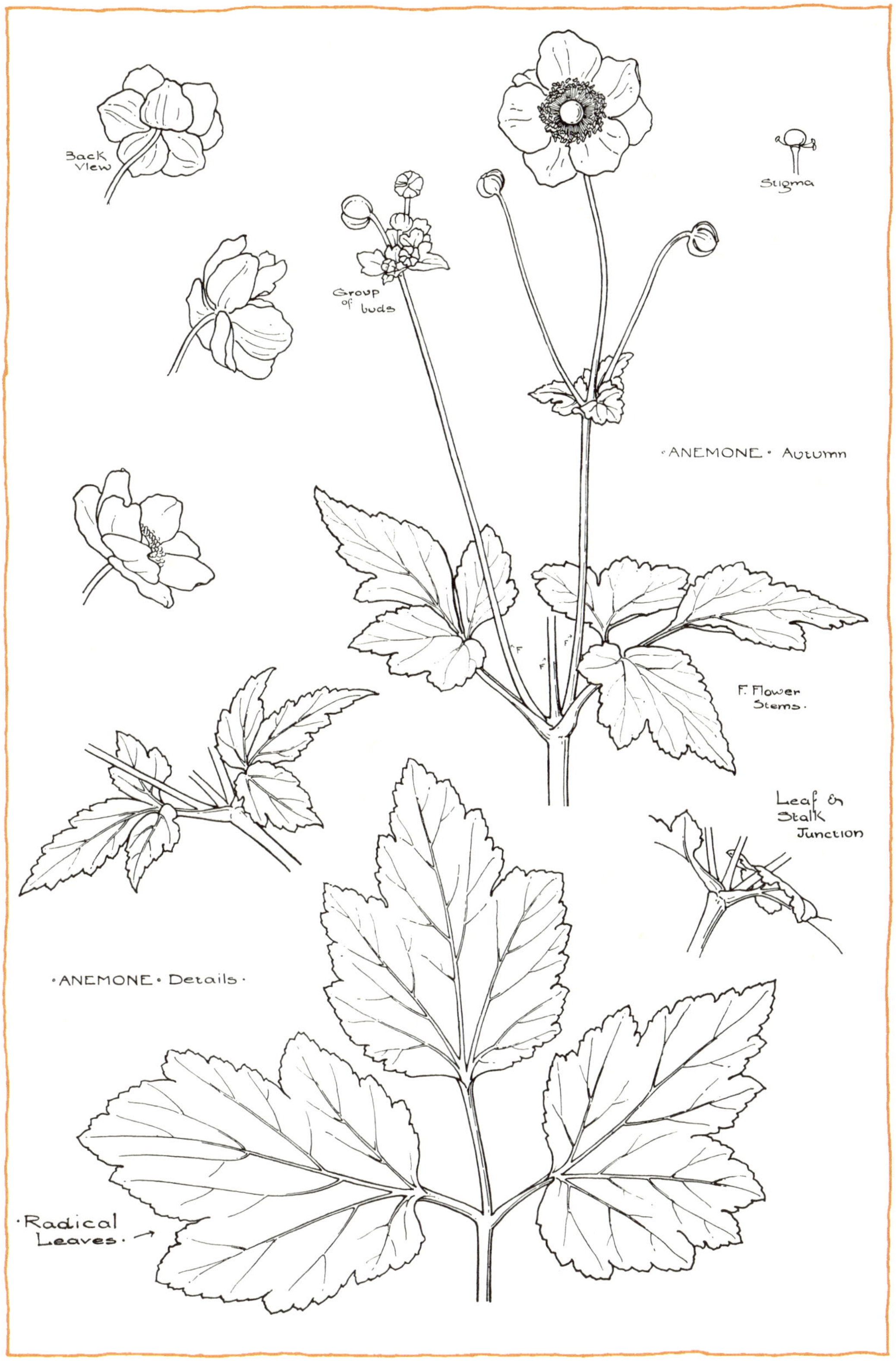
Back View
Group of buds
Stigma
·ANEMONE· Autumn
F. Flower Stems.
Leaf & Stalk Junction
·ANEMONE· Details·
·Radical Leaves·

Japanese anemones

Anemone hupehensis var. *japonica*

This painting of Japanese Anemones was the artist's fifth assignment while working for her Diploma, about two-thirds of the way through the course. She says that she spent so long on the flowers that she ran out of time to work on the leaves, which was unfortunate. However, although there are areas which could be improved, such as leaf-joints and the minutiae of tiny leaves and veins, the artist has done particularly well in achieving such a clear, fresh magenta pink for the flowers and shading them without muddying the effect; pink is not an easy colour to shade and can soon be made to look dirty. The slightest hint of grey and the clarity is lost.

The delicate hints of purple combined with stronger pigment has worked well for the petals and the cast shadows help to create a very pleasing result. The stems are also well drawn and shaded, bearing in mind that curved or twisted stems are harder to control than those which are upright and straight. A good drawing exercise involves sets of parallel lines at varying distances apart, straight, curved and linear with kinks in them, as all will be encountered in one flower or another.

This is altogether a very natural composition which captures the style of the plant, but it could have been improved by finishing the stems at different levels rather than in a straight line. This straight and rigid base can work well with stiff flowers such as lilies or gladioli but seems contrary to the happy-go-lucky nature of Japanese Anemones.

Watercolour, Kamiko Kambe-Gang

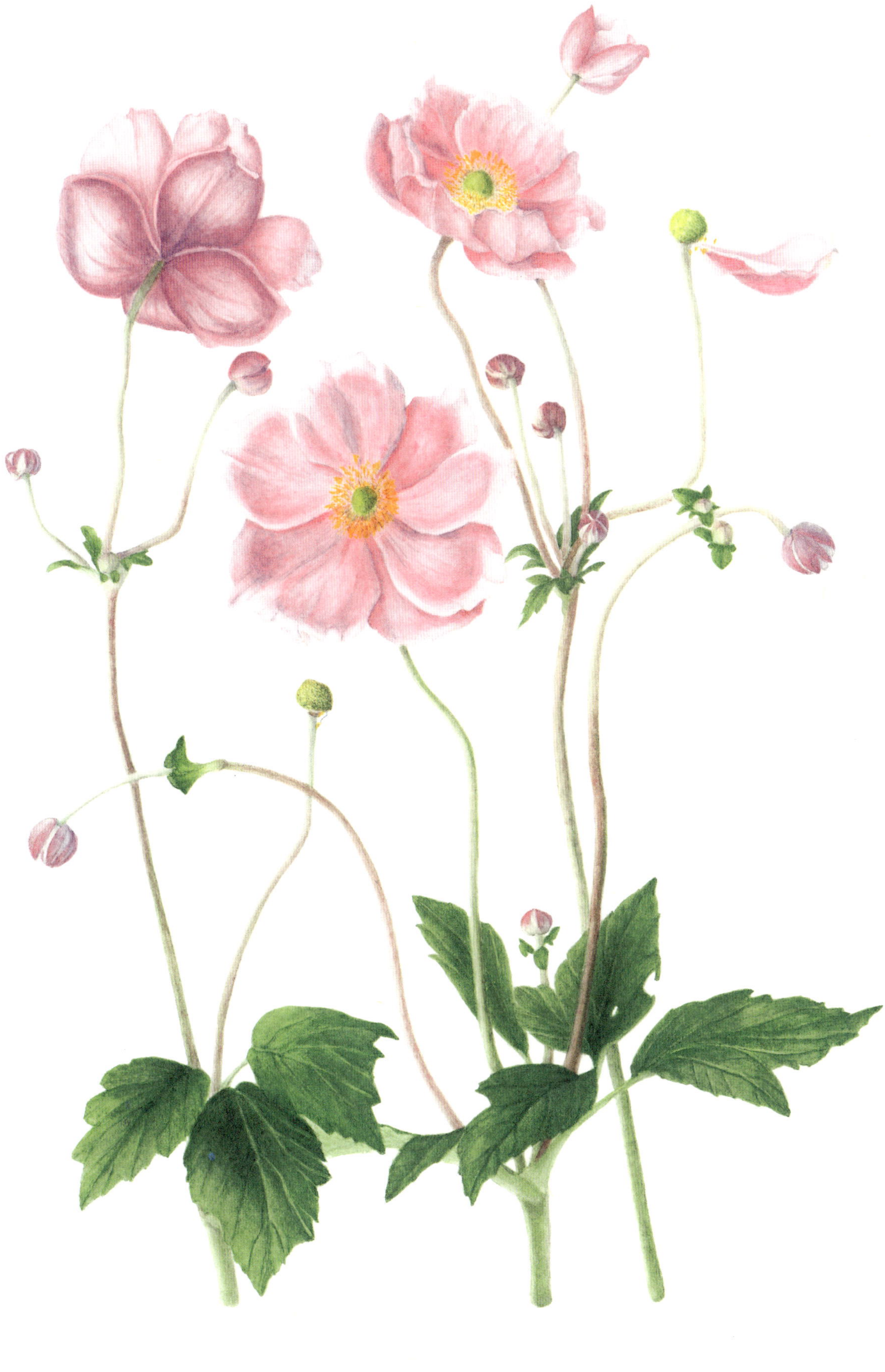

Aquilegia

Aquilegia hybrids

It is currently fashionable to breed bigger and showier plants for our gardens and these hybrid aquilegias are far removed from the small and simple 'granny's bonnets' still found in many a cottage garden. Their stems belie their delicate appearance by supporting very large flowers and the artist has succeeded in making a graceful composition while abiding by the rule of three – not only three stems, but three open flowers, three red buds and a blue flower with two attendant buds creating its own lop-sided triangle.

Good observation and drawing is essential when tackling aquilegias as their arrangement of spurs, sepals and petals is ready to trap the unwary. Sometimes it is a good idea to take a flower to pieces in order to discover exactly how it is formed and I would certainly advise this when working on aquilegias for the first time.

One of the colours the artist relied on for this painting was Winsor & Newton Thioindigo Violet, sadly no longer available. Colours come and go at the whim of the manufacturers and usually those that disappear are the ones that are most highly valued by the flower painter, as in this case. However, the artist took careful notes of the pigments used and they are as follows: for the blue flower he used a wash of Permanent Rose on the sepals overlaid with a mix of Permanent Rose and Cobalt Blue (all Winsor & Newton). The white petals were shaded with the same mix and the stamens were painted with Winsor Yellow shaded with Indanthrene Blue. The dark red sepals were glazed with Schmincke Ruby Red and Thioindigo Violet, while the petals required a shading of French Ultramarine and Light Red with a touch of Ultramarine Violet. The stamens were painted as previously described. For the flame-coloured flower he used variations of Quinacridone Red on a wash of Cadmium Scarlet with added Perylene Maroon on the spurs. Winsor Yellow and Indanthrene Blue made up the foliage colour with shading of Thioindigo Violet.

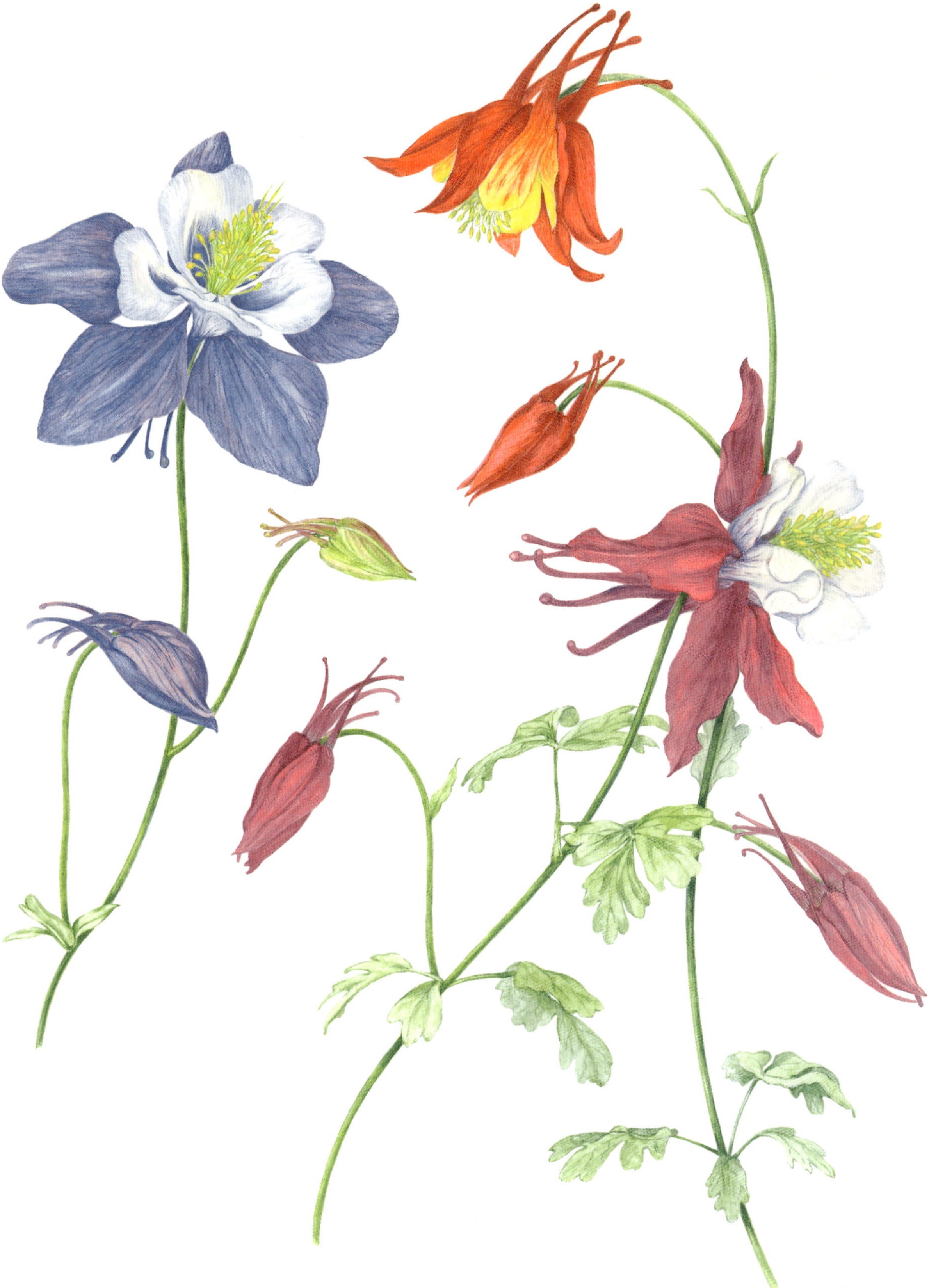

Marsh-marigold

Caltha palustris

Marsh-marigold, *alias* Mayblob, *alias* Mary-bud, is a strong healthy-looking plant, appearing in the early spring and lighting up marshy land and the banks of streams. Its flowers are a rich gold in colour, and its leaves are kidney-shaped, large and glossy, and crenate. Most of the leaves grow from the root, but some from the flower-stalk junctions clinging round the stem, from which point also fibrous stipules grow. In the language of the botanist the flower is a perianth, the petals and sepals being alike, not being differentiated into calyx and corolla. It grows in masses from six to twelve inches high. Petals five or more, stamens indefinite in number, and the same colour as the petals. EC

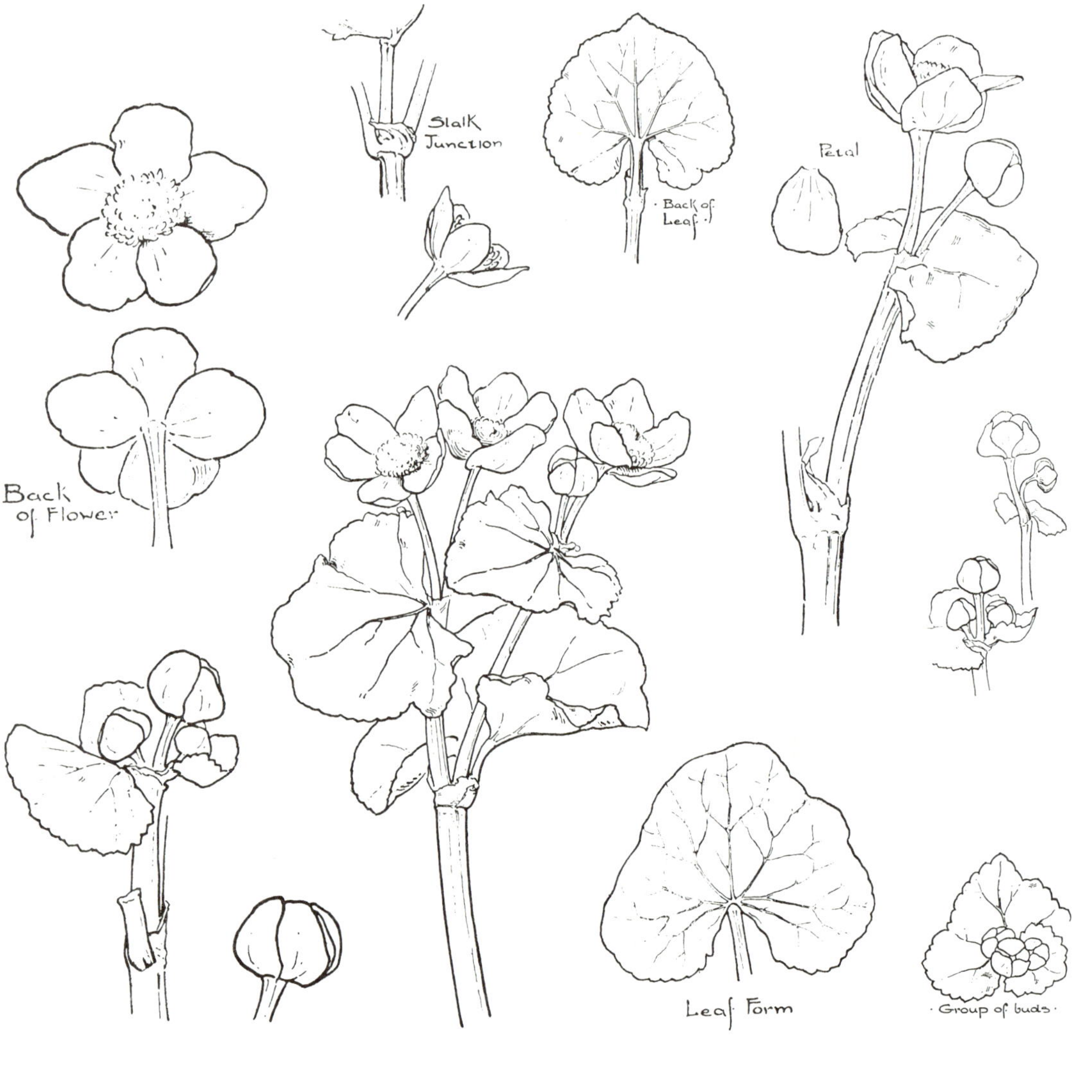

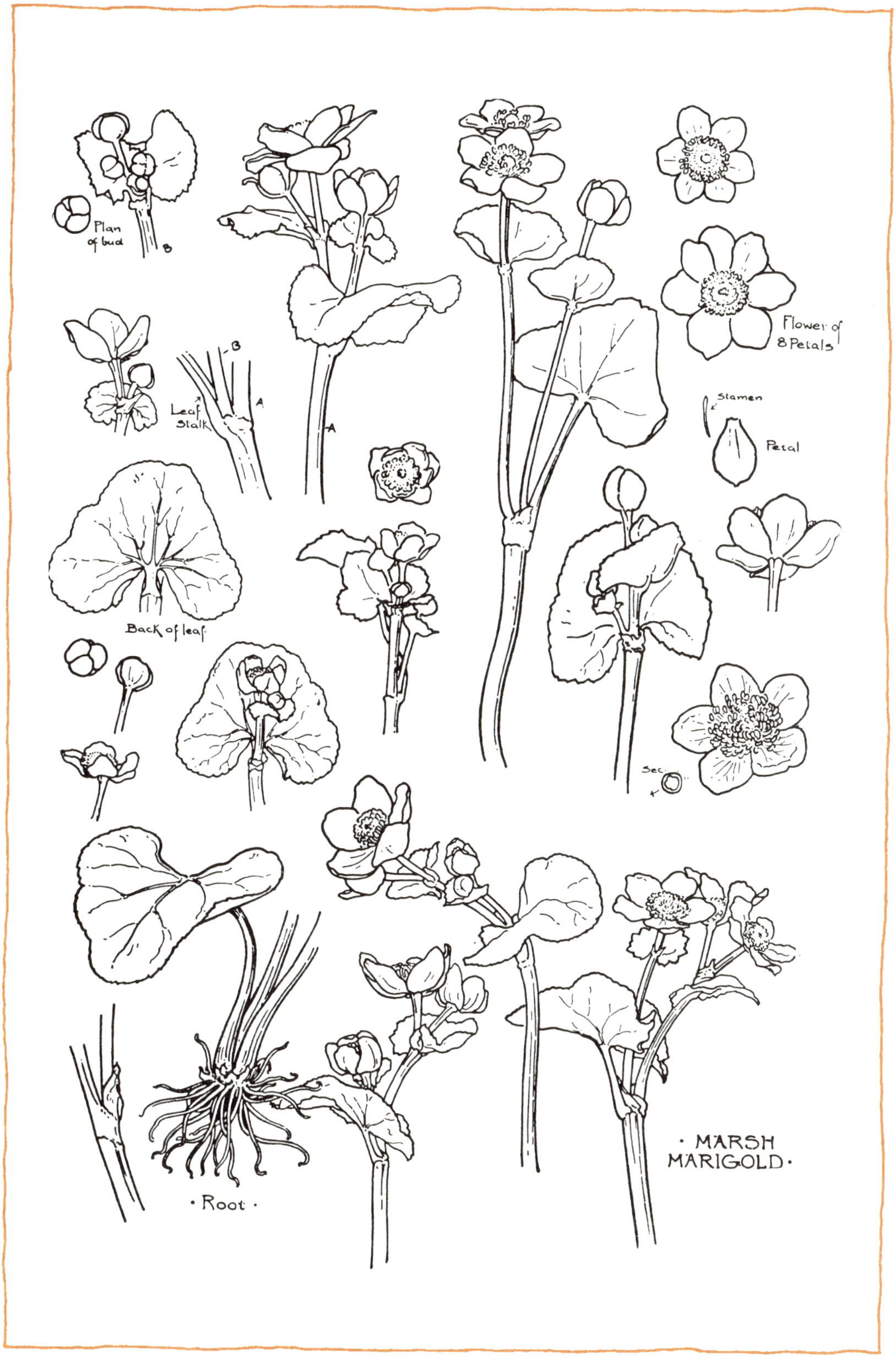
Plan of bud
B
B
Leaf Stalk
A
A
Flower of 8 Petals
Stamen
Petal
Back of leaf
Sec.
· Root ·
· MARSH MARIGOLD ·

Marsh-marigolds

Caltha palustris

This portrait of the Marsh-marigold has quite a contemporary layout and several things are particularly noteworthy. Large leaves are always challenging, but the artist remained undaunted and has handled the green washes extremely well, creating a good tonal range with fine venation and a crisply serrated edge. The stems are shapely and ribbed, with the cut edges exposing the hollow interiors. This is a good example of why it is best to finish off the stems in a true botanical study, rather than fade them out; here it emphasizes their structure and shape. A pink tinge has been gently washed in at the base of the stems to pleasing effect.

Each flower has retained the brilliance of the yellow pigment without being muddied by too much shading and the centres have been worked with care. Only in the lateral half section, in the style of Arthur Harry Church, has a common error been made. Five sepals have been shown, whereas two and a half would be correct for a five-petalled flower.

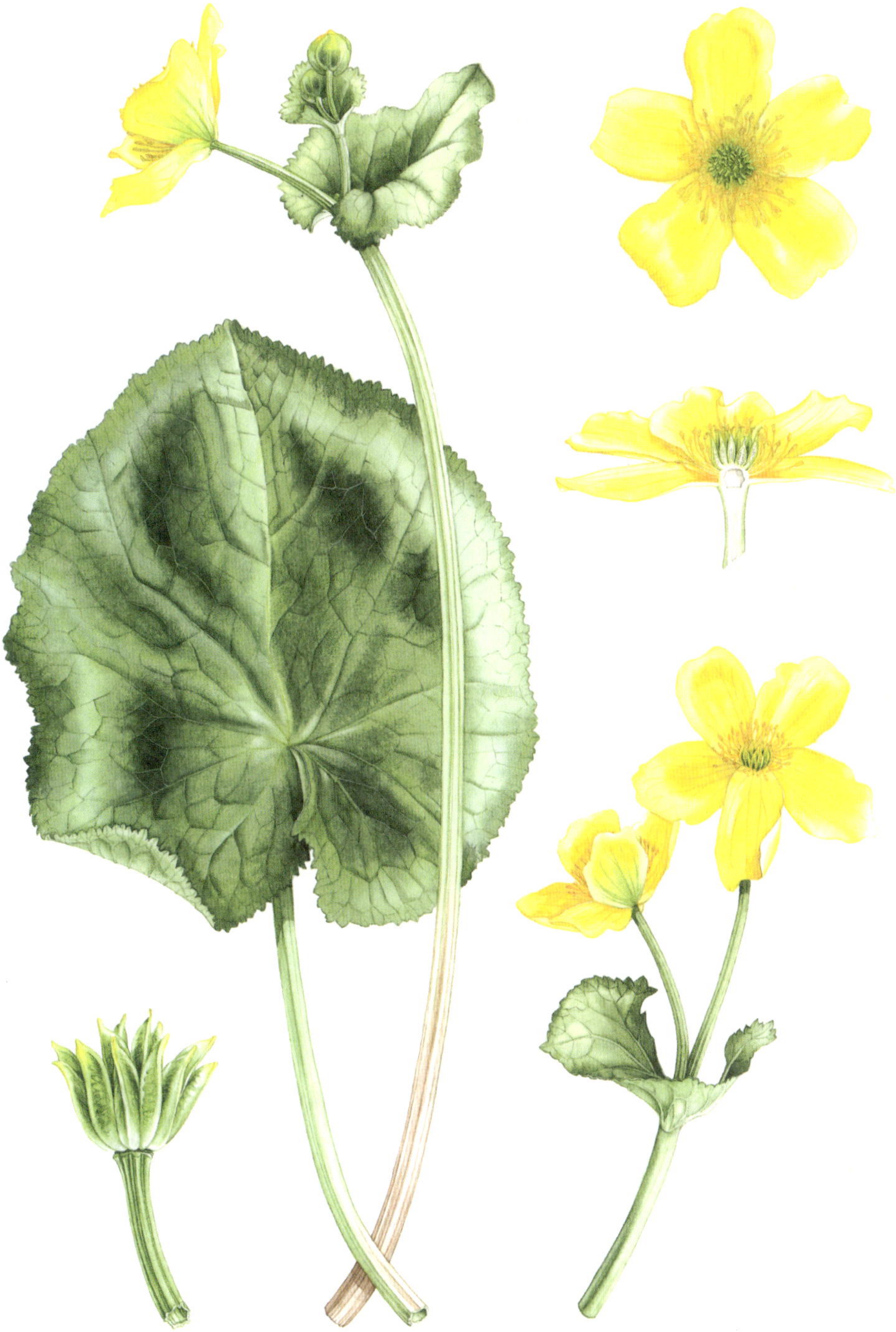

Watercolour, Chris Taylor

Clemats

Clematis viticella

A climber that makes rich with its purple blooms any trellis or house-front up which it is trained to climb. It has only four petals or sepals – some varieties having six or eight – and is a perianth. Its leaves are bold and entire, and grow in pairs and opposite, its stamens and carpels are numerous. Beginning to flower in the early autumn, it lasts until winter commences. There is also a wild member of this family, *Clematis vitalba*. Its petals are four in number, small and are reflexed, the stamens or filaments are long, giving the name of Old Man's Beard, another and more common name being Traveller's Joy. The petals are whitish-green. It is to be found abundantly in the South of England. The Clematis is one of those plants that climb by means of their leaf stalks and not by tendrils. EC

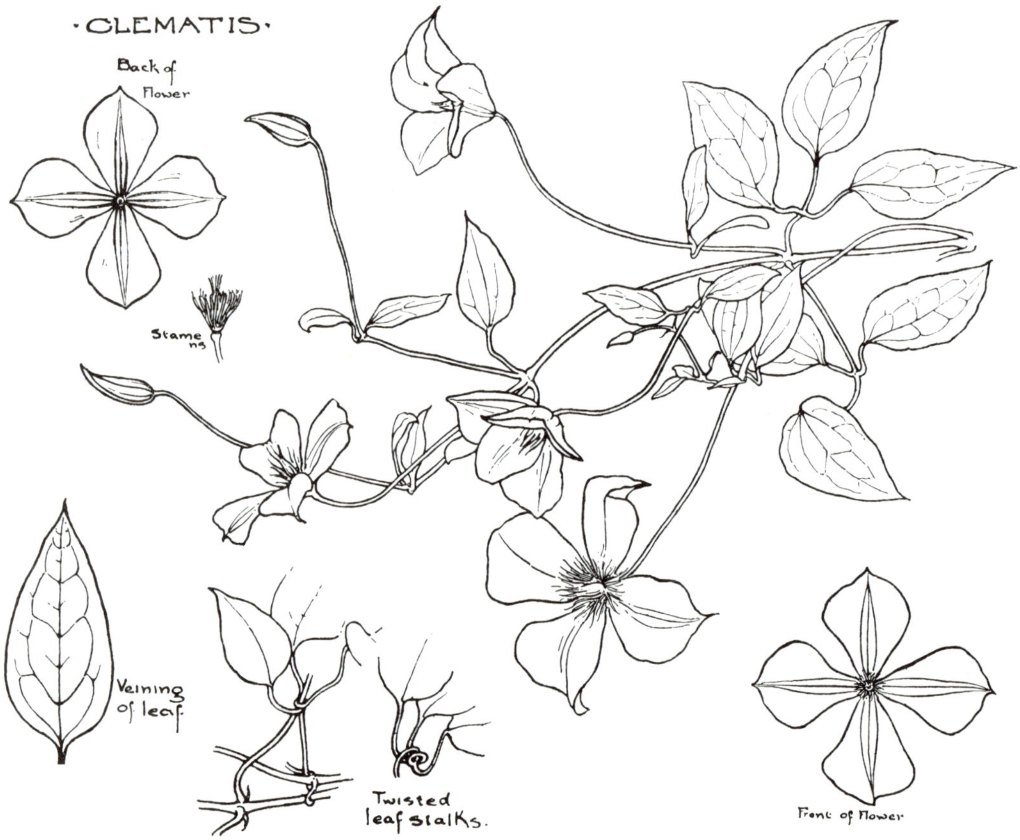

Clematis

Clematis 'Bill MacKenzie'

The long-lasting flowers of the *Clematis tangutica* hybrid 'Bill MacKenzie' appear in late summer and continue into the autumn. Their cheerful yellow lanterns have the same distinguishing feature as *C. tangutica*, namely the thick sepals that earned it the common name of Lemon Peel clematis, for that is exactly what they suggest. The contrasting purple filaments and delicate cut-leaf foliage make this a cheery plant for scrambling over fences. As always, the artist was thorough in noting her choice of pigments, which were Schmincke unless otherwise stated: for the flowers she used Vanadium Yellow and Lemon Yellow shaded with Green Earth. Olive Green Yellowish was mixed with Chromium Oxide Green. For the leaves she used Daniel Smith Dark Sap Green, Green Yellow Shade, Daler-Rowney Midnight Green and Sennelier Sap Green. The stems required Sennelier Sap Green, and Schmincke Sepia Brown Tone and Quinacridone Violet, with just a touch of Mauve.

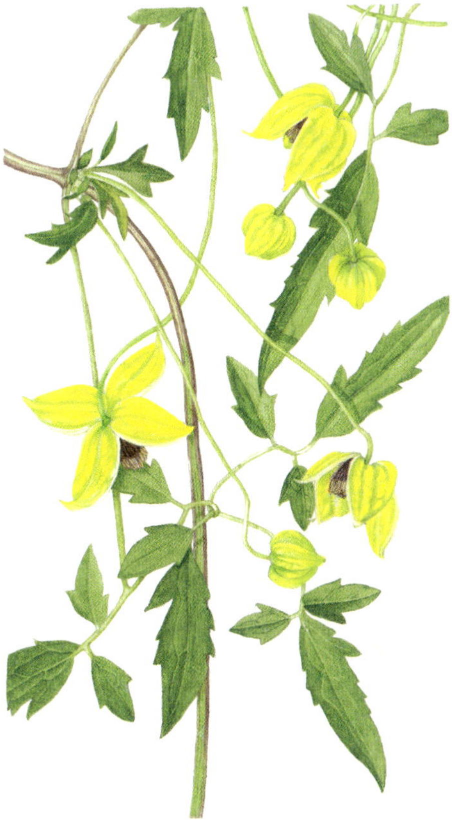

Watercolour, Kay Rees-Davies

Pulsatilla

Pulsatilla vulgaris 'Red Clock'

I couldn't resist this brilliant new hybrid pulsatilla when I saw it at the garden centre, although I knew from past experience of painting the usual purple and white varieties that it would not be the colour but the hairy petals that would be tricky. Sure enough, in parts this specimen was very whiskery, with some petals displaying a silvery down, others with long individual hairs and still more apparently smooth. For the most densely hirsute areas (the large flower, left-hand petal) I allowed the edge of the petal to blur and then flicked the fine hairs over that with the very tip of the brush. The flower at 11 o'clock displayed more individual long hairs, so here I kept the petal outline sharp before drawing them in with a very pale pinkish-lavender mix.

The light area between the top of the stem and base of each flower shows how dense the hairs were at these points. Foliage was sparse at this time as it grows up when the flowers have died down, a typical characteristic of chalk grassland species. Being an instinctive painter rather than a methodical one, I dart around the palette taking a little pigment here and a touch there, so it is never easy to recall exactly what I used. It is no bad thing for students to cultivate the same exploratory way of working and while honing their skills they can always make note of successful colour mixes. As two flowers are rarely alike some adjustment is always likely to be needed, but overall I think this can add to the liveliness of the interpretation. In this case I used a combination of Schmincke Magenta, Purple Magenta and Deep Red, with small amounts from the Sennelier range of artists' colours as required.

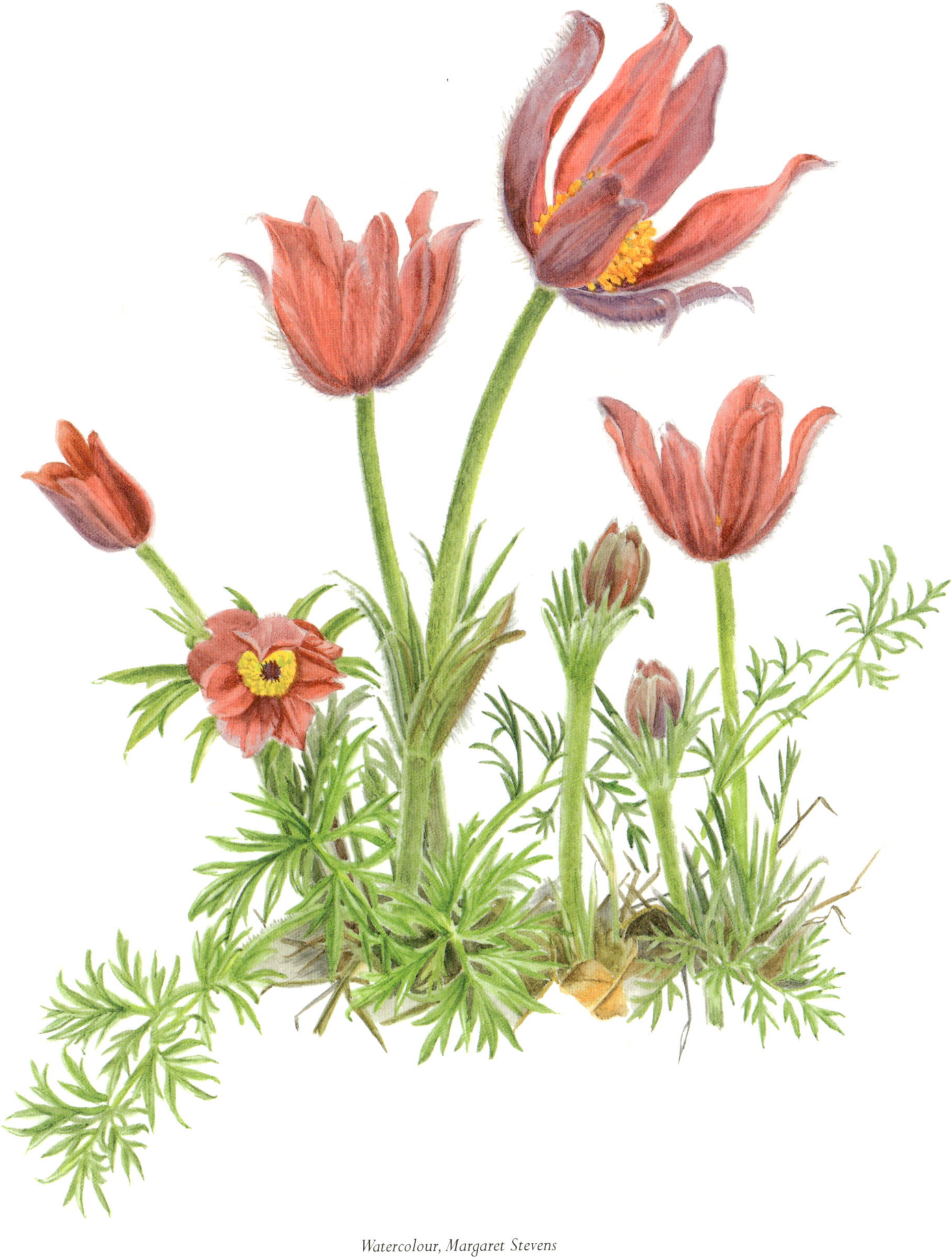

Watercolour, Margaret Stevens

Columbine

Aquilegia vulgaris

The colour of the Columbine varies from a white to a deep purple; the sepals are same colour as the petals, which terminate in a horn-like spur; these and the sepals alternate. The leaves grow chiefly on long radical stalks, and are generally divided into three very distinct segments, which are again lobed and serrated. It grows from one to three feet high, and flowers in June and July. Some of the radical leaves are several inches across, the flowers about one and a half inch across.

EC

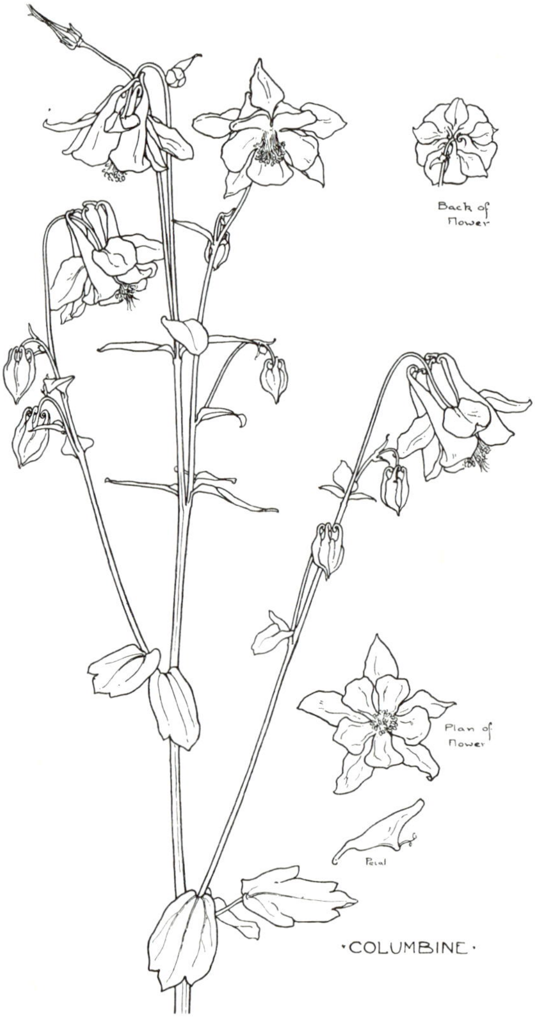

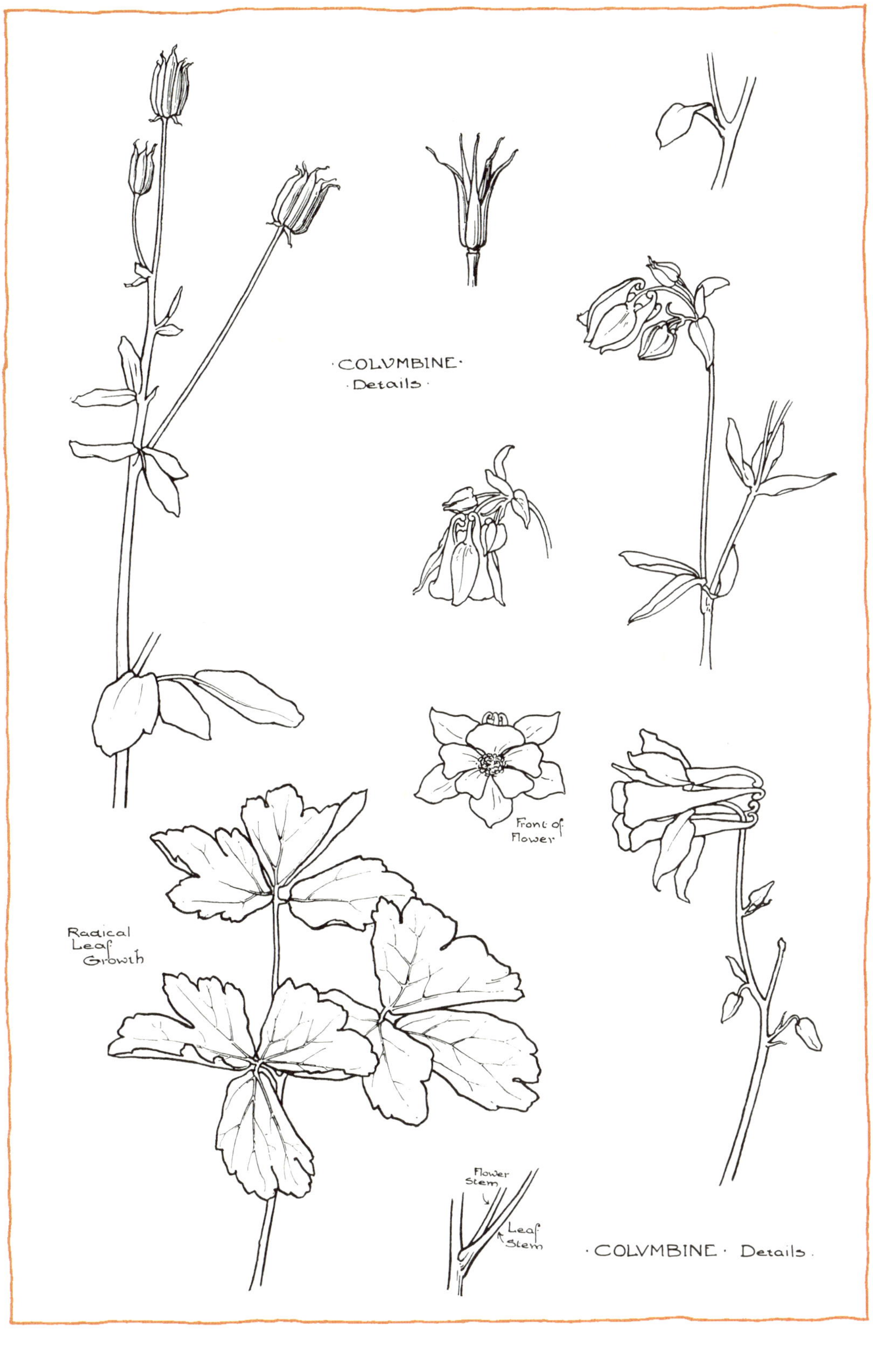
·COLVMBINE·
·Details·
Front of Flower
Radical Leaf Growth
Flower Stem
Leaf Stem
·COLVMBINE· Details.

Buttercup

Ranunculus bulbosus

There are some half-dozen species or this plant, all of which are common in England. The one figured here is the bulbous Crowfoot, which, along with the Meadow Buttercup, is perhaps the most abundant in our meadows. The flower has five bright yellow petals and five pale green sepals, which, in this case, as soon as the flower is fully developed, are reflexed or thrown backwards on to the stem. Sometimes they may be found with more than five petals, this author once found a specimen on the banks of the Trent with no less than 30 petals; it is shown in the plate, but of course is quite exceptional, and must therefore not be taken as representative. The root swells out into a kind of bulb, which is the chief characteristic of this variety. Its leaves near the root are large and many lobed, deeply divided and serrated; those higher up the stem are longer and thinner. Long leaf-like bracts are found at the junction of the flower-stalks. The stamens are numerous and yellow, surrounding the pale green stigma. The plant is erect and branched, growing to a foot or more in height. It is one of the typical flowers of late spring and early summer, and may be found from May to July.

EC

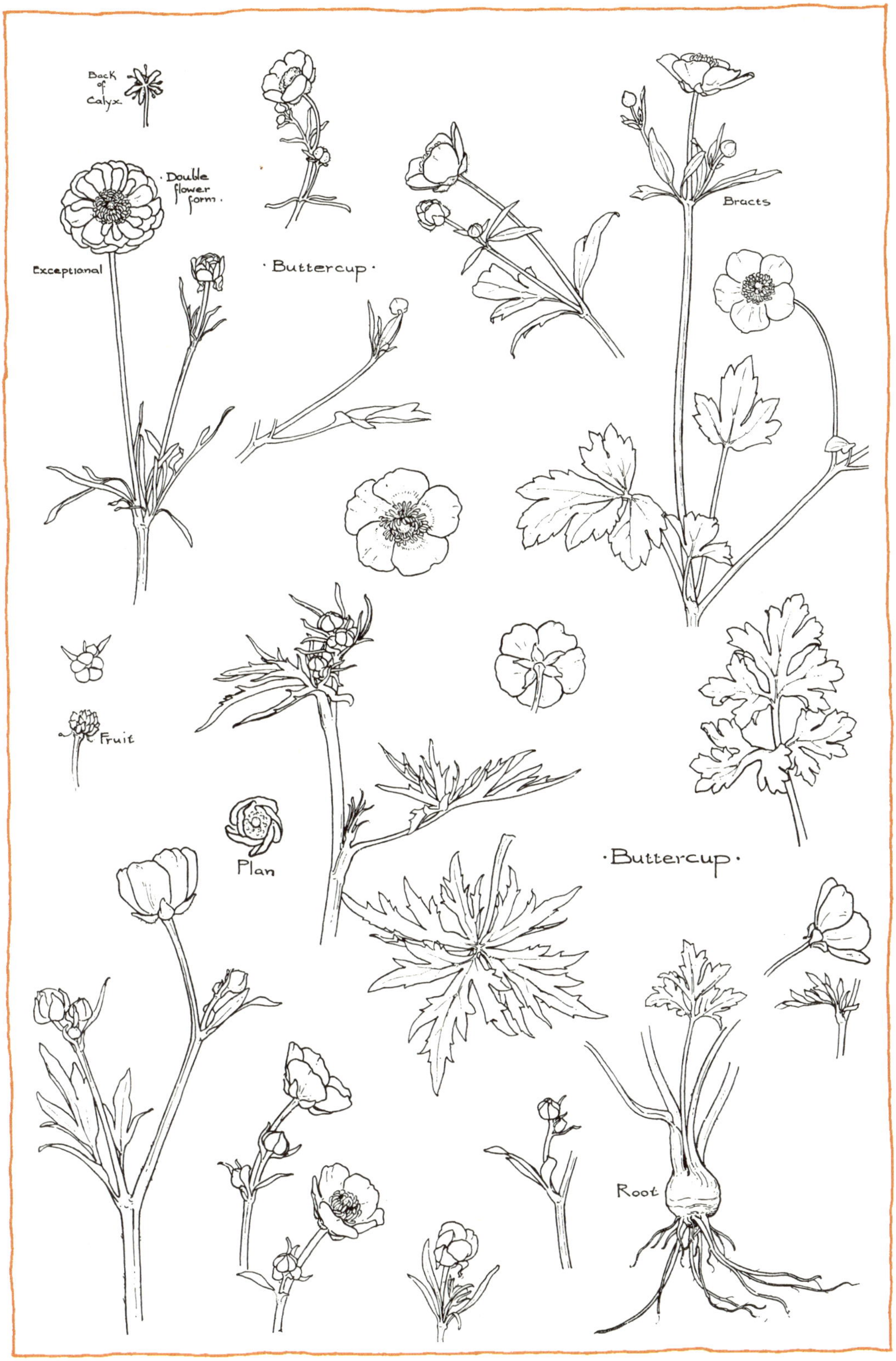
Back of Calyx.
Double flower form.
Exceptional
·Buttercup·
Bracts
Fruit
Plan
·Buttercup·
Root

Buttercups in Mixed Spring Flowers

Ranunculus acris

This charming painting of a simple bunch of Buttercups with other spring wild flowers such as a child might gather is a move in the direction of flower painting rather than true botanical illustration. In spite of this the flowers are no less accurately depicted, and this type of painting calls for additional skills in composition.

In the Bluebells there is that hint of pink without which the colour would not be true. Winsor & Newton Permanent Rose and Cobalt Blue are both likely to be used for this. The blue of these flowers and the gold of the Buttercups will always look good together as they truly complement each other. However, the introduction of the pink Clover was essential – you only need to cover the clover flowers with your fingers to see how much the painting relies on their inclusion. Even in this aspect of composition an odd number of colours will work better than an even one, particularly as the pink in the Bluebells joins in harmoniously. The White Dead-nettle, as a non-colour, does not affect this, but its placement adds height and lightness without introducing a fourth colour. The stems are allowed to fade out, which is perfectly acceptable for this type of decorative painting.

In a detailed mixed bunch of this type the artist builds up gradually, flower by flower. She painted the Buttercups first, trying to show all aspects of each particular flower. Each flower-head was painted in detail, leaving the stems in pencil so that she could superimpose more flowerheads or change the way stems overlap as the work progressed. This method of working, flower arranging on the paper, allows the structure of the composition to evolve while keeping the colour balance true. Extra flowers can then be added to give depth or fill any gaps.

Watercolour, Barbara McGirr

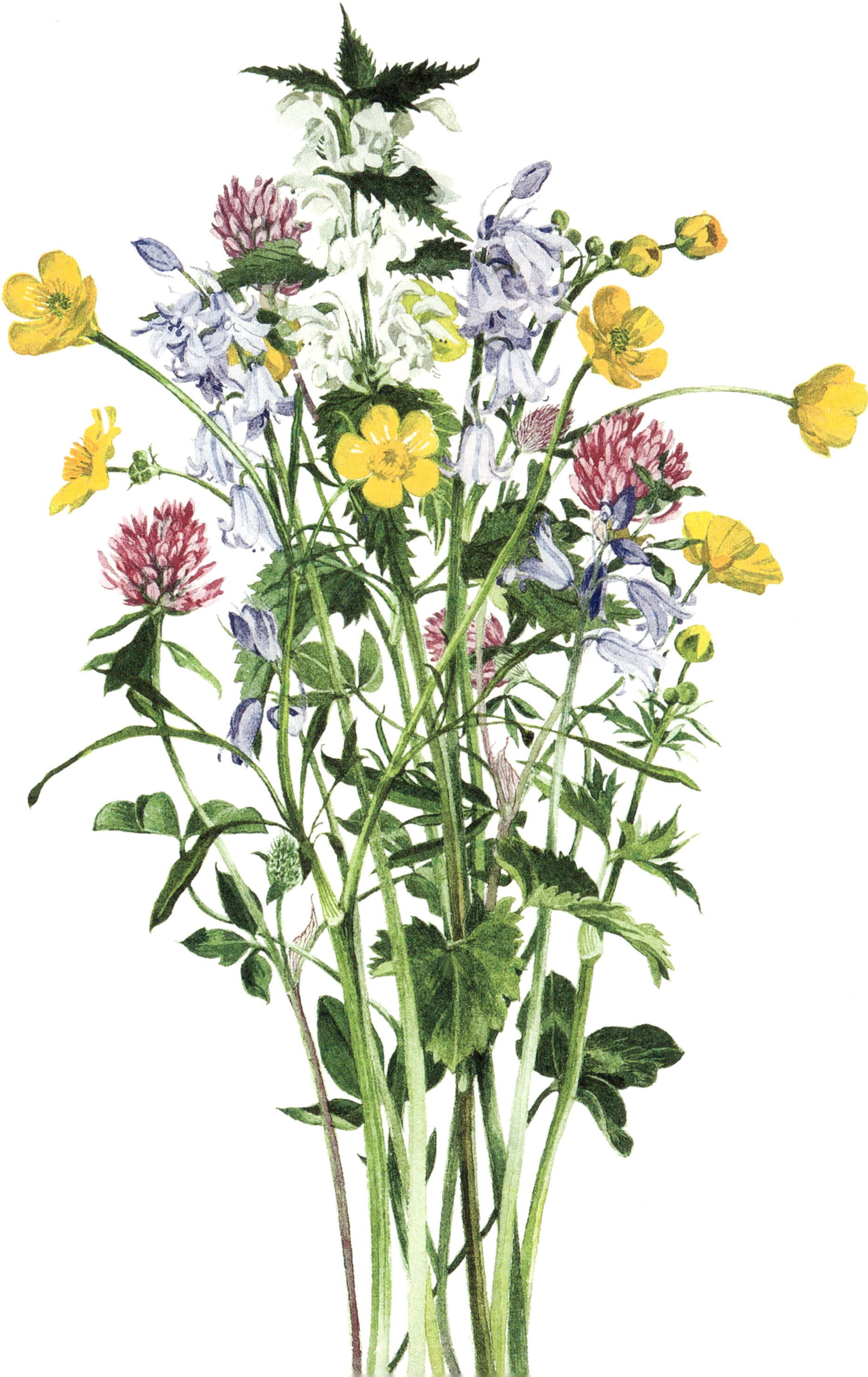

Lesser Celandine

Ranunculus ficaria

'Spring is coming, thou art come', writes Wordsworth of this little flower, which accurately describes its early appearance. There are few more welcome or brighter blooms that usher in the early spring than the little Celandine coming ' 'ere a leaf is on a bush'. Its golden star-like blossom lights up the hedge banks and moist shady places in most pastures and lanes. Belonging to the Buttercup order, it consists of from six or eight to ten or more bright yellow glossy petals, and a calyx of three sepals of a pale green. The leaves are mostly radical, and are cordate and sometimes angular in form, slightly thick, and dark green in colour. The flowers are borne singly, on stems that are a little longer than the leaf-stalks and are slightly channelled, and also taper rather quickly to the flower, broadening very much at the root. The root consists of a number of oblong or cylindrical tubers and fibres. The height of the plant is from three to eight inches. Although looked upon as a common weed, it inspired the above quoted poet to sing its praises often, and a copy of it is carved upon his tomb.

EC

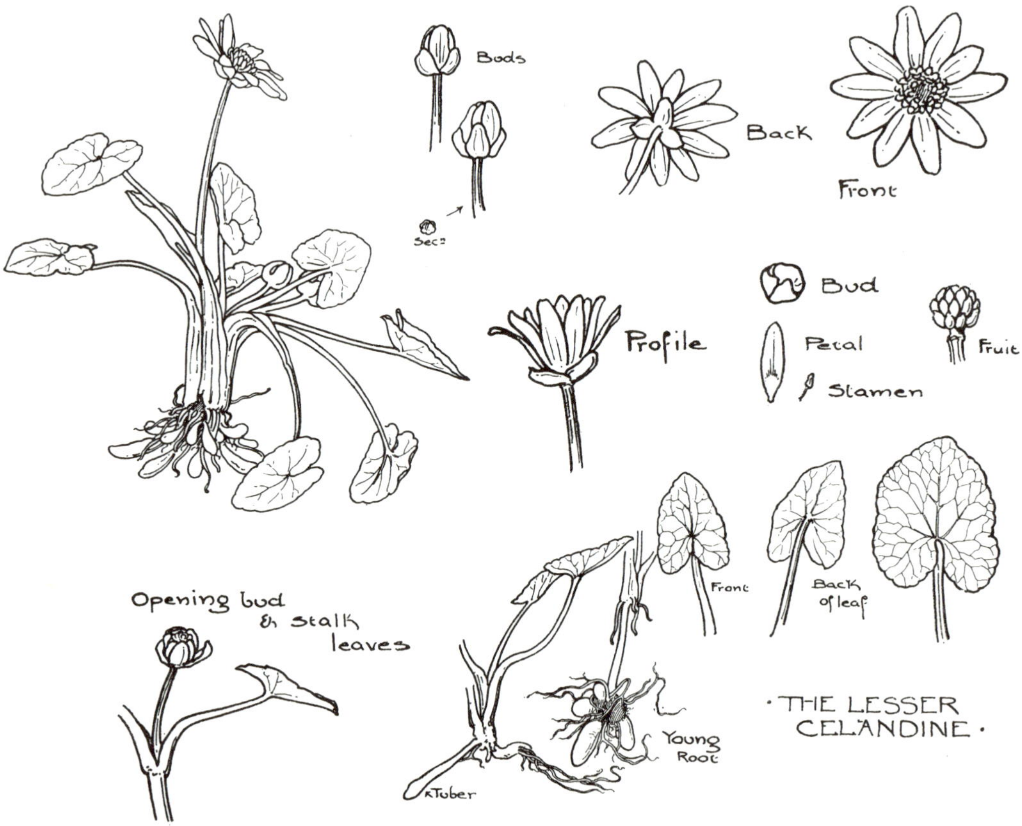

Lesser Celandine

Ranunculus ficaria

This artist has used several plants to build up an attractive composition, using pencil to balance what would otherwise be a preponderance of green and yellow, also the fine roots at the bottom of the page. According to the ancient herbalists' philosophy known as the doctrine of signatures, the fleshy roots seen on the main plant, resembled haemorrhoids, so not surprisingly they were used in a concoction for the treatment of piles, giving it the alternative and less attractive name of Pilewort.

As with Buttercups, the yellow of the petals is intense and very shiny and the underside may show a reddish-brown staining. The beauty of the leaves lies in their heart shape and mottled green colours. Each of those shown here has been observed individually, areas of highlight noted and maintained while building up patches of quite dark green pigment. You can of course lift off paint before it dries too thoroughly and sometimes this is easier on small leaves. The student needs to practise both methods, because what is natural for one will not suit another.

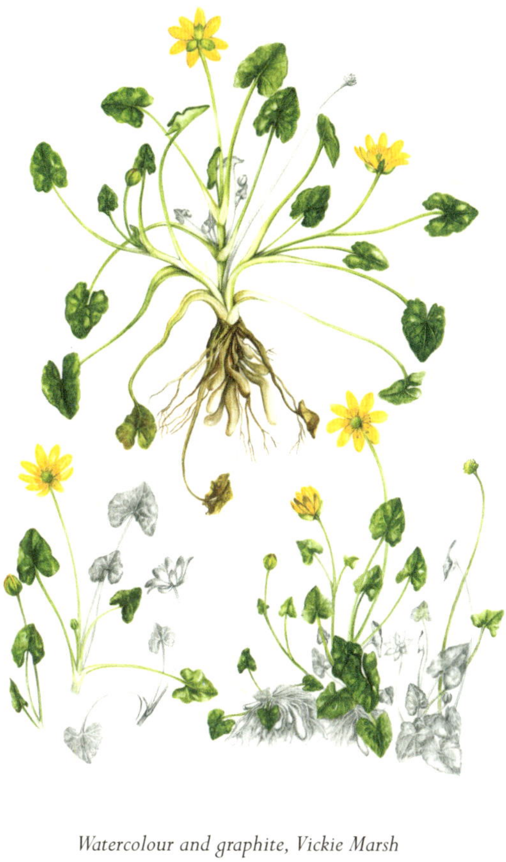

Watercolour and graphite, Vickie Marsh

ROSE FAMILY *Rosaceae*

Blackberry or Bramble

Rubus fruticosus

Blackberry is a conspicuous plant or shrub in English hedgerows. Its flowers may be seen from July to September, varying in colour from white to pink. The inflorescence is what is known as a compound panicle; the flowers growing in little groups at the ends of short stalks which branch from the main stem. Petals five and six, with the corresponding number of sepals forming the calyx. Stamens numerous. The fruit may be had from August to October. The leaves grow alternately with, as a rule, five or three leaflets, each on a separate short stalk, and are often lobed. Bracts and stipules grow at the junctions of the flower and leaf stalks with the main stem. One variety of this shrub is called the Dewberry, in which the sepals clasp the berry. Buds, flowers, and fruit may be found on the same plant at the same time. EC

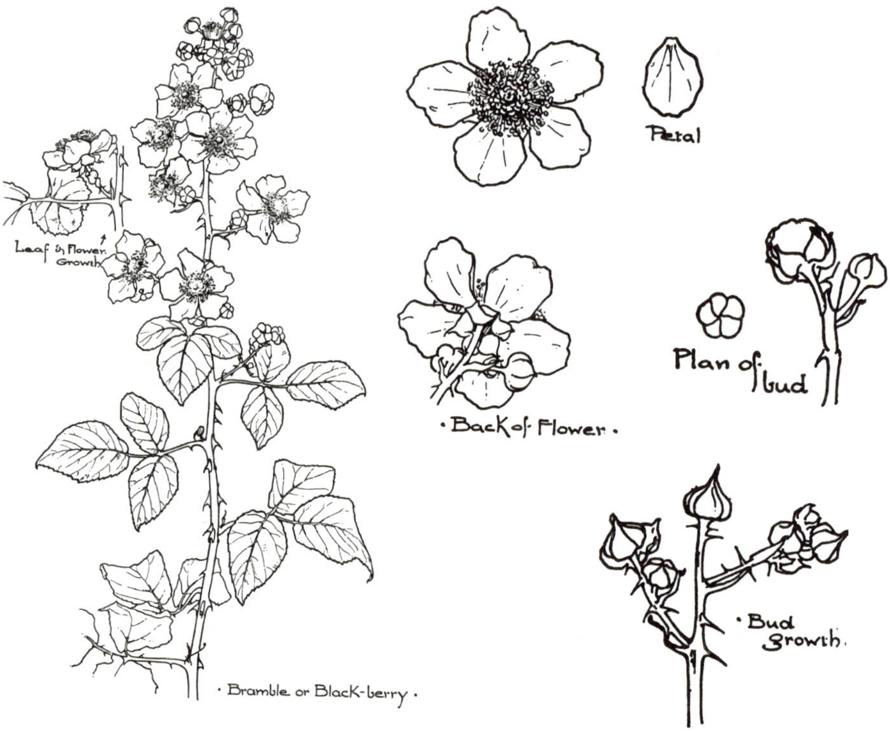

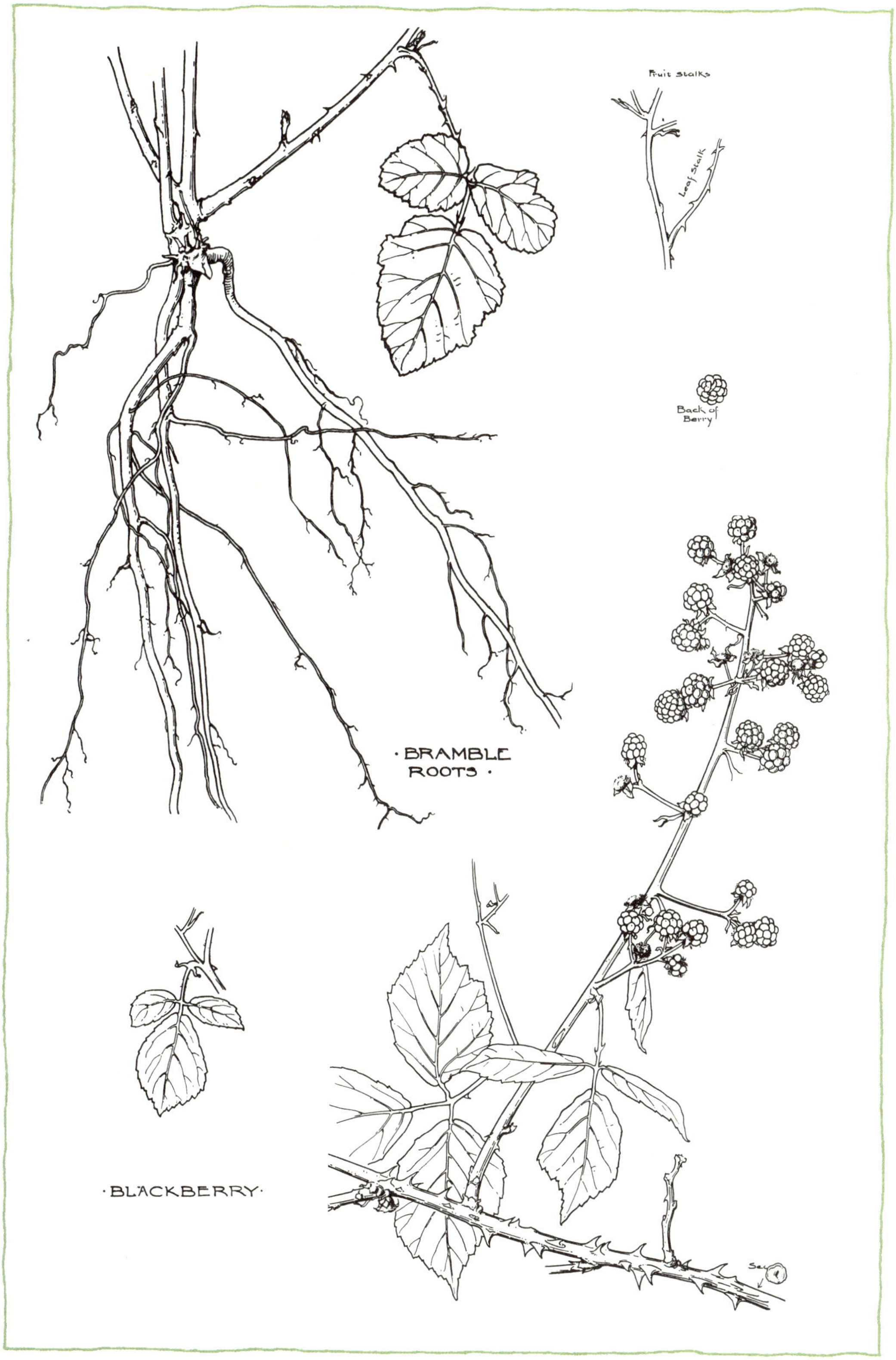
Fruit stalks
Leaf stalk
Back of Berry
·BRAMBLE ROOTS·
·BLACKBERRY·

Hawthorn, May or Whitethorn

Crataegus monogyna

In May the hedgerows are white with this hedge shrub. Its groups of white-and-pink blossoms are not only attractive, by their particular form and sweet odour, to the ordinary flower lover, but by their possibilities to the artist also. The flowers grow in the form of what is botanically known as a corymb; they are five-petalled, with calyx of five divisions, stamens many.

The leaves are divided into three and five lobes, deeply serrated as a rule. Stipules large and leafy. The fruit or haws are found through the autumn, forming groups of red ovate berries. Flowers May to middle of June. EC

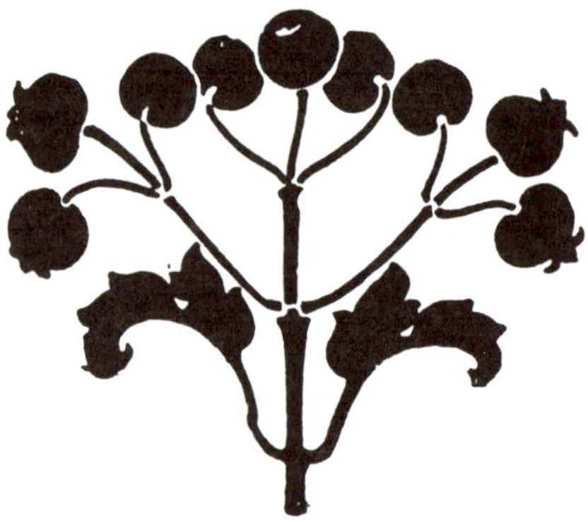

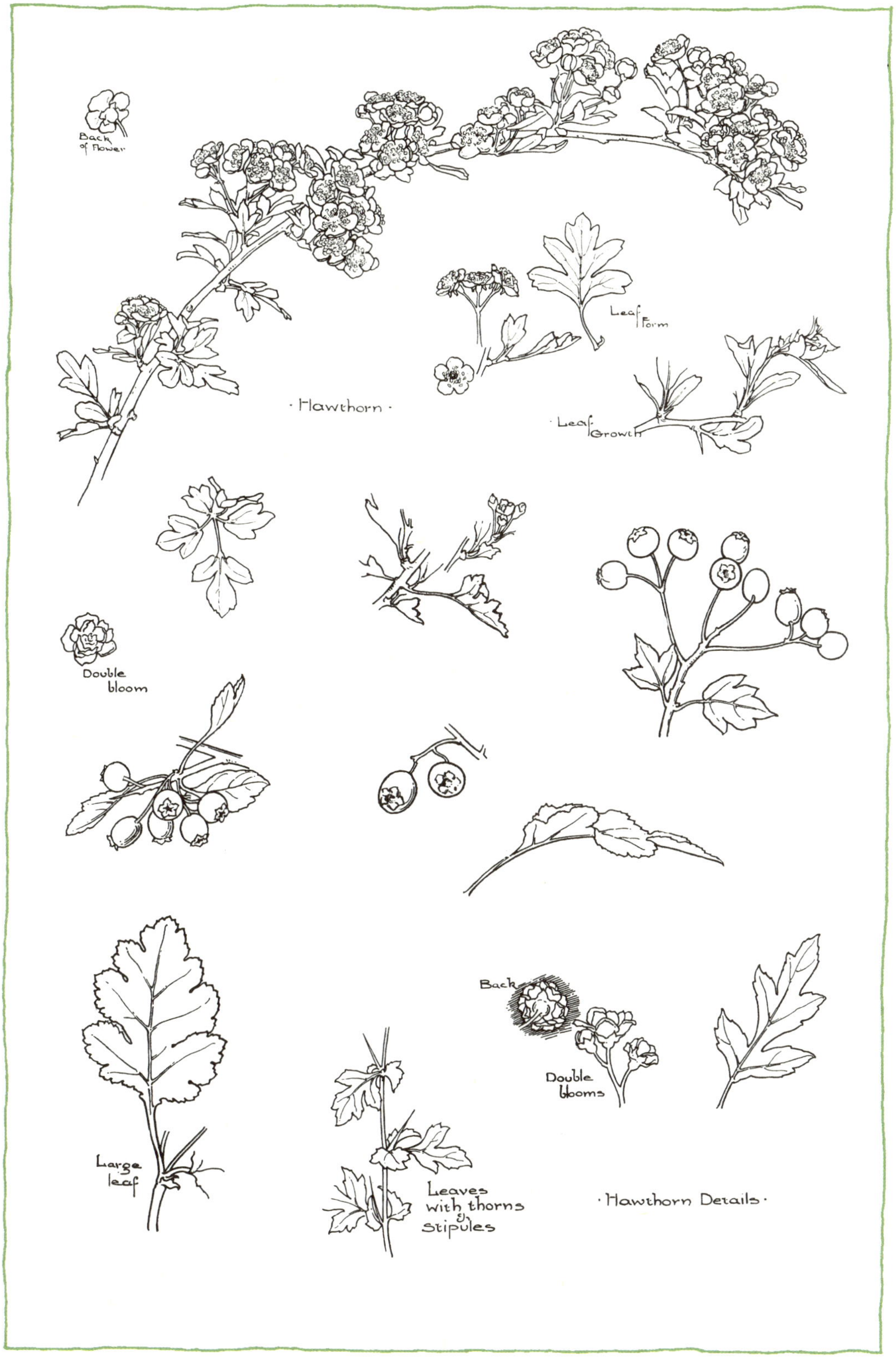
Back of Flower
Leaf Form
· Hawthorn ·
· Leaf Growth
Double bloom
Back
Double blooms
Large leaf
Leaves with thorns & stipules
· Hawthorn Details ·

Hawthorn

Crataegus laevigata

In this study the artist has shown the tangled growth of Hawthorn very well, something that is not always easy to achieve from a compositional point of view. It is best to paint the fruiting branch first and wait until the following spring for the delicate blossom to appear, then one can choose a small sprig to fit into whatever gap has been left for the purpose. When one works this way round the composition somehow dictates itself with, in this case, the stronger element of lichened bark and scarlet berries providing the dominant note.

The artist used Winsor & Newton Cadmium Red Deep and Brown Madder and Daler-Rowney Transparent Red Brown with a touch of Winsor & Newton Thioindigo Violet for the glowing berries. The number of times that Thioindigo Violet is mentioned throughout this text shows how much it will be missed by botanical artists. For the greens she mixed Indanthrene Blue with Transparent Yellow, both Winsor & Newton, and also Winsor & Newton Permanent Sap Green with Daler-Rowney Midnight Green for the darker tones.

Notice the care with which the artist has painted the complex array of pedicels from the berries to the twig. All of these have a beginning and an end, which may seem obvious but all too often the student loses the way and one finds unfinished stems which leave the fruit unattached. Equal care has been given to the multitude of stamens that speckle the creamy flowers. All combine with the varying textures of the bark and lichen to create an interesting portrait of a familiar hedgerow tree.

Watercolour, Kay Rees-Davies

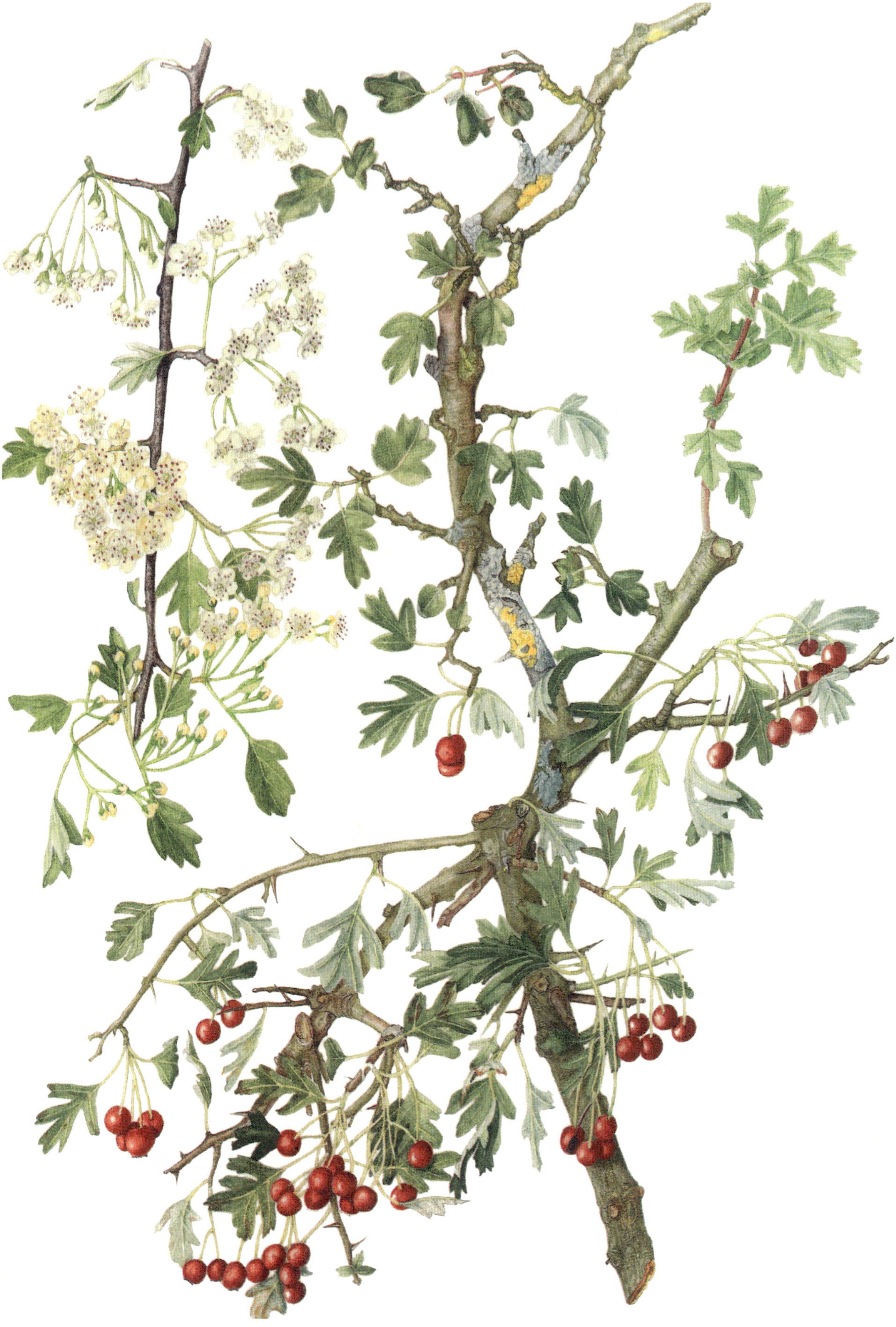

Crab Apple

Malus sylvestris

Apple blossoms in the month of May form a picturesque sight in the hedgerows and fields when in bloom. The flowers grow in little tufts or umbels along the branches. The leaves are egg-shaped and serrated. The flowers are succeeded by small fruit, which vary in shape according to the particular variety of tree, some being quite spherical, others are elongated. The flower bears five petals, and varies in colour from almost a white to a deep pink. The calyx has five sepals or small teeth; the stamens numerous and yellow. EC

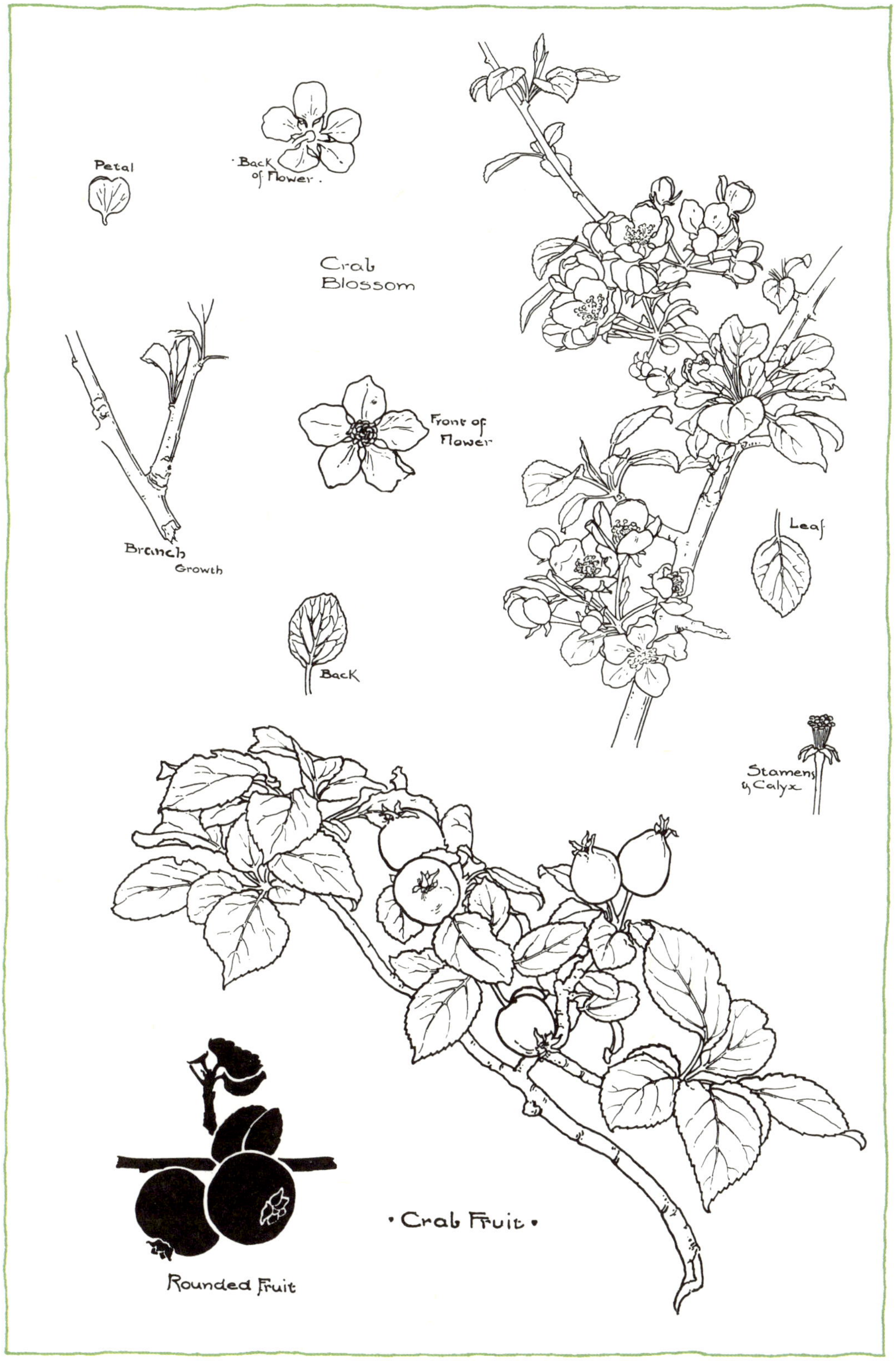
Petal
· Back of Flower ·
Crab Blossom
Branch Growth
Front of Flower
Leaf
Back
Stamens & Calyx
Rounded Fruit
· Crab Fruit ·

Crab Apple

Malus sylvestris 'John Downie'

This cheerful painting shows 'John Downie' Crab Apples at their colourful best, and I like to think that something similar was known to Shakespeare when he wrote of roasted crabs hissing in the bowl, conjuring up a warm image of Christmas and Wassail. Such historic imagery is appropriate for work on a traditional surface such as vellum – the skin of a calf or other young animal – which allows pigments to glow in an unbeatable fashion. Now one of the most expensive supports available to the modern artist, it requires fastidious technique since there is none of the forgiveness shown by paper. As it is not absorbent, the paint sits on the surface and must therefore be applied with great care, all the time striking a balance between wet and dry. Layers of colour are built up with small brush strokes or stippled – really wet washes cannot be applied as too much water will harden the vellum and it will curl up.

The artist's branch is weighed down with fruit which creates a natural diagonal composition, leaving triangles of space at opposite corners where blossom could have been shown. In this case it is pleasing to see the apples without any extras and the result is a painting which would add a little spot of warmth to any room. The artist drew all the fruit first and then the leaves, which she painted quickly before they deteriorated and fell off. She then went back to the long-lasting fruit and gave them lots of attention, seen in terms of highlights, blemishes and colour variation. For the fruit the artist used a pale wash of Winsor & Newton Naples Yellow then glazes of Indian Yellow blended in with Winsor & Newton Quinacridone Red and Schmincke Permanent Carmine.

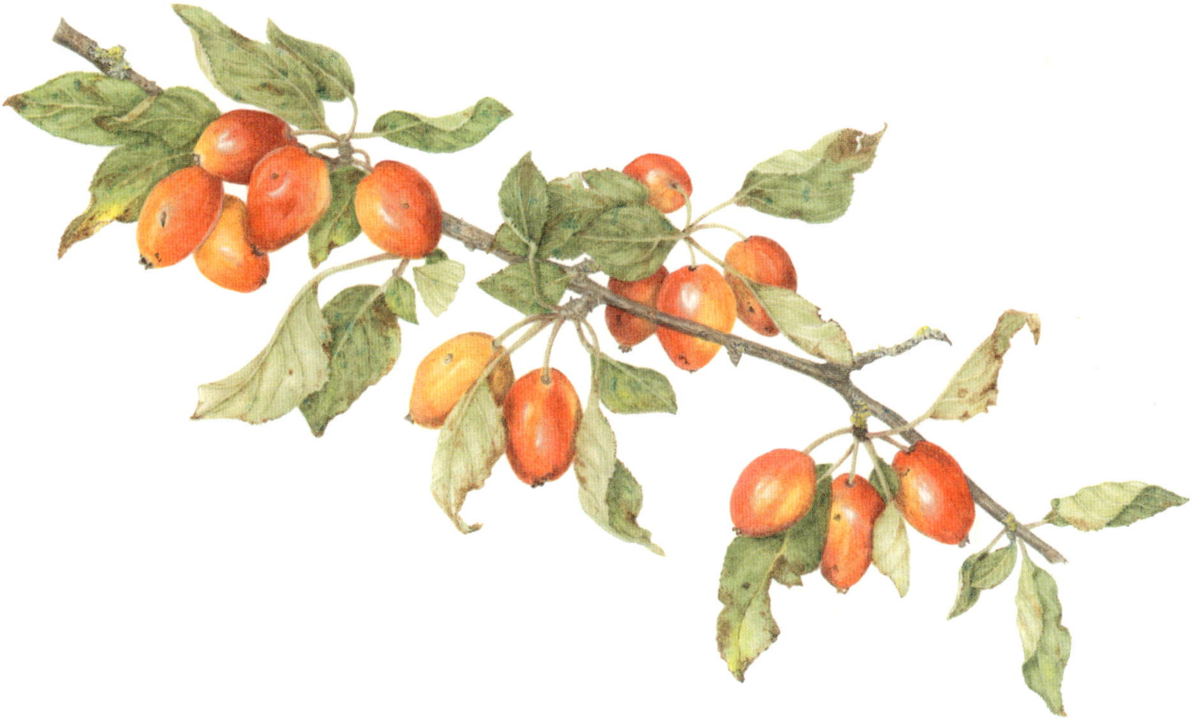

Watercolour on vellum, Gillian Dudley-Smith

Sloe or Blackthorn

Prunus spinosa

Sloe is another of the hedge shrubs, and though not so well known as some others, is not by any means the least beautiful. It is known in the spring during its term of flowering as the Blackthorn, when its pure white flowers contrast strongly with the black thorny stems; at this time it is without a developed leaf. When the fruit appears, with the leaves, later in the year, it is then known as the sloe. The perfectly rounded fruits are a deep purple, covered with a rich bloom. Its leaves are small and elliptical, finely serrated. The flowers have five petals and five sepals; stamens numerous. The shrub is much branched, some of the smaller branches ending in a sharp thorn.

EC

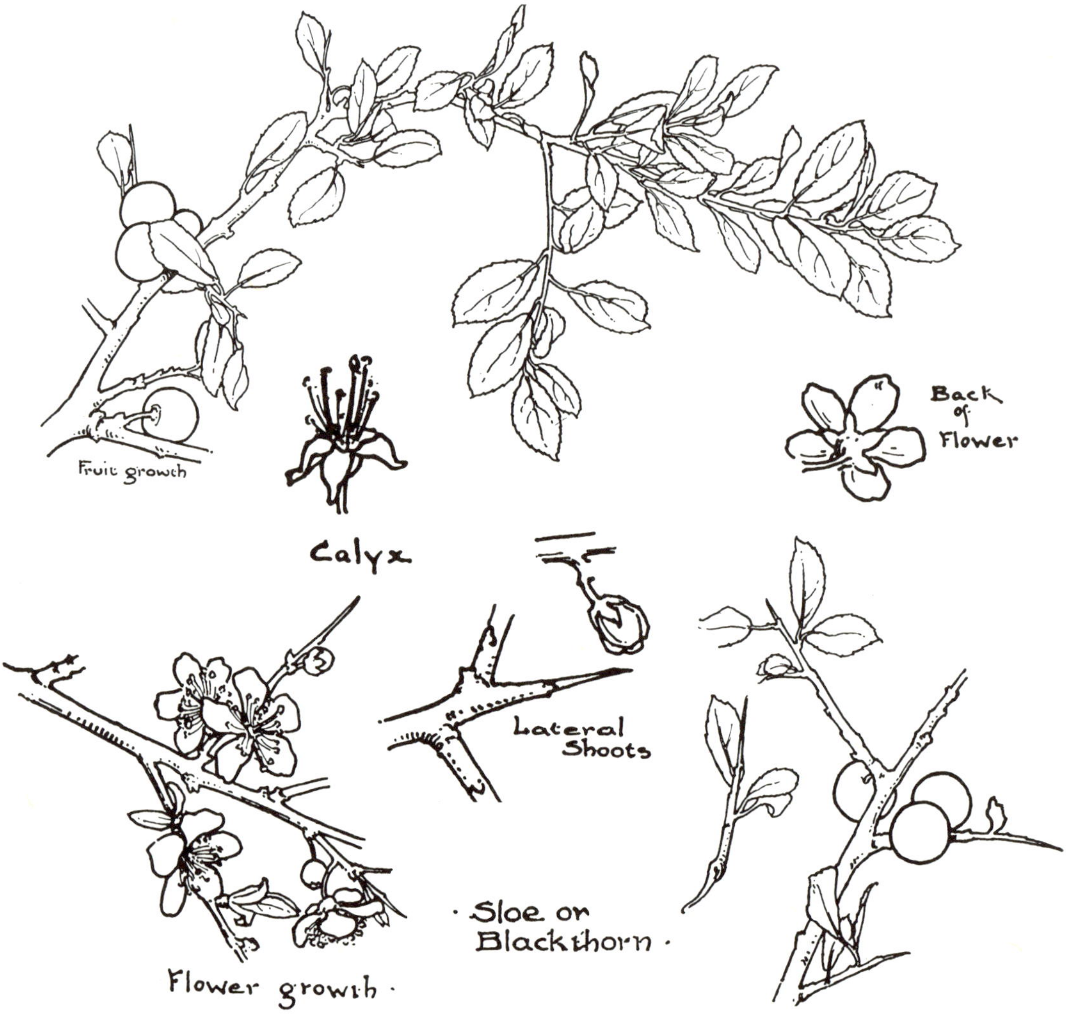

Blackthorn

Prunus spinosa

The sight of a snowdrift of Blackthorn blossom in the hedgerows gladdens the hearts of all those who make sloe gin since it forecasts a good crop of fruit later in the year.

Here the artist has shown both the delicate flowers with their central boss of gold-tipped stamens and the dull purple-black fruit. The supporting twigs, although dark, also have a chestnut-red touch which extends to the leaf pedicels. She will have taken time and care to paint the finely serrated leaves and the vicious thorns, a natural armoury that helps to create many a cattle-proof barrier. Careful brush drawing enables these fine details to be achieved, provided the brush, regardless of its size, has a really fine point. Note also the careful way in which the cut ends of the twigs have been shown, which adds to the overall finish of the study.

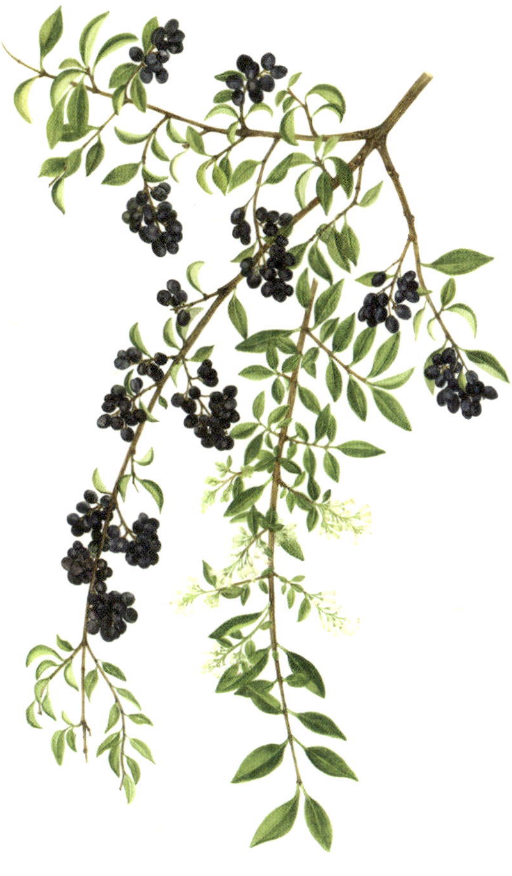

Watercolour, Vickie Marsh

Wild Rose

Rosa canina

There are several native species of this plant or shrub, which forms such a glorious hedge covering in June. Probably the one figured here is the most common, but the white variety, or Field Rose, runs it pretty closely for beauty and popularity, and may also be found in flower much later. It is almost unnecessary to enter into any kind of description of it, as the least observant lover of flowers finds himself drawn towards it, both on account of its sweetness and its lovely form. The artist especially knows it well as a rule; but it is just one of those plants that 'age cannot wither, nor custom stale, its infinite variety'. Its petals are five in number, from a delicate pink to a much deeper tint; as a rule they are cleft. There are five sepals, sometimes entire, very often divided. Stamens are numerous and bright yellow, surrounding the small sessile stigma. The leaves are of the pinnate order, that is, five or more leaflets of elliptical form, are arranged on each side of a central stem, which is terminated by one of the leaflets. They are sharply serrated, and at the base of the leaf-stalk are wing-like stipules. The flowers grow in twos or singly, branching from each side of the main thorny stem. They are succeeded by the fruit or 'hips', which appear in the autumn and winter, turning from a green to a brilliant red. EC

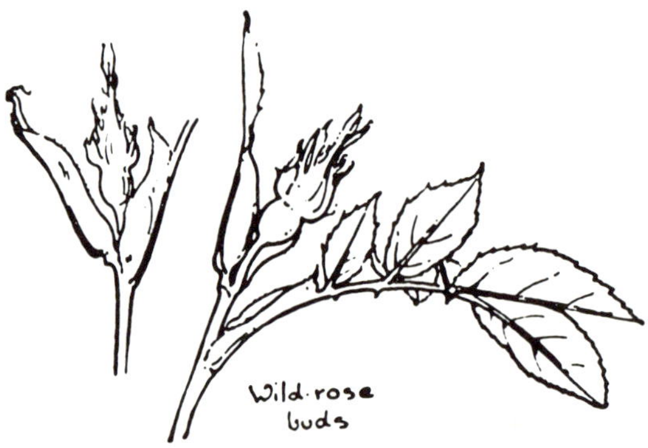

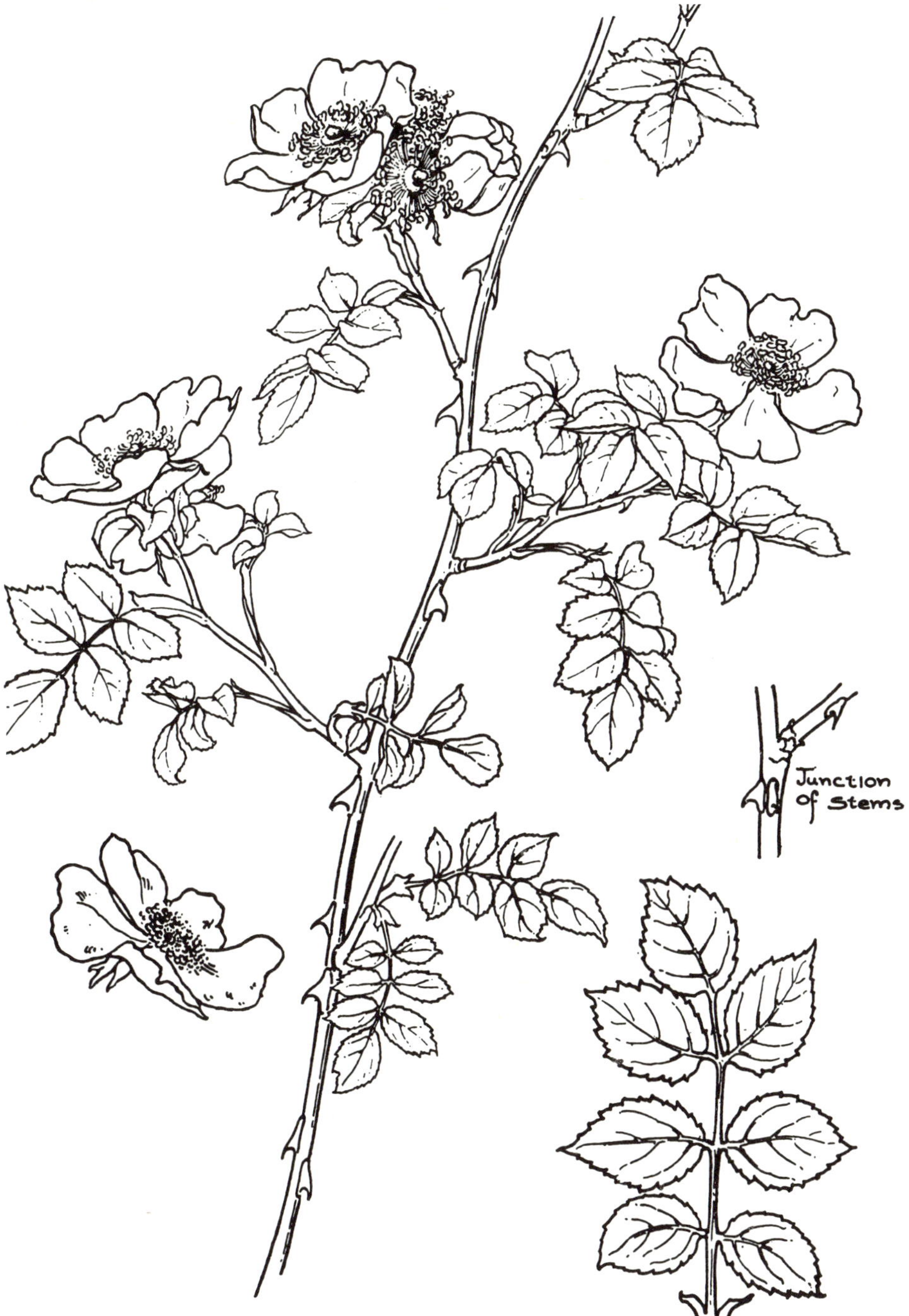
Junction of Stems
· Wild Rose ·

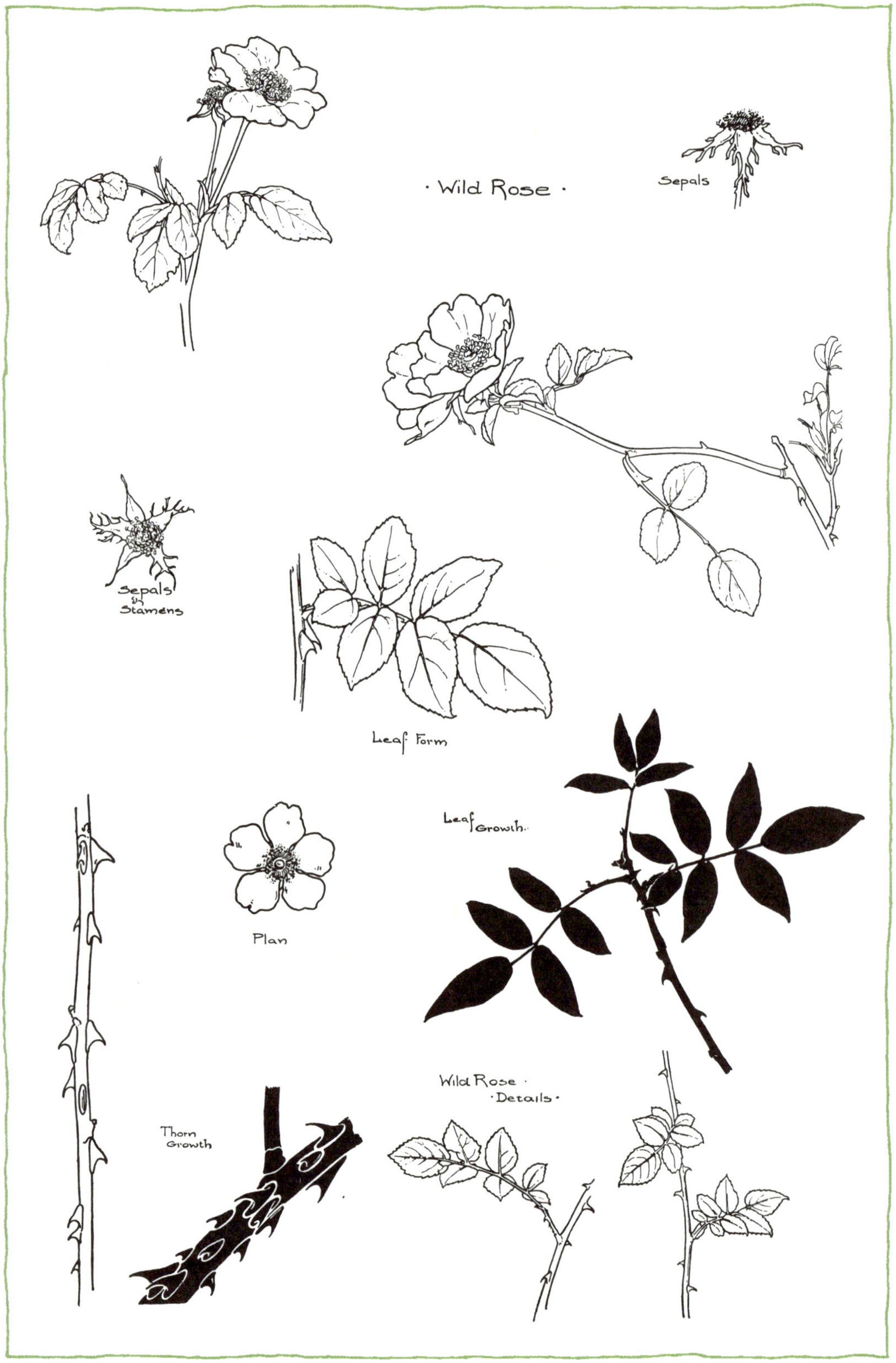
· Wild Rose ·
Sepals
Sepals & Stamens
Leaf Form
Leaf Growth
Plan
Thorn Growth
Wild Rose · Details ·

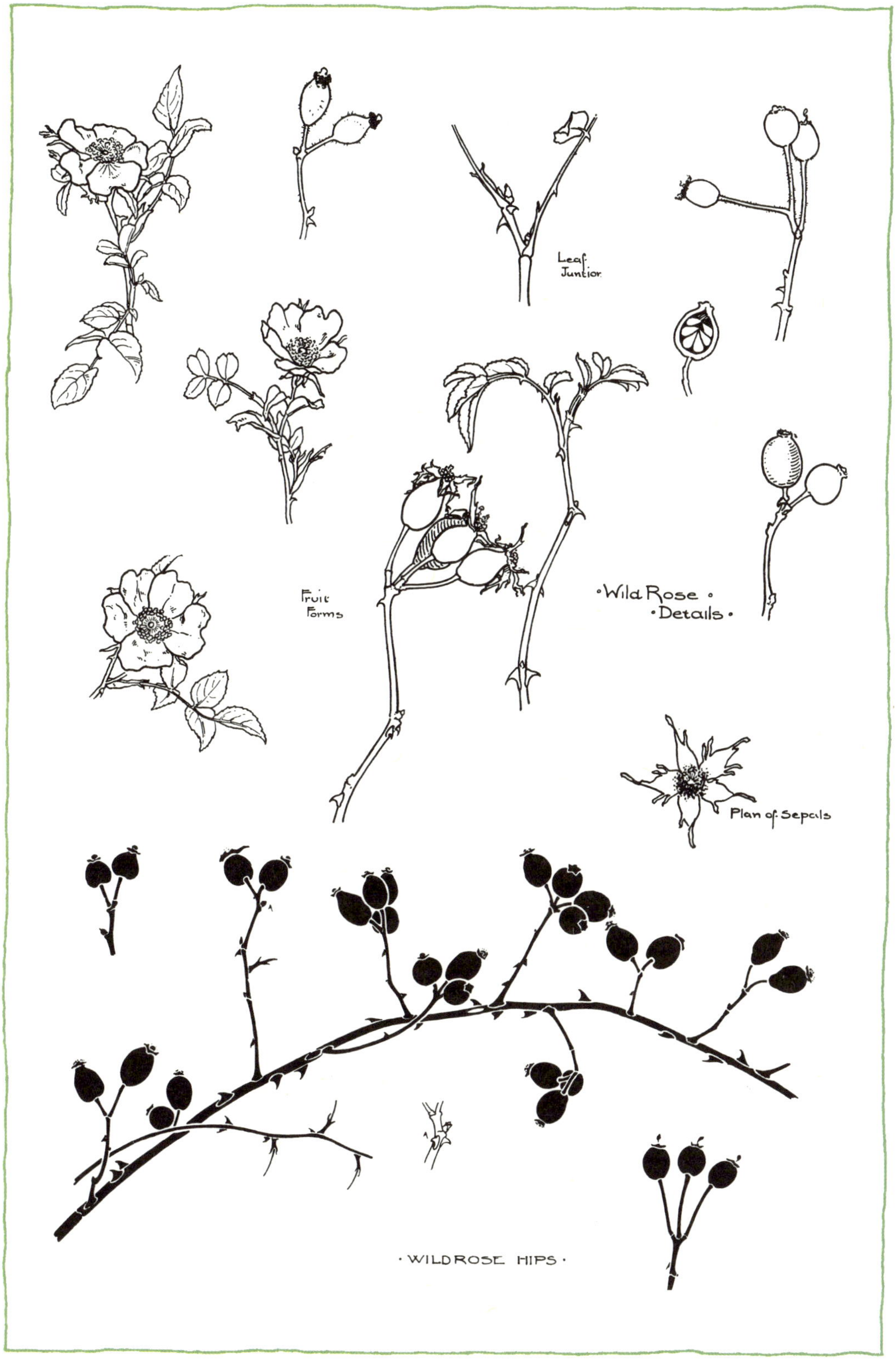
Leaf Juntion
Fruit Forms
·Wild Rose·
·Details·
Plan of Sepals
·WILDROSE HIPS·

Rose

Rosa 'Flower Carpet Coral'

It is time consuming to paint on vellum but I know of no other support which allows the paint to glow with such brilliance and this ground cover rose was a deserving case. I prefer not to use graphite to draw the outline on vellum although errors with pencil or paint can be erased by rubbing gently with '000' emery paper. For my initial drawing I used a pale mix of the appropriate colour and drew with the very tip of the brush. As always I selected a foreground flower, the one on the left,and painted the pale rose outline, then added a delicate wash of Naples Yellow for the centre and on the lower petals that showed a golden flush beneath the red. Permanent Rose and Quinacridone Red gave me most of the strong colour and this was built up using the miniaturist's technique of thousands of tiny brush strokes. This enables the colour to be smoothly blended. Purple shadow tones were added last of all. The right-hand flower was painted next and then the opening bud at the top. Finally, the leaves were painted in the same fashion, making sure to reserve the palest areas of highlight.

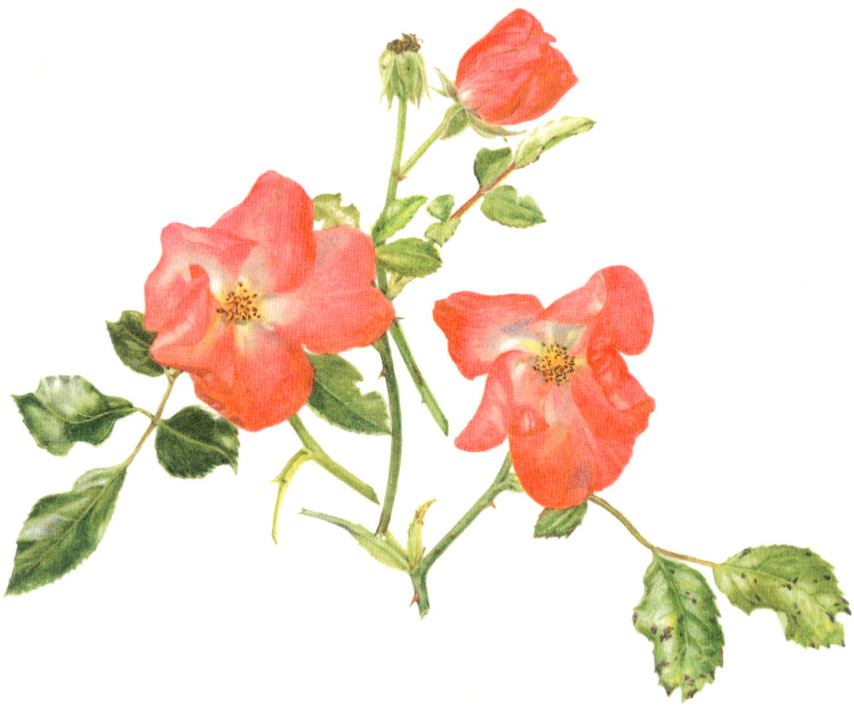

Watercolour on vellum, Margaret Stevens

Sherard's Downy-rose

Rosa sherardii

The artist found this species rose growing on mixed scrub and woodland near her home in North Wales. From the colour of the flowers and shape of the thorns it would appear to be *R. sherardii,* or Sherard's Downy-rose, although this is more commonly found in the wild in Scotland. However, garden escapees account for the movement of many plants away from their usual territory. The brilliant rose hips are rich in Vitamin A, C and E, and also, unusually, fatty acids; the seeds were once added to bread as a vitamin supplement.

Permanent Rose will have been the perfect shade to capture the vibrancy of the petals and any of the opaque Cadmium Yellows and Naples Yellow would enable the stamens to stand out (all Winsor & Newton paints). This painting called for a great deal of patience in order to give each leaflet the attention needed to portray the finely serrated edges and clear venation. Leaf-joints, thorns, buds and developing hips as well as those in full crimson glory have all been minutely observed and described so that the life cycle of this plant is encapsulated on the page.

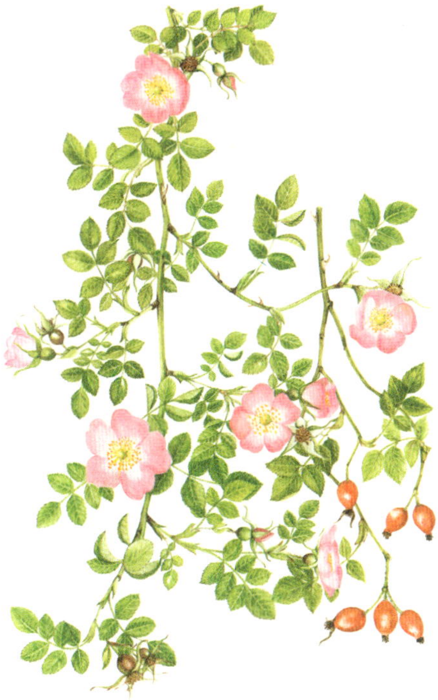

POTATO FAMILY *Solanaceae*

Woody Nightshade

Solanum dulcamara

Nightshade, or Bitter-sweet, is one of those trailing or climbing plants which, not being self-supporting, leans and crawls over the thick vegetation of the hedgerows. It is most conspicuous when bearing fruit in the autumn, its berries being egg-shaped or oval, turning from a bright green to a bright red, and growing in bunches with a very decorative growth. The flowers are small and of a purple colour, having five pointed petals, which are usually reflexed, i.e. turned backwards on to the flower stalk, the anthers are united and form a pointed yellow centre, the calyx has five divisions; there is also a small green spot at the base of each petal. There are five stamens and a pistil. The leaves vary in shape considerably, commencing at the lower part of the stem by being heart-shaped; they gradually become more lanceolate, having often a pair of wing-like lobes at the base, giving the leaf the hastate form. The groups of flowers grow as a rule from the opposite side of the stem to the leaves, but from the same point on the stem. This fact makes it rather difficult to get a satisfactory view of both leaves and flowers or berries from the same piece. Its flowering period is a long one, being from June to September, so that both flowers and berries may be found growing together on the same plant, as is the case with the blackberry. EC

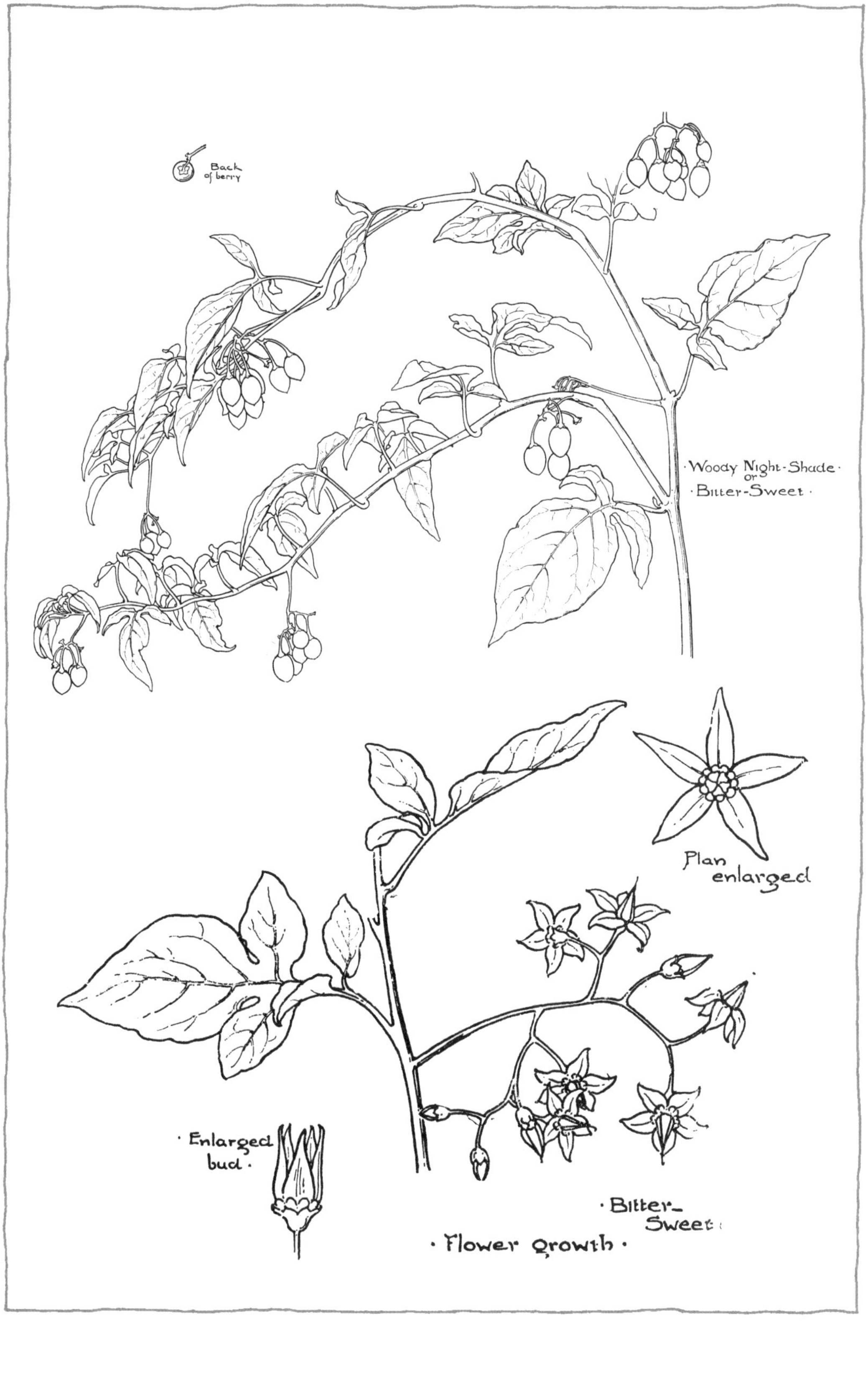
Back of berry
·Woody Night-Shade·
or
·Bitter-Sweet·
Plan enlarged
·Enlarged bud·
·Bitter-Sweet·
·Flower growth·

Woody Nightshade

Solanum dulcamara

The artist was attracted to the natural decorative line of this plant, commonly known as Bittersweet or Woody Nightshade, when she was required to paint it for an exhibition commemorating the work of the Massey sisters, who recorded the wild flowers of Anglesey in the 19th century. In *Flora Britannica* (Chatto & Windus, 1996), Richard Mabey comments that the seeds are bitter with a sweeter aftertaste and the crushed leaves smell like burnt rubber; although not as dangerous as some of its relatives, it would appear to have only its looks to recommend it. The Solanaceae family is one of extremes, with aubergines, potatoes and tomatoes providing food while other cousins such as Henbane and Deadly Nightshade are poisonous.

This depiction of Bittersweet harks back to Clark's day, as the artist has used a crisp, illustrative style with all parts outlined with the brush and this would not have looked out of place a century or more ago. She has also used the brush to draw very fine detail, not least the thread-like purple stems and calyces of fruit and flowers. If you look really closely you will find that not a line is out of place and indeed, because of the painting's simplicity, fudging a mistake would have been out of the question. For the student it is a reminder that time spent practising brush control will pay off in the future.

Watercolour, Linda Dearden

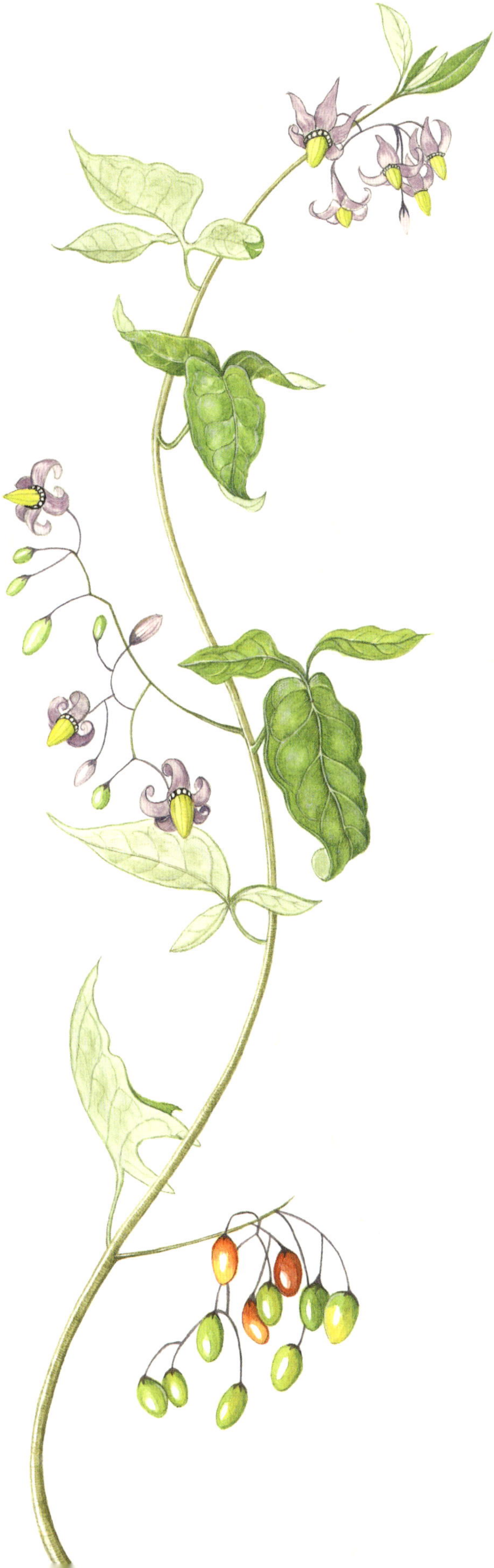

Aubergine

Solanum melongena 'Slim Jim'

This friendly member of the family, which allegedly caused a sultan to swoon when served as a tasty dish, comes in a variety of shapes, sizes and colours including white, speckled, lavender and green, with many new cultivars on offer. A native of India, it can be grown outdoors in milder climates in the northern hemisphere or in a cool greenhouse.The artist likes this variety, which is prolific in flower and fruit as well as being an attractive subject to paint. It is rather dominated by the outsize mature leaves, which have attractive and prominent purple veins. In order to create a pleasing picture the artist allowed the leaves in the lower quadrant to fade out, resulting in a well-balanced composition both structurally and tonally. She finds Winsor Violet a lovely colour to work with, cooled with French Ultramarine or warmed with Alizarin Crimson. Her green palette comprised Winsor & Newton's French Ultramarine, Indanthrene Blue, Perylene Green, Transparent Yellow and Aureolin.

Watercolour, Yvonne Edwards

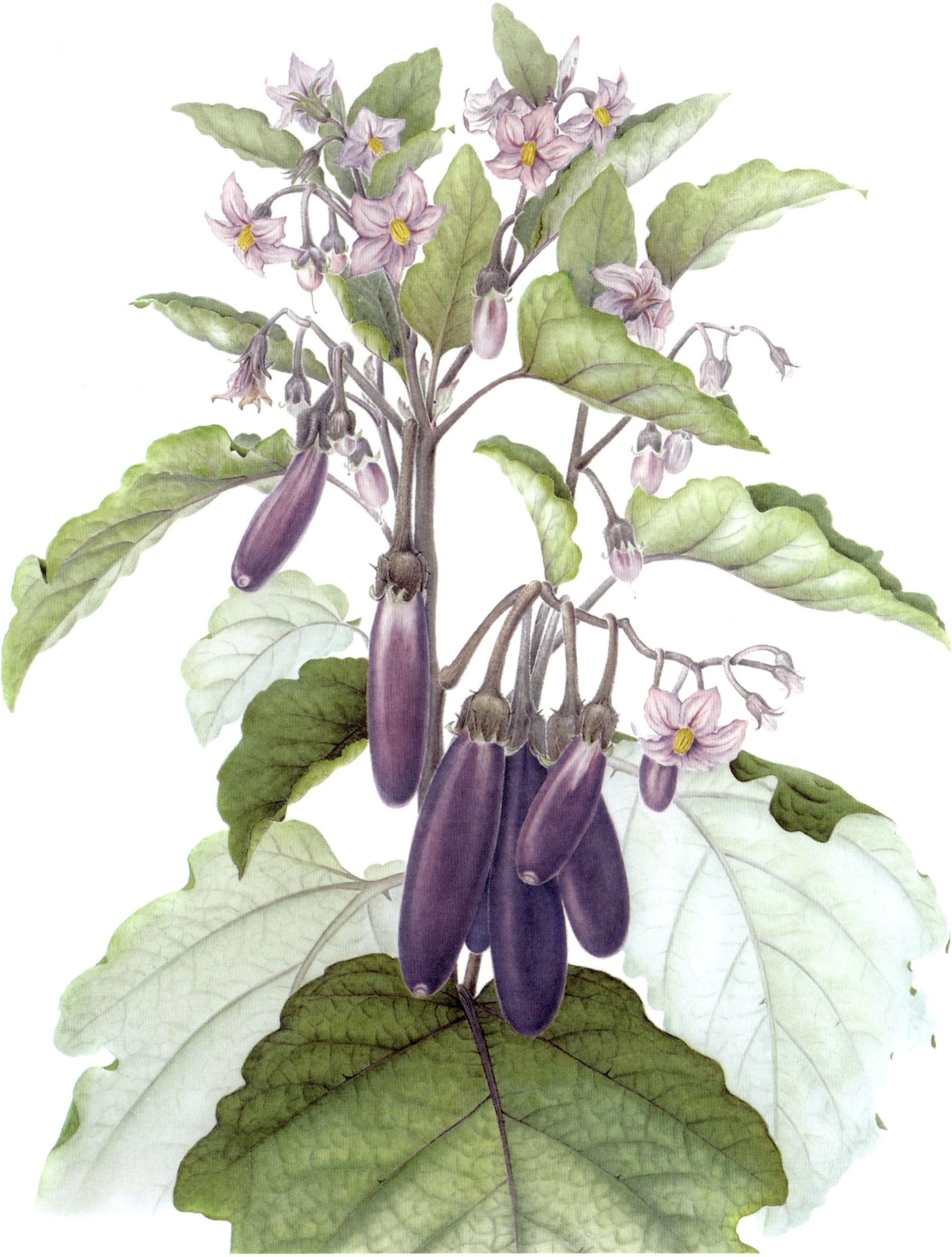

VIOLET FAMILY *Violaceae*

Violet

Viola

One of the several wild varieties of Violet, one or other of which colours the hedgebanks and woods from March to July. The flowers and leaves grow practically straight from the root on several varieties, but on the one figured here, they grow from the stems also. The usual height is from about three to five inches. The flowers have five petals and five sepals, the centre petal being the largest and ending in a spur at the back of the flower. The colour varies from a pale blue to a deep purple. The leaves are broad and heart-shaped or cordate, and serrated, rather dark green in colour. There are five stamens, the anthers of which and the pistil are united. The stipules are long and pointed. The fruit is a capsule of three divisions. Found on hedgebanks, in thickets, and pastures. EC

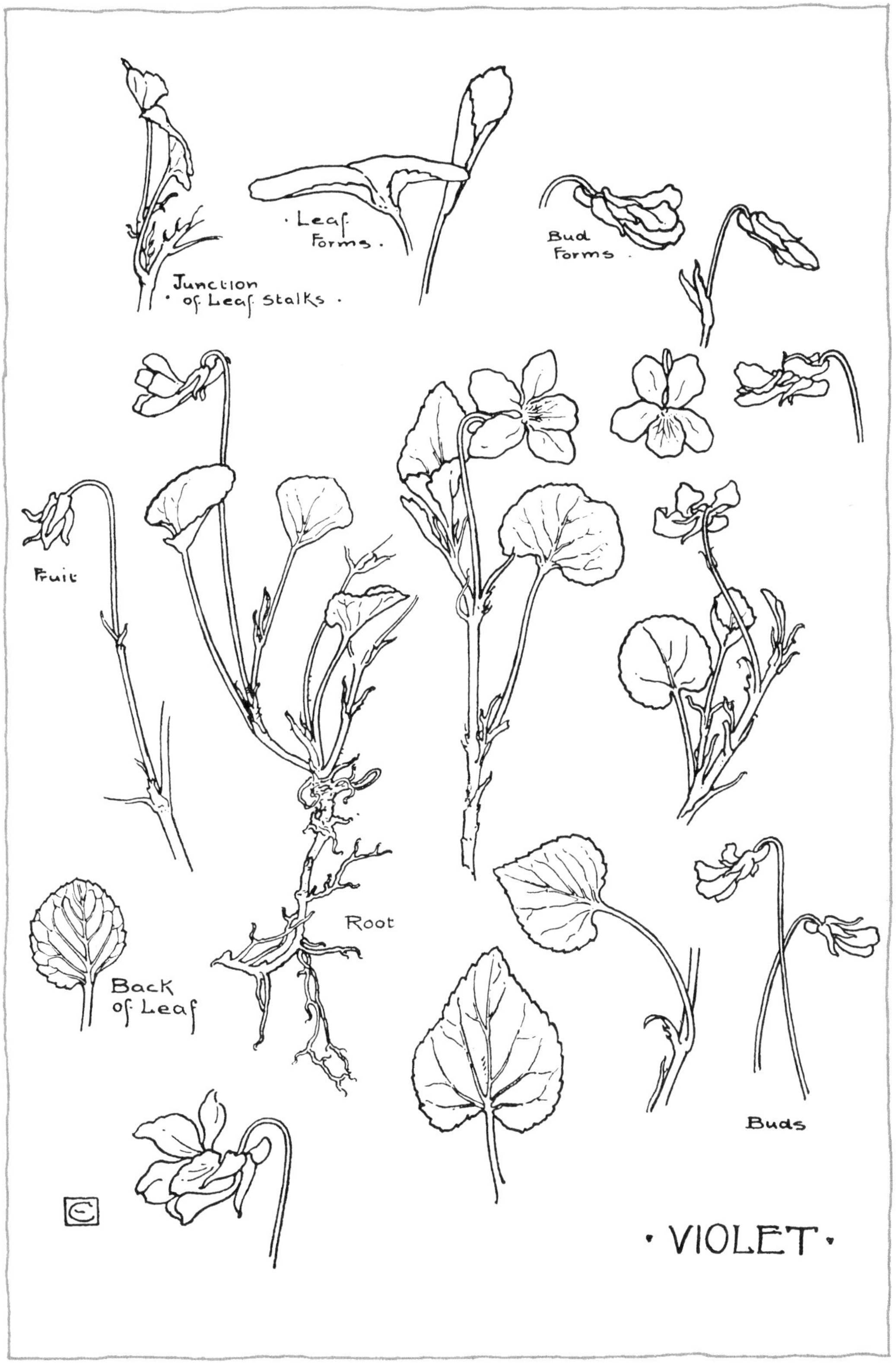
Junction of Leaf Stalks
Leaf Forms
Bud Forms
Fruit
Root
Back of Leaf
Buds
VIOLET

Violet

Viola 'Queen Charlotte'

Since classical times violets have been cherished first as a medicinal plant, then for their perfume in confectionery and for display as a cut flower. Here the artist has painted a delightfully simple portrait of a clump of 'Queen Charlotte', one of the many hybrids raised over the last few centuries which has surprisingly survived to the present day when many have been lost.

True violets differ from pansies in the presence of the spur, the leaf shape and root system. The artist has kept the leaves looking fresh by applying the wet-on-wet technique in the early stages before picking out a few areas in greater detail where the veins are most conspicuous; she favours this method when plants have a numerous overlapping leaves as it stops the painting becoming too dense. Touches of blue and pink were added to Winsor Violet for the flowers.

INDEX